Challenge of a Liberal Faith

Third edition

George N. Marshall

SKINNER HOUSE
UNITARIAN UNIVERSALIST ASSOCIATION

Seventh printing.
Copyright © 1966, 1988 by the Unitarian Universalist Association.
Copyright © 1970, 1980 by George N. Marshall.
All rights reserved.
Printed in the United States of America.
ISBN 0-933840-31-4
UUA item code 9000001

Acknowledgments
The author expresses appreciation to many persons and agencies making up the Unitarian Universalist Association for material included. Special acknowledgment is hereby made to many ministers, living and dead.

The Unitarian Universalist Association gratefully acknowledges those individuals and publishers who have granted permission for use of their copyright materials. Every effort has been made to trace the ownership of copyright material. If any infringement has been made, the Unitarian Universalist Association will be glad, upon receiving notification, to make appropriate acknowledgment in future editions of this book.

Permission has been granted from the following: from "The Hollow Men" in *Collected Poems 1909–1962* by T. S. Eliot, copyright © 1936 by Harcourt Brace Jovanovich, Inc., copyright © 1963, 1964 by T. S. Eliot. Reprinted by permission of the publisher. From "Ten Mills" and "Not All There" from *The Poetry of Robert Frost* edited by Edward Connery Lathem. Copyright © 1969 by Holt, Rinehart and Winston, Inc. Copyright © 1962 by Robert Frost. Copyright © 1975 by Lesley Frost Ballantine. Reprinted by permission of Henry Holt and Company, Inc. "Evening Meal in the Twentieth Century" from *Address to the Living* by John Holmes, © John Holmes. Reprinted by permission of Mrs. Doris Holmes. "The Prayer" by Rudyard Kipling. Reprinted by permission of Doubleday and Company, Inc.

Library of Congress Cataloging-in-Publication Data
Marshall, George N.
    Challenge of a liberal faith.
    Bibliography: p.
    Includes index.
    1. Unitarianism.   2. Universalism.   3. Liberalism
(Religion)   I. Title.
BX9841.2.M28 1987   288'.32   87-13930
ISBN 0-933840-31-4

CONTENTS

Preface to the Third Edition

When this book comes to my mind, I think of such phrases as "Why try?," "Easy does it," or "Accidents will happen," because I never tried to write a specific book on Unitarian Universalism. On the other hand—like most other Unitarian Universalist ministers—I did want to write books on liberal religion. But there was no time when I said, "I'm going to sit down and write an introductory book to our movement for newcomers that can double as a refresher for old-timers," which is how some people have described this volume.

Like other ministers dealing with many people new to our movement, I was often asked, "We've read the pamphlets—what's the next study effort, short of enrolling in a college course or a theological seminary?" We had Earl Morse Wilbur's weighty two volume *History of Unitarianism*, the first volume called *Socinianism and its Antecedents* and volume two entitled *Unitarianism in England and America*. And there was Richard Eddy's massive study of *Universalism*, and more recently Russell Miller's two thorough and meticulously researched volumes on the history of Universalism, *The Larger Hope*, (underwritten by the Universalist Historical Society). Our neophytes would say, "Hey, but after the pamphlets, what do you have for people who don't have a PhD?"

While serving as minister of the Church of the Larger Fellowship, I developed an introductory program, a directed reading course, which evolved into *Challenge of a Liberal Faith*. Through our home program for religious education at the C.L.F. we had the organizational experience to realize that a traditional correspondence course would place impossible responsibilities on the staff by asking them to correct lessons, etc. We were already devising courses where the student (or the parent or partner) was his or her own monitor, and that is how our directed reading course worked.

This was easy to do. I'd slap down a few ideas, glibly write them up, and add some questions, quizzes, or tables to mull over. I then added materials from my colleague ministers and religious educators, thus broadening the scope of inquiry. Nothing weighty, just something to make a point, to give away or mail out, and forget about. With a mimeograph machine in those days, as with a photocopier today, there was no weight of the world riding on every sentence; nothing to be compared with the great thinkers of our movement, (just something to run off on a mimeograph and throw away) so that there never was the intellectual baggage we would bring to writing a book. Nathan Keats, an editor with Pyramid Books (who wrote me that his wife and daughter attended a UU church in Stamford, Connecticut) got hold of the assorted mimeographed lessons and wanted to print them as a book. It's the best example of serendipity I know!

The ten lessons became chapters, and the study aids were incorporated into an appendix at the end of the book. The ten lessons may be divided into only four divisions: (1) (first four chapters) attitudes and scope of Unitarian Universalism as a viable religious alternative; (2) (two chapters) Unitarian and Universalist history in the Old World and in North America; (3) Unitarian Universalist beliefs, (or what other churches might call doctrines or theology—terms we tend to avoid); and (4) how the individual can fit into this scheme of things—through religious educational opportunities, church participation or the opportunities for establishing local societies through the ministry-at-large offered by the Church of the Larger Fellowship. These four divisions have often been used as the basis for four study sessions in local churches or fellowships. Since the study guides developed as companions to particular chapters are no longer clipped to the relevant lesson in the published format, we suggest the reader work in tandem with the appropriate study guide for each chapter.

If I took myself seriously as an author (that is, tried to write something of enduring quality), you'd not be reading this. Perhaps it comes from dashing off a sermon after supper Saturday nights. (I often wondered if I wrote a second draft of a sermon how it might have come out! But ministers are like this; we write at feverish pitch just before going into the pulpit and then spew forth our current ideas before sanity or probity sinks in. This may be what keeps our congregations stirred up and on the edges of their seats.)

Since these ensuing words were written not for the ages but for those in need of immediate assistance a few years ago, there has been need for updating and keeping abreast of changing patterns of thought and expression. It may sound strange to a younger generation, but only a few brief years ago we gave little thought to degenderization: "man" referred to the human race and humanity could be described as "he" rather than "he or she." It was commonplace to talk about Negroes rather than blacks, and even though we had only recently emerged from the Second World

War, we still thought as Americans or Canadians rather than in global terms, making necessary adjustments internally in our own minds rather than externally on the printed page. The revolution in awareness that occurred in the 1960s led us to see that humanity was both masculine and feminine; that "blacks" was a more inclusive and honorable designation than "Negroes," while the democratic world community was broader than our provincial American terminology indicated. In like manner, our Christian/ Protestant rootage is no longer as evident as it once was. Now we are more conscious of our interrelatedness with the Oriental world religious community and the secular humanist movement, since it is essential to religious liberalism that it reach out to other religious traditions and expressions.

To note these changing points of emphasis is not to describe shortcomings in the earlier manuscript. On the contrary, it is an indication of a major thesis of this volume: namely, that change or evolution in the religious sphere is not only inevitable but desirable. Newer social issues involve us: gay and lesbian rights once were hardly mentioned in straight society while today they are high on the agenda in sensitive circles. Human rights around the world are highly visible concerns. Along with abortion rights, birth control, and the exploding world population, goes world hunger, which marks a high priority on the agenda of liberal religious organizations. Ecological concern, environmental issues, and acid rain have called our attention to the broader linkage in the great chain of life and environment. This linkage includes the salvation of endangered species and the urgency to find sensible, sound, and safe means of disposing of chemical and nonbiodegradable waste products, including nuclear and industrial waste. Today religion is much more concerned with the ecosphere and biosphere than in the past, so that traditional concerns over the conservation of nature make sense of Schweitzer's reverence for life as the ethics for ecology.

Resolutions on many moral, ethical, and societal needs are considered annually at the movement's General Assembly. They serve as a guide for a social concensus. The Unitarian Universalist Service Committee seeks to represent the desires of the liberal religious community for direct action in the world's trouble spots. A Unitarian Universalist Peace Network is both spokesperson and clearing house for the importance of structuring a viable peace program in today's world. An effort is made to interpret the manifold needs, opportunities and avenues of action open for the religious liberal through the *Unitarian Universalist World*, the denomination's journal. Its pages will show the deep commitment to the religious, ideological, moral and spiritual perspectives which enrich the lives of Unitarian Universalists. In all these ways it is hoped that we can practice what other religions preach.

Add to this the human issues of terrorism, apartheid, war, political and military aggressive actions, the growing illiteracy that condemns the illiterate to second-class citizenship, and the political and economic injustices in today's world, and we see the vital necessity for a stronger, larger, more committed religious liberalism. Consequently there is more, not less, need for such a volume today.

—George Marshall

Before Reading

Before reading Chapter 1, we suggest that you turn immediately to the Study Guide to Chapter 1 and check your religious ideas. At the conclusion of the book, you may find it interesting to compare your attitudes again. Also, maximum value of this book will be derived if you acquaint yourself with the Study Guides and by keeping a thumb in the back of the book, refer to the guide for each chapter as you progress. It will increase your interest and your knowledge as you read the exciting story of *Challenge of a Liberal Faith*.

1

Why Pick A Church?

"Choosing a church or synagogue can be a difficult decision when a family moves to a new neighborhood or decides that its present church is unsatisfactory. What should you look for in a church?" wrote Rev. Ernest Campbell of the Riverside Church, New York City, in *The Reader's Digest*, June, 1969, in an article entitled "How to Pick a Church."

The difficulty with this article is that the wrong question is asked. For most people today, it is not "how to pick a church?" but rather, "why pick a church?" There are increasing numbers of people whose concern for a church affiliation is minimal and who, when they are free of previous involvements, give little thought to a church affiliation when they move away. To them, the question is not "how to?" but "why?"

Dr. Campbell goes on to say, "The basic doctrines of each Protestant denomination are really quite similar. The differences may come down to church organization and sacraments—the way baptism is administered, for instance. But some of the historical differences have paled considerably." Accordingly, he lists and suggests various considerations in "how to choose," which range from congeniality of people, qualities of the minister, social connections, to adequacy of building, *et cetera*. These reasons show just how shallow church membership is for the large majority of people who are involved in the great central denominations, which Campbell suggests have jaded or blurred the distinctive historical commitments which made them relevant at one time.

Today most people are looking for relevant connections, associations, relationships, and opportunities. Relevancy for most people is found outside of the churches. Any number of surveys show that there is both a resistance and a protest against organized religion. This is clearly the major factor concerning the churches today.

Perhaps that protest begins with one of two feelings. First, religion should deal with the inner life of a person and how he or she relates to others. Instead, most churches put the primary emphasis on the life of the church, on its dogma, doctrines, beliefs, and worship, and the individual must adjust or accommodate himself to the institution.

But in a day and age of freedom, of individuals grasping the right (often calling it a God-given right) of individual freedom and self-expression, why should not church people? Christians have long talked about the sheep and the lambs and the sheep and the goats, but should they as people be sheeplike themselves and not assert their own right to nurture their own religious life?

Another term once almost entirely restricted to church use was "love," when used in other than a romantic way. Now the word love stands out in graffiti (scribbling) on walls, sidewalks, souped-up automobiles, and wherever the young, the disenchanted, the dropouts and students gather. One does not any longer have to go to the Gospel hymns or the writings of St. Paul to discover the significance of love ("Now abideth faith, hope and love, these three, but the greatest of these is love."—I Corinthians 13:13) or the social driving power ("Love beareth all things, believeth all things, hopeth all things, endureth all things; love never faileth."—I Corinthians 13:7-8) it can unloose to change the cynically cold and calculating world in which we live. The power of love marks the beginnings of the social revolution of today.

When the church is performing its task, it often will make the uncomfortable comfortable and the comfortable uncomfortable. Another way of saying this is lamentably to recognize that for the majority of persons, religion is a comfortable, conforming experience used to make people conformists, uncritical, and unthinking. To the religious liberal, on the other hand, the church is important because it offers an alternative approach which strengthens, builds resistance, enhances courage, and challenges life's easy platitudes. Thus the religious liberal may be the best hope for salvation in the church if it successfully creates this new sense of "mission." Otherwise the church is following the path to its own destruction.

Such a quick look around us shows that the signs of the times are changing and that a social revolution is in danger of taking pure religion outside of the churches. Free people are expressing free faith. Are the churches in the process of being bypassed?

Some people will laugh and say, "Much of this idealism is not structured, organized, fundamental, or well-reasoned; it does not fit into a systematic pattern, and it will not give a consistent world view." Very well, but some well-trained thinkers have the same thing to say about the church. For instance, Rabbi Nathan Gaynor wrote,

> Much of contemporary religion is immature and irrelevant. It does not humanize or educate the conscience.
> All too often it succeeds only in generating smugness, without offering a vision of things as they might be. If it does direct eyes to the future, it does so by fostering the illusion that utopia can be achieved without human effort.
> If religion is to become relevant, then we need to alter its direction. A mature religion looks at the world with open eyes. It affirms that there are no short cuts to a better tomorrow. It prepares us for the possibility of failure. At no time does it make peace with injustice or tyranny.
> In a word, if religion is to play its proper role in contemporary society, it must again assume the task of social criticism on behalf of a better tomorrow for mankind.

And David Poling, an ordained minister formerly editor of the prestigious *Christian Herald* magazine, surveyed the contemporary church scene in his book, *The Last Years of the Church*,[1] and described it this way: "Buildings, annual budgets, twelve choirs, not including bell ringers, scouts, youth groups, women's circles, relocation problems, church parking lots (an entire book has recently been published on this alone . . .)." He later continues, "The churches have nothing to say because they are panting under the loads and burdens of housekeeping projects. We live in the biggest building-and-grounds, construction-and-shrub-trimming period of Christian history. We have stained more glass and hung more drapes and gilded more crosses and plated more chalices than any era of Christendom." He continues again to tell us, "This is not a special sin of Protestantism. Long ago our Catholic brethren, from bishop to parish priest, learned where the action is. Not the prayer book. The Bankbook. This is what it takes to build cathedrals, extend missions, et cetera . . . . " Poling's verdict is that these might be "the last years of the church" not because "the church is failing, but because it is too successful." Material success often leads to spiritual failure. This is "Poling's law of churchmanship," and to this millions of people outside of the churches say Amen.

Even the great liberal spokesperson the late Bishop James A.

Pike, gave his reasons to *Look* magazine (April 29, 1969) for "Why I'm Leaving the Church," stating. "Ours is the last major nation in which the Christian Church appeared to be strong and healthy, but finally, here, too, the standard-brand denominations have started 'down the slippery slope . . . '" He discusses a fast-growing "credibility gap" between the church's doctrines or teachings and the facts of modern science and then adds that there is also a "relevance gap." He stated, "Many of us know of scores of efforts to make the Church and its message 'more relevant,' but the increase in these efforts falls far short . . . "

We can go on and talk about the underground church and the great struggle to modernize ancient practices within the Roman Catholic Church, growing out of the fresh breeze of the Ecumenical Council and of the current backlash against the Americanization of the Church, or the Protestantization of Catholicism, as the opponents of change within the Catholic Church call it. Such books as *A Modern Priest Looks at His Outworn Church* make the best-seller list. All admit and point to certain weaknesses within the Roman Church which need to be rectified. The only question is whether the liberal proposals of the Second Vatican Council will do it, or whether the church should retreat into its ancient forms and traditions and wait for the current storms to pass. In this, it is precisely like mainline Protestantism

However, that the Roman Church made the effort is much to its credit, even though it too feels a backlash that may defeat the liberal elements within it. A decade earlier, for instance, it would have been inconceivable that the Vatican would have convened a five-day meeting on the culture of unbelief under a newly devised Vatican Secretariat for Nonbelievers. News reports stated it was attended by 4,000 persons in sessions at the Gregorian University in the spring of 1969. The Associated Press reported on those sessions, stating,

> Institutional religion is on the way out, a German expert on the sociology of religion told a symposium on atheism sponsored by the Vatican and the University of California.
>
> "I suggest we live in a period of transition in which a particular social form of religion, institutional specialization, is on the wane," Prof. Thomas Luckman, of the University of Frankfurt, said today.
>
> "This doesn't mean all the churches are going to be boarded up. Such institutions," Luckman said, "still will have some use if they can help individuals articulate their subjective beliefs.
>
> "One characteristic of the period of transition is that 'belief' in the traditional sense in which sociologists use the term is under-

going a radical transformation," Luckman said. "'Unbelief,' on the other hand, is about to disappear entirely as a social fact."

Luckman said that everyone has beliefs attached in some way to what he terms "the sacred cosmos" and that as institutional religion dissolves, the categories of "believer" and "nonbeliever" will merge.

"Two types of religion will result," Luckman continued:

"1. One individual will construct his own private system of ulti-mate values that will not fit into an already established church.

"2. Another individual, after a phase of doubt, will arrive at a system of ultimate values that can be expressed through an existing church."

The formidable bluestocking journal, *Manas, A Journal of Philosophy*, opened an editorial on formal religions with this sentence: "We seem to be in the midst of the disintegration of the institution of the church. Hardly a month goes by without some new disclosure, usually by a clergyman, reporting a decline." The *Manas* article goes on to recommend a natural religion in place of the formal, sterile religion of institutionalism.

We propose to show there is a religion in existence, with deep roots, and we invite your inspection. It is a religion that challenges the institution and attracts those who want to have a do-it-yourself religion, to "do your own thing," and to attract the anti-institu-tionalist in our midst.

Unitarians had a remarkable spokesman a century ago, who proposed a chart for a modern, liberal religious movement. Theodore Parker wrote,

> The church that is to lead this century will not be a church creeping on all fours, mewling and whining, its face turned down, its eyes turned back. It must be full of the brave, manly spirit of the day, keeping also the good of times past. There is a terrific energy in this age, for man was never so much developed, so much the master of himself before. Great truths, moral and political, have come to light . . . It demands, as never before, freedom for itself, usefulness in its institutions, truth in its teachings, and beauty in its deeds. Let a church have that freedom, that usefulness, truth and beauty and the energy of this age will be on its side. But the church which did for the fifth century, or the fifteenth, will not do for this. It must have our ideas, the smell of our ground, and have grown out of the religion in our soul. The freedom of America must be there before this energy will come; the wisdom of the nineteenth century, before its science will be on the churches' side.
>
> A church that believes only in past inspirations will appeal to old books as the standard of truth and source of light, will be

antiquarian in its habits, will call its children by the old names and war on the new age, not understanding the man-child born to rule the world. A church that believes in inspiration now will appeal to God; try things by reason and conscience; aim to surpass the old heroes; baptize its children with a new spirit, and, using the present age, will lead public opinion, not follow it.

Let us have a church that dares imitate the heroism of Jesus, seek inspiration as he sought it, judge the past as he; act on the present like him; pray as he prayed; work as he wrought; live as he lived. Let our doctrines and our forms fit the soul, as the limbs fit the body—growing out of it, growing with it. Let us have a church for the whole man: truth for the mind, good works for the hands, love for the heart; and for the soul, that aspiring after perfection, that unfaltering faith in God, which, like lightning in the clouds, shines brightest when elsewhere it is most dark.

But that was Theodore Parker a century ago. Has Unitarian Universalism lost its relevancy in the intervening century? We think not. In April, 1960, Joseph Poling wrote in *Pageant* magazine, "Perhaps more than any other denomination, Unitarian ministers are likely to speak out bluntly on controversial issues, firmly backed by their flock. In Lincoln's day, the Unitarian church was a militant leader of the antislavery movement. Today its churches—including the southern ones—open their doors to blacks and actively support integration.

"When Senator Joseph McCarthy was at his most influential, the Unitarian-controlled Beacon Press was the first publishing house to issue books attacking his practices as demagogic. Unitarians are active out of all proportion to their numbers in United Nations associations and in the World Federal Government movement. They do not hesitate to question what they deem to be religious folly—even if it means challenging the world's most popular evangelist, as A. Powell Davies did when he publicly asked Billy Graham to justify his assertion that 'Heaven is a 1,600-mile cube containing trees that produce a different kind of fruit each month.' Nor do they hesitate to oppose any movement, theological or political, which they feel threatens the freedom of the individual.

"Their lack of fear of controversy may stem from the fact that their church was born of disputation. The name 'Unitarian' was coined in the 16th century for certain Protestant dissenters from the doctrine of the Trinity. (Actually, Trinitarian doctrine became church orthodoxy only by a divided vote of the General Council of Constantinople some 375 years after the death of Christ.) Mi-

chael Servetus, who in 1533 was burned at the stake in John
Calvin's Geneva for his 'Unitarian heresy,' is generally considered
the founder of modern Unitarianism. His followers profited from
the first great edict of religious freedom, issued in 1568 by King
John Sigismund of Transylvania (Hungary). By 1600, there were
425 Unitarian churches in Transylvania.

"In England during the 17th century, men like the poet John
Milton, the philosopher John Locke, and the physicist Isaac Newton fostered the church's growth. As the 18th century grew to a
close, Joseph Priestly, a Unitarian minister and the discoverer of
oxygen, was forced to flee to the United States to escape the attack
of mobs protesting his liberalism. Encouraged by Benjamin Franklin, he established the first Unitarian church in this country at
Northumberland, Pennsylvania, in 1794. Soon after, Boston's
famed King's Chapel left the Anglican fold. And, in 1802, the
church founded by the Pilgrim Fathers, the First Parish in Plymouth, became Unitarian."

Thus, he clearly shows the relevancy of Unitarian Universalism to be both contemporary and in keeping with its historical
antecedents, as a religious fellowship which has not blunted its
driving power. Perhaps that is because, while dedicated to broth-
erhood and understanding, it has had the courage to continue
walking alone. Poling continued, "Although the denomination has
grown steadily, it is not a member of the National Council of
Churches of Christ. When the National Council was formed by
American Protestant churches at the turn of the century, the three
Unitarian delegates to the organization meeting in New York were
denied admission as heretics who would not recognize 'Jesus
Christ as Lord and Saviour.' The three 'heretics' turned away were
Massachusetts Governor John D. Long, Charles W. Eliot, president
of Harvard, and Dr. Edward Everett Hale, author of *The Man
without a Country* and then chaplain of the United States Senate.

"The Unitarians accept their maverick role with wry good
humor. Heresy, they say, is a relative charge, since, after all, the
Catholics regard all Protestants as heretics. As far as they are
concerned, there is no such thing as a heretic; just man, entitled
always to his own belief, imperfect but not inherently bad, capable
of rising by slow degrees to even higher planes. To aspire to
contribute to the ennoblement of his life is a goal, they feel, which
no name-calling can demean."

Those within the Unitarian Universalist movement may even
enjoy the name-calling, for we recognize and enjoy the role of
being heretics in a conventional sense, in being the mavericks of

the religious landscape. This is the challenge of liberal religion, which frees us from old stereotypes so that we can develop in freedom a modern religion that is increasingly naturalistic, humanistic, idealistic, and realistic. If you have ever doubted traditional faith; if you have ever wondered about ideas that others do not question; if you have ever felt revulsion at concepts of life and death that are so trite they become meaningless banalities of the religious life; if you have a tendency to reject the clichés of religious institutionalism, and been appalled by its sentimentality; if your mind refuses to accept nonscientific teachings, you may be a Unitarian Universalist without knowing it and on the road to religious liberalism. This volume is meant to help you explore whether you have that different quality of religious sensitivity that makes you a religious liberal. If you do, the following chapters will show that you are not alone, but a member of an increasing band of people who claim a heritage which has long existed as a minority in the culture of the West and now is coming into its own.

Note
[1]Doubleday, 1969, pp. 61, 69.

2

An Alternative Religion

Most people have a faith by which they live. Many have a church to which they belong, in which they would choose to educate their children, or where they would christen or dedicate them. They turn to this church for a marriage, or for a funeral, requiem, or burial service. The two—the faith one lives by and his church affiliation—are not necessarily the same, however. That faith may be nothing but a belief that tomorrow is worth experiencing. It could be merely a conviction that while life may be meaningless, one is curious enough to want to know what comes next.

This sense of faith was behind the imagery used by Ralph Waldo Emerson when he said: "The gods we worship write their names on our faces, be sure of that. And a man will worship something—have no doubt about that either." Emerson showed that worship of material things leads to ultimate selfishness, just as love of power leads to loss of mercy. We may think, he says, that we can hide this basic faith in things from others, but our actions reveal it. All people love something, just as all people have a faith by which they live. This love determines the true goal of worship.

We, too, need to find what it is we truly love and worship, what it is that determines our faith. Emerson calls us to the realization that worshipping is far more personal and much deeper than the formalized rituals of a closed church sanctuary. Worshipping is the identification and absorption into the things of personal merit and value. What is it that we, in turn, value the most? It is not the church we attend, the creeds we recite, or the hymns we sing. Religion should be the focus of worship, but for most it is not.

The kind of things a man loves helps determine the kind of person he is, wrote Dean John Murray Atwood of St. Lawrence University. This underlies the justification of religion and shows why its primary emphasis should be highly ethical. Yet too often faith is tied up with pale light, subdued music, and softly spoken words of comfort.

Thus Emerson, the nineteenth-century Unitarian preacher and lecturer, and John Murray Atwood, the twentieth-century Universalist preacher and educator, join forces to say that we are molded by what we worship, toward what we aspire, and become greater or smaller, depending upon our vision of the good life. In this sense, our worship is our culture.

To the religious liberal, worshipping—religion—becomes more than the Sunday morning practice. Religion includes, but is not limited to, Sunday morning worship. For instance, Henry T. Hodgkin wrote in his book, *Lay Religion*, "A man's religion is not the creed he professes, or the things he can postulate about God. It is the few simple and elementary convictions by the strength of which he lives." This is our first claim. Beautiful ideals, which are creeds, not deeds, are religious window dressing and are meaningless. The test of faith is life. Too often life is a long battle between the beliefs by which we live and the beliefs by which we would like to live, or by which we would like to be thought to live.

As we consider the nature of faith, we are led to the realization that the things we say we worship and the things our lives show we value may be quite different. A scientist works with facts and knowledge which must be proven at each point by experience, testing, verification, measurements, and retesting. The scientific method may be one's entire mind-set five or six days a week in the laboratory. On the seventh day, one may very well worship in a church where great assumptions are accepted on faith, where Divine Revelation and the authority of a council or scripture is taken as beyond human wisdom or examination. If one believes in one's work on weekdays and in church doctrines on Sunday one may recognize that faith and church are two different compartments of life.

Long ago in the Counter Reformation, at the close of the medieval and the beginning of the modern era, St. Thomas Aquinas offered the "two fold path" whereby faith is supreme in doctrinal matters and mind in secular affairs. The dichotomy of faith and thought has continued as an artificial boundary for Christians from that day on. It is an iron curtain of the mind, just flexible enough to be pushed one way or the other, depending on the pressures exerted. Some people seemingly can live by it, whereas others, confused or upset by the contradictions raised, give up organized faith and live as skeptics or nonreligious. On the other hand, others give up all reliance on knowledge and science and retreat into an anti-intellectual vacuum. Still others try to resolve the conflict and come to terms with it.

In doing so, they quite often have an alternative faith by which they live. The young lady who has typed many of the thoughts included here observed, even though she considers herself a good Episcopalian, "I don't really disagree with anything you say; I just don't find it necessary to leave my church even though I hold the same beliefs as you."

The late A. Powell Davies, a Unitarian preacher in Washington, D.C., once noted that this duplicity between faith and affiliation tended to be a general condition among many liberal-minded people, who were liberal in their religious outlook, but were not identified with the liberal religious movement. He sums up a position, which is held both within and without our movement. He wrote, "There are millions of Unitarians in America today, but not in Unitarian churches. There are millions of Unitarians who don't know that such a church exists. They do not know its history. They do not know its basis. They do not know its purposes. They do not know that they themselves are Unitarians." Writing from a slightly different perspective from my young friend, he is saying substantially the same thing: many agree with us whether they know it or not. Of course, the one speaks from inside the Unitarian Universalist movement and the other from outside it.

Protestants are not the only ones who feel this way. A Catholic author, whose book, *Christian Denominations*, bears the imprint of the Bishops of Fort Worth, Cleveland, and Toledo, summed up a section on Unitarianism by noting that Unitarians and Universalists numbered 100,000 in the early 1940s, "but there are, alas, millions of nominal Christians of their type."[1]

A Roman Catholic book, *Separated Brethren*, written in 1961, tells us that "Perhaps one Unitarian out of a hundred has actually affiliated with the Unitarian and Universalist churches. Certainly the combined membership of 170,000 for these two denominations hardly represents the number of Americans who hold rationalist and deistic positions."[2]

This is a saw that cuts both ways, of course. Many ministers in other churches and church members find it necessary to give increasing attention to the persons who hold an alternative religion rather than the faith of the fathers. One distressed adult, through a series of events, found herself slowly becoming involved in the affairs of a community church. In consequence, it seemed only natural that she yield to the gracious, howbeit persistent, urgings of its minister to become a communicant. The process seemed easy. She merely needed to attend a few evening sessions and then be welcomed with the other communicants on a designated Sunday morning. After attending the classes for several sessions, she reported telling the pastor that she could not go through with it because she did not believe the Creeds. "My dear lady," he responded, "we do not ask that you believe them, only that you memorize them." *Touché* for the clergyman, but this bit of brilliant repartee lost him a member. Undoubtedly there are sophisticates who would have responded, but, in this instance, the prospective neophyte was old-fashioned enough to believe that integrity is still part of the morality of churches. Her mouth could not say words that her heart could not affirm and her intellect accept. She had almost bypassed her alternative faith for social convenience and good company; but in a moment of truth, when alone after confirmation class, she confronted herself on her own Mount of Temptation and realized that her alternative faith must now become her primary faith for the sake of intellectual honesty.

This type of experience, more than any other, accounts for the fact that Unitarian Universalism in the post-war years (1949-1964) was the fastest-growing denomination in the United States and Canada. How else explain that a nonmissionary body grows more rapidly than the denominations that spend millions on both home and foreign mission programs? Here is a church that does not convert, but merely receives those who come to its doors seeking acceptance. It welcomes such, because most of its members have come out of other religions. They know what it is like to struggle alone with the fears and frustrations of being a nonconformist in an orthodox church that demands one's total acceptance of beliefs and that often glories in the knowledge that its beliefs are out of context with modern ideas.

We say this is happening because of a universal element in religion that is caught up and made important in Unitarian Universalism. Ralph Waldo Emerson, in his essay *The Preacher*, summed it up this way: "I see that sensible and conscientious men and women all over the world are of one religion." He goes on to say, "We are commanded at every moment and in every condition of life to do the duty of that moment and to abstain from doing the wrong." This is greater than all other commandments, he says. This point will be made over and over in presenting the liberal religious way of life: religion in its essence is simple and can be simply stated, but the theological complexities of the churches have made "pure religion and undefiled" impossible to grasp. To most it becomes not this straightforward "commandment," but begins with ten, goes on to the catechisms, confessions, creeds, doctrines, and dogmas, until the simple God and the religious purposes becomes lost amid a million words and abstractions. Religion is simple and elemental and involves a one-to-one relationship, the relationship of person to person, of oneself to one's conscience, and to universal relationships (usually summed up as one's relationship to God).

In this essay, Emerson sums up: "My inference is that there is a statement of religion possible which makes all scepticism absurd. Worship changes its forms from age to age, but the reality endures. We no longer recite the old creeds [remember, he began and ended his long career as a Unitarian minister—first at the Second Church in Boston and later at the Follen Church in East Lexington] but the heart remains as ever with its old human duties. Truth is simple and will not be antique; is ever present and insists on being of this age and of this moment. Speak the affirmative; emphasize your choice by ignoring all you reject, seeing that opinions are temporary, but convictions uniform and eternal."

We must, as Emerson points out, come through as individuals:

> Every human being has a choice between truth and repose. Take which you please, you cannot have both. Between these, as a pendulum, man oscillates. He in whom the love of repose predominates will accept the first creed, the first philosophy, the first political party he meets—most likely his father's. He gets rest, commodity and reputation; but he shuts the door on truth. He in whom the love of truth predominates will keep himself aloof from all moorings and afloat. He will abstain from dogmatism and recognize all the opposite negations between which, as walls, his being is swung. He submits to the inconvenience of suspense, and imperfect opinion, but he is a candidate for truth, as the other is not, and respects the highest law of being.

We say this is a fair statement of the choice between a religion into which one is born and one which must be found or, more likely, developed. There is a safe anchorage for a person willing to drift with the prearranged patterns of life around him, unthinking, unchoosing, uncritical. However, for the person of integrity there is a demand to make a personal decision and personal choice. In doing so, many find the need to go beyond the first creed, the first party, the first philosophy to a second and a third, always examining the alternative choices.

Unitarian Universalism is a religious liberalism precisely because at no point does it settle down into being a static faith, a building-block philosophy, but is a quest for values which each individual must develop. In this light, it has been said that a Unitarian Universalist church is not one where an individual comes to learn a faith, but rather to develop a faith of one's own. It may differ from that of the person sitting in the next pew, but they will hold in common something infinitely more precious than conformity: they will be completely honest with one another. Each will hold a faith clearly seen and intensely felt, a faith based on experience, not the handed-down clothing of others' theological vestments. It will not offer repose (although it can bring a great peace of mind), because it is based on the experience of a worshiper who has not stopped living. Faith will grow and change with new experiences. Hence, it will have the capacity to always be adequate. When William Ellery Channing, the aged man who in his youth had been the flaming leader of the Unitarian revolt from Calvinism, met an old colleague, he noted a new danger that the younger men in the pulpit were "making an orthodoxy of the liberalism of our youth." Already Dr. Channing had passed beyond the position of his youth, and he recognized that once liberalism became static and systematized, it, too, would become an orthodoxy, like all other religions. Liberal religion must not settle for repose, must not shut the door on new truths, must not rest, but rather must "submit to the inconvenience of suspense and imperfect opinion." Yesterday's insight is hindsight today. The bible of tomorrow has not been written, is not completed.

The temptation is strong to go on and say that Unitarian Universalism is everybody's alternative faith, but the facts are otherwise. It may be, but it may not be. Enthusiastic discoverers of this liberal faith often assume that everyone shares this initial fervor. Actually, while it is true that one may choose either a formal faith of church creed and liturgy or the alternative faith of what he lives, there are choices of alternatives. Some, for instance, as Emerson stated, choose greed and profits. Others choose Communism or Fascism. For some, nationalism is the alternative. Some choose a great cause: freedom, civil rights, women's rights, just as in the past they chose prohibition and abolition. A great cause can become a second religion; a selfish interest may; and, as Emerson suggested, repose may. There are many people, however, who want a faith that involves their expectations and idealisms; a faith that enhances their concerns for great causes by a meaningful philosophy that encourages individual action and thought, yet nevertheless makes sense. Some of these people, perhaps many more than we realize, find this new orientation toward making life meaningful in the Unitarian Universalist movement.

When one breaks free of old moorings, one turns to immediate activities that engross one and keep one from feeling useless, rootless, and hollow. Social, professional, business, and cultural activities on a dizzy round of frenzied living often break all sense of connection with a vital, cultural stream of life. Some people recoil by almost pitiably clinging to old religions and will not allow themselves to think about the cleavage between content and form. They go through the outward form knowing that it does not make sense to them; but, inasmuch as it does to someone, it might have meanings and uses they do not comprehend. The tragedy is that it is not a living faith for them—not a part of their lives.

Others, equally pitiable, cling to a person to give meaning to life, but inasmuch as people are growing, responding, and constantly changing, they have only an illusionary substitute for a faith. Many a family situation ends on the bitter rocks of lost illusion when one adult tries to make the other the center of meaning. People, however, must be individualities, with the rights to solitude, growth, and independence. No person can go through life forced to remain a constant element which holds together an otherwise floating life of a partner, sibling, parent, or offspring. Hence, people cannot permanently take the place of faith in an individual's life.

Nor can a cause. I have known people who went through the final period of life as lost souls, inasmuch as the cause to which they related no longer existed. For some in former days it was states rights, prohibition, or suffrage. They had never related their cause to a larger way of life, to a more inclusive philosophy enabling them to move on from one interest to another as part of a consistent social pattern. The cause had taken the place of old orientations beyond which they had once gone, but for each there had been a failure later on to develop a basis of a new faith that would reorient their lives for broader living.

Persons sometimes say to Unitarian Universalists, "Why is it that you make so much of great men and women in the past who represent your faith?" A possible excuse for pointing them out is because we believe that faith defines one's life, that the argument for our faith is the example of our lives. Those who have visited our churches or have written for literature to the Church of the Larger Fellowship of the Unitarian Universalist Association in Boston, know that Unitarian Universalists are proud of such men as the American Presidents John Adams, John Quincy Adams, Millard Fillmore, Thomas Jefferson and William Howard Taft. They honor the memory of the great writers—Longfellow, Lowell, Hawthorne, Whittier; they are proud of great women—Clara Barton, Mary Livermore, Dorothea Dix, Julia Ward, and Florence Nightingale. Great leaders in the mental health field, such as Dr. Brock Chisholm in Canada, former head of the World Health Organization of the United Nations; great surgeons, such as Dr. Paul Dudley White, noted heart specialist; and scientists such as Linus Pauling and Charles Steinmetz show the effect of faith on life. This is the justification for mentioning that such people are, or were, Unitarian Universalists, and it is very much to the point to note that they were and that their religion defined or redefined their lives. An article in the *New York Herald-Tribune* noted that "Unitarians have from the first exercised an influence out of all proportion to their numbers" (Nov. 6, 1946). In the publication *Factors in Eminence*, one reads, "A check of persons listed in *Who's Who in America* reveals that those holding Unitarian beliefs number twenty-eight times more than their proportion in the population." It then lists more than twenty eminent Americans who are regarded as Unitarian Universalists.

Unitarian Universalism is no sterile intellectual religion, in spite of efforts to so characterize it by unsympathetic observers. It moves people to notable action, and wherever Unitarian Universalist churches are meeting the challenge of faith those communities are uplifted and improved. The late Democratic Presidential candidate in 1960 and 1964, Adlai Stevenson, for many years a noted American leader, and Ambassador to the United Nations during the administrations of Presidents Kennedy and Johnson, speaking impromptu at a church gathering in Colorado, paid the following tribute to his fellow Unitarians: "I believe I can offer one important testimonial; and that is, that having spent the last twelve years in public life, I've become more and more conscious of the importance of Unitarian groups, Unitarian communities. I don't mean just our church services, just our worship, but Unitarian people—who appear in my life constantly. They're the sort of people who do the advance thinking, who are, for the most part, rocking the boat, who are cutting the furrows, who are ahead of the procession in contemporary thought in our country about our great social and political problems, as well as our theological discussion. This is the active agent in the body politic that is most necessary."

Another way to sum up the sense of urgency motivating Unitarian Universalists was that used at an annual assembly of the denomination when the venerable Dr. Curtis Reese, for many years the executive of our mid-continental offices in Chicago, spoke. Dr. Reese said, "This is not a time for liberals of the genteel tradition who are frightened in the presence of explosive issues that blast their world and shake the earth. It is not a time for liberals of the pious tradition who believe that all is right with the world and that all things work together for good. It is not a time for confused liberals who move simultaneously in all directions without arriving anywhere in particular.

"This is a time for liberals who believe that the only form of society worth building and perpetuating is one grounded in respect for the integrity of persons, committed to critical inquiry and devoted to abundant freedom."

There have been times when liberals have been of the "genteel tradition," timid and frightened, unable to take a stand or hold with resolute hands and feet to the rocky course of a hard voyage through life.

Gone are the days of the pious liberal who can affirm "God's in his heaven, all's right with the world!" With Browning's Pippa, this concept passed from the stage of decision long ago.

The confused liberal, rushing in all directions, a veritable Don Quixote dueling with windmills, merely added to the confusion that was so baffling.

Liberalism is no longer an "easy faith." Liberal religion makes its demands of its followers, and presents its challenges, so that today there is need for courage to be liberal.

It used to be said that it was easy to be a liberal. This undoubtedly meant different things to different people. To some it meant they could join a church without doing a lot of memorizing. To them it was bad enough memorizing all the Bible verses required of certain lodges without having to do so to join a church as well! Some might have thought there were too many important demands on the mind without cluttering it up with such nonsense as memorizing creeds and catechisms.

In comparison it might seem, superficially, to be easier to be a liberal, and short-circuit all these requirements.

But once the average church member has gone through the steps of joining the church the religious requirements are over. One might be required to do certain minimal things, such as observe the Sabbath, give an hour a week to services, observe Holy Days of obligation, but the creative and compelling requirement of religion will have come to a climax. From this point it tapers off, and creativity, challenge, and growth are no longer required.

When the average church member in America puts on a hat once a week and starts for the door, he or she is in the process of performing a major requirement as a member of a church. The strength, the prestige, the status of the church are entirely dependent and determined by this one activity of the week and this one requirement.

For the religious liberal, this is simply not so. Going to church, taking down one's hat, and starting for the door is not the means of fulfilling religious vows, but the indication that a process is starting that cannot be fulfilled in one hour, one week, or one year. It is a process which will require every hour of every day for the rest of one's life. There will never be an hour or a day or a month or a year in which religious responsibility can be avoided.

When a religious liberal joins a Unitarian Universalist church, a challenge has been accepted to make life religious in the broadest sense of the word. One says, "There are no compartments to life in which religion can be shut off. There is no cubby-hole where I can any longer keep religion and only let it out for occasional airing."

In joining the Unitarian Universalist Church, we have recognized that there are no Holy books, but that all ideas that are creative and inspiring and lead to a better life are religious. We have accepted the proposition that instead of Holy Days and Sabbaths, all days are holy in that every day is the day and the time for the fulfillment of religion.

We have agreed that all are sacred, rather than that a few are saints, and all life is inviolate. The primacy of the individual raises all to the divine and enhances the dignity and respect that in former times was reserved for a few elect and chosen saints and prophets. In like manner, we have come to the acceptance of the priesthood of all persons of goodwill and of each as his or her own priest, so that the minister is a guide and a helper rather than a member of a class divinely set aside for the sacred functions. The minister has become a friend and counselor rather than a pastor, priest, and confessor.

The religious liberal has abolished the separations between the sacred and the profane, the secular and temporal. Life is a unity, and, in this sense, the name Unitarian Universalist has proper meaning: it is the emphasis on the unitary nature of life and religion, which is a universalizing process. If life is a unity, then God is likewise. Then no number of attributes or persons can subdivide and violate that unitary principle. But the world's superficial emphasis fails to grasp the fundamental reality of the Unitarian Universalist position that the prime sense of oneness of life makes religion inseparable from life. From this premise come the basic religious liberal concepts of the dignity of human beings, of the reliance upon reason, and of a faith grounded in the natural rather than the supernatural. It will be a faith that exposes the fallacy of reliance upon external props so that there is no need for mediators or atonement. One has and should have a one-to-one relationship to life and the divine.

Unitarian Universalism challenges its adherents with the courage to be liberal. It means that there are, therefore, no props by which one can be supported in this religion. There is no crutch on which one may lean. A religious liberal must stand in all nakedness before one's God and with only one's own power confront life. Nevertheless, we find that as individuals we are more than sufficient. Ours is a creed we have not memorized only to forget. Ours is a faith that cannot be taken from us; nor can it be lost. We discover that sufficient unto the needs of the soul are the powers of the soul and that a free religion is the greatest power in all the world for confronting the issues, the pitfalls, the crises of life.

Consequently, we can withstand conformity without defeat. We can be free to be detached from the things of this world and the things of the institutional world in order to hold fast our integrity in the face of the grave and great challenges of life.

This liberal religion, however, becomes easy in a different way. As we accept its challenges, it becomes easy to fulfill. Gov. William Bradford, of the Pilgrim founders, wrote in his journal of the awful rigors of the first winter and then, summarizing the losses, the fears, the weakness of the group, he added, "But we had through it all an answerable courage." The religious liberal finds an answerable courage. Courage is the indispensable substance of religious liberalism. It makes "the spirit live" when "the word killeth." It takes courage not to settle for a religion "once for all delivered to the Saints." It requires the courage to be unwilling to accept the proposition that God, having spoken at some time remote in antiquity, is now aloof and distant, as though one were dead, as though religion were merely an antiquarian interest. The religious liberal accepts the proposition and responds to the challenge that religion is a universal expression of the human spirit which everywhere seeks to break forth in new, fresh expressions. It cannot be stifled by institutionalism, conformity, complacency, blindness, and fear of a new reorientation of values. The religious liberal has the courage to stand for the new, the fresh expression, to listen to the oracle in one's own breast, and to express the religion of one's own heart and mind.

There is, thus, the challenge to exalt religion as a living force, not merely a repetition of times past. Religion becomes an uplifting experience which brings freedom, new dignity, new energy, and power to life. Religion makes possible fuller, greater, more creative, and imaginative lives. It raises us to greater heights, so that in the words of Isaiah we "can rise up on wings as eagles, run and not be weary, walk and faint not."

There is the challenge for more creative art forms, for new venturing in the esthetic realms, for the creation of a new liturgy. Such a new faith will be expressed in new hymns, tunes, words, art, and architecture.

The real fulfillment of liberal religion comes as we respond to the challenges it presents with moral courage to measure up to the demands of faith. It comes with the intellectual courage to think clearly in terms of the ends and means of life and the dedication and commitment to fulfill those ends. It comes as social courage to fulfill hopefully our roles in the arena of everyday living, to measure up with strength, value, and integrity in our relationships as we apply ethics and morality to daily life.

If we lack the courage to carry out our faith it withers. "Without vision the people perish" wrote the ancient Old Testament writer. Without the courage to be liberal, Unitarian Universalism will perish. Courage can prove that we are sincere in what we profess to stand for. Through social action Unitarian Universalism is often assessed by the public. For we say that only in terms of moral action can a religious liberal show that religion counts. In terms of the intellectual courage to speak up, to stand up, for the truth as one sees it, one can show the ideas for which we stand. Unitarian Universalism has grown and prospered in human history when it bore witness through courage to a religion that is expressed in action. If it becomes stagnant, or where it does not grow, it is because it lacks that example of answerable courage. The same holds for individuals. Only by answerable courage can we be liberal. Horace Traubel, that great newspaper crusader of the end of the nineteenth century knew this well when he penned his "Chant Communal": "What can I do? I can talk out when others are silent. I can say man when others say money. I can stay up when others are alseep. I can keep on working when others have stopped to play. I can give life big meanings when others give life little meanings. I can say love when others say hate. I can say every man when others say one man. I can try events by a hard test when others try it by an easy test.

"What can I do? I can give myself to life when others refuse themselves to life."

Notes

[1]Pp. 207, 210, Rev. Virgilius H. Krull, C.PP.S, *Christian Denominations*, 1943, Carthagena, Ohio: The Messenger Press.

[2]William J. Whalen, *Separated Brethren*, 1961, N.Y., The Bruce Publishing Co., as serialized in *The Pilot*, Boston Archdiocese, Mass., April 8, 1961, page 15.

3
The Need for A Contemporary Religion

"Universalism: the biggest word in the language!" exclaimed Elizabeth Barrett Browning upon seeing a Universalist tract for the first time. That was in London. In Lynn, Massachusetts, the formidable Dr. James M. Pullman was challenged: "You Universalists have squatted on the biggest word in the English language. Now the world is beginning to want that word, and you Universalists must either improve the property or move off the premises."

In Monticello, Virginia, more than a half-century earlier, Thomas Jefferson wrote to James Smith, of Ohio, on December 8, 1822, "I confidently expect that the present generation will see Unitarianism become the general religion of the United States." Earlier, Dr. William Wilberforce, writing in England in 1797, had hurled the thundering invective, "Unitarianism is the halfway house to infidelity."

At different times and in various places a lively and vigorous discussion pro and con the liberal religious movement was taking place in the Western world. Many great figures of the Enlightenment expressed Unitarian ideas, and Locke and Newton (as were their predecessors, Copernicus and Erasmus) were all suspect. (See Robertson's *Short History of Free Thought*.) John Murray, the founder of the American Universalist movement, was publicly attacked as a Deist; and the books of his teacher and spiritual counselor, John Relly, were destroyed. Fortunately a copy of his major book, *Union*, made its way to the old fishing town of Gloucester, Massachusetts. Thus Relly's views were transplanted to these shores.

This message, which was the seed of modern Unitarian Universalism, has had a long and honored history, albeit a stormy and tempestuous one, whose story is seldom told. Consequently, once they discover it, most people are surprised to learn that Unitarian Universalism is deeply rooted in Western culture. Yet here is the faith of members of the Pilgrim band at Plymouth;[1] of Ethan Allen,[2] whose Green Mountain Boys wrote an epic of human courage; of Captain John Parker who drew the line on Lexington Common where his Minute Men assembled to face the redcoats in 1775.[3] It was the faith of three of the first six Presidents of the United States—Jefferson, Adams and John Quincy Adams. Professor J. Franklin Jameson, respected for his persistent objectivity in reporting historic developments, writes in his book, *The American Revolution Considered as a Social Movement*,[4] that he is "not competent to discuss at length the influence of the Revolution upon theological thought in the United States. But," he adds, "I will, in mere passing mention, call attention to the fact that, of the religious bodies which in this period were growing in numbers and zeal, four (that is to say all but one) were anti-Calvinist— namely the Methodists, the Universalists, the Unitarians, and the Freewill Baptists. This is not without its significance." Historians recognize that Unitarianism and Universalism were vital, growing forces at the time of the American Revolution.

Our concern here is with the contemporary nature of a modern faith with deep roots. What is the essence of this modern faith? In 1961, a new denomination, the Unitarian Universalist Association, came into being, uniting the Unitarian and Universalist heritages into a single ongoing stream. Some may laugh at our clumsy name but so far we haven't found anything more honest or descriptive.

Unitarian Universalists accept the universe, the natural world, and mortal life as a major arena of living. Their faith proclaims that the basic concern of religion is human existence on earth rather than in an afterlife. It focuses on the irrepressible conflicts of the mid-twentieth century just as our forebears dealt with the controversial issues of their times.

Its interests are the moral and ethical issues of living and the requirements for conduct these issues inspire. It has tended to seek our religious messages and inspiration from texts that emphasize, "Be ye doers of the word, and not hearers only." It is inspired and impressed by "deeds not creeds."

Unitarian Universalism believes in "salvation by character," that is, we are capable of achieving more ideal lives as the result of our own efforts to strengthen and sensitize ourselves. It does not rely on some supernatural intervention. It believes in the supreme worth of every human personality, in the individual man and woman as the purpose and the instrument of the struggle for a better society.

This modern faith asserts the goodness of all; it sees each as the child of God or, as many of us would say, as the child of the universe. Humanity stands high on the evolutionary ladder, with great potential for further growth, and, theologically speaking, even now possessing evidence of the divine and at best being just "a little lower than the angels." The moral struggle lies within each person to control and win and is not a responsibility that one can scuff off or pass over by pretensions of unworthiness, guilt, or sin. There is no such passive element in our religion. Edwin Markham, a poet who discovered for himself the Universalist church and frequently attended its services in New York and Brooklyn, wrote:

> We men of earth have here the stuff of paradise.
> We have enough.
> We need no other stones to build the stairs on to the Unfulfilled,
> No other ivory for the doors, no other marble for the floors,
> No other cedar for the beam and dome of man's immortal dream.
> Here on the common human way is all the stuff to build a
>   heaven.
> Ours the stuff to build eternity in time.

The complex structure we call religion is really not one system, but a number of categories, each with its own structure. Thus, we need to clarify some basic meanings to understand what we mean in using different terms, which are not synonymous, but are each distinctive. Such terms as theology, ethics, philosophy, and philosophy of life need clarification before we undertake our exploration into the nature of contemporary religion. Brief explanations follow.

A person's way of life, or philosophy of life is important. While there are people without a creed, as Emerson and Atwood said, there is no one without a philosophy of life.

A theology is a systematic organization of the concepts or the doctrines which one holds as expressing his religion. Many thoughtful people do not have a theology. Religions can exist without theology.

A system of ethics is the organized principles of human conduct by which an individual can determine what course of action he should follow and which may at the same time enable him to make such judgments as are necessary of the actions of others. One can have ethics without conventional religion.

A philosophy is the system of knowledge by which the principles one lives by can be explained and organized.

A philosophy of life, on the other hand, is the working principles by which one does live. Hence, it is the way of life, the way one does live.

Our topic is the liberal religious way of life as represented in the Unitarian Universalist movement. It must be pointed out that, while what we say applies to Unitarian Universalism, it has a wider application.

Unitarian Universalism offers the individual the opportunity to find the focus of attention needed in his life as he moves away from the formalities of structural and theoretical expressions of religion to a personal way of living. There is more fluidity to life than can be allowed by doctrines, and this flexibility is the hope for religious fulfillment, indeed, for personal fulfillment.

One of the quandaries of modern life has been that the individual needs to find the elements of meaning and fulfillment, but lives in a society which minimizes the person so much that one loses oneself in an external world. T. S. Eliot was an authentic voice which protested this loss of individual meaningfulness. This is suggested in his lines,

> We are the hollow men
> We are the stuffed men
> Leaning together
> Headpiece filled with straw. Alas!

They somehow sum up the frustration and protest of people who lack a life of substance in these times, when it is difficult to achieve personal value and meaning. There is an urgency which is significant as, through the experiences arising out of the stress and tension of existence, we create the content which enriches individual living. Unitarian Universalism—any liberal religion—seeks to help the individual become something more.

The orthodox religious way of life is also aimed at helping its followers to bring meaning into life and to escape the verdict of hollowness. Our response in this regard is that there are people to whom orthodoxy can never become the vital substance of contemporary living. We say that truth once found adequate in bygone ages may have served those eras admirably, but in our day and age we must find truths which make us free, can enmesh our lives, pick us up, reorient us, and set us down pointed in a direction in which the view is certain and the course clear.

Our orthodox friends wear what Thomas Carlyle called "Hebrew old clothes." These are the external religious props of life. Often such people call the religious liberal's worship service the "Sunday edition of the *Ladies' Home Journal*." They say, "What you call religion may be ethical, but it is not spiritual; it may be good mental health, but it is poor gospel truth; it might be psychiatry, but it is not theology. It sounds like sociology, but it is not spirituality."

They are surprised if we do not think it too important to press the argument. Indeed, we find a satisfaction in the close approximation of our religious concepts with related fields of endeavor, inasmuch as we believe that religion should not be separated from the world of practical affairs, nor from the insights of the intellectual disciplines.

The religious liberal, whether or not he or she can convince others of it, is aware, however, that this philosophy of life is religious, although it may not be theology.

The Rev. Harry Meserve suggested that certain aspects link in common the unique position which Unitarian Universalists hold, and I quote them because I think they apply to all religious liberals: (1) religion is understandable in terms of human experience; (2) religion makes its impact in ethical terms on society; (3) in freedom the rationale of religious liberalism may be discerned; (4) religion is a universal experience, rather than one limited to a segment of the human race for either cultural or ideological reasons; (5) Jesus of Nazareth stands out in our minds because he rightly belongs in the class of the great saviors of mankind; and (6) religious fellowship is a means of helping us mutually deepen and strengthen our own lives and those of our companions of the way.

Does Unitarian Universalism work? Can it accomplish these ends? Jeannette Hopkins has done a wonderful service in her newswoman's reports which are presented in *Fourteen Journeys*, published some years ago, describing the reactions of new members to what the liberal church has meant in their lives. There was, for instance, the printer, who characterized himself a rebel, but who after joining with Unitarians learned to say, "I don't hate capitalists any more." He said, "I had no religion really, until I was fifty years old. But now I do not think religion is hokum."

The entire point of the Unitarian Universalist church, he pointed out, was that it did not require belief in something he couldn't believe. "They let me come and give what I could."

Then there was the Midwestern lawyer, who broadened the vistas of his narrow life so that he could say, "This church has also given me an incentive to do things I have always known I should do. I had bitter prejudices toward anyone who was different from me—Catholics, Jews, Negroes, foreigners . . . I feel friendly now, and I believe in racial equality." The universalism of his religion is inclusive.

There also was the school supervisor who called herself "a religious renegade" who discovered: "Prayer is more a way of clarifying your own feelings than anything else—gathering strength to abide by your ideals . . . I had rejected orthodox religion without putting anything else in its place. I was afraid of getting false answers . . . But I feel a need now to understand why I'm here . . . It's not enough to be against something . . . The church, the simplicity and beauty of the service, give me a sense of serenity. I go early on Sunday to collect my thoughts."

Or, there was the mother and musician from Vassar College: "This church has helped me to be less inflexible than I used to be, toward myself and to other people . . . I think I'm easier to live with now; I'm growing into quite a different person."

And she added: "I'm glad in a way that I didn't find the Unitarian church any earlier. I don't think I had developed my liberalism and tolerance enough. But now, Unitarianism gives me something real. I can live and die by it."

Is Unitarian Universalism as a way of life workable? Indeed it is. Fourteen case histories collected by Jeannette Hopkins in a single church could be repeated in almost any of our churches. Ours is so often a church of "come-outers" who have made their own religious journeys to religious liberalism.

One should bear in mind that the whole point of our church is not to build up an organization, but to help people escape the nightmare of being hollow men and women; to help people make their own lives bearable and meaningful, so that they are worthwhile to have around as well as good company for themselves.

One good example of this was the sense of religious commitment with which the eminent writer, Pierre Van Paassen wrote, "My joining the Unitarians in this day of grave historical crisis is an act of Christian affirmation, an act of faith in the possibility to sensitize the conscience of America through the Unitarian spirit and to humanize the social order, before the combined forces of clerical and political reaction gain the upper hand and turn this 'land of the Pilgrims' pride' into a moral leper colony."

Great social concern and cultural crisis drive many to our churches and fellowships. Others come for ethical, moral, intellectual, and spiritual hunger and needs not otherwise met. Emanuel Angelow wrote a few years ago in *The Universalist Leader*, "Although I learned of the Universalist religion by accident, it was no accident that made me a Universalist, for I found this religion and approach to life identical to mine. Like many other Americans I believe that if there is any authority in the world it resides in the mind of each individual person. Our institutions, religious or governmental, derive their authority ultimately from the individual . . . The Universalist church upholds and nourishes my conviction that man has the ability to solve the problems of the world through the free and unrestricted use of intelligence."

Roy Litton, when a member and officer of our Universalist church in Eldorado, Ohio, criticizing the religious scene in America, noted, "This new streamlined version of orthodoxy, this hot water bottle variety of faith, offers us a synthetized, vitaminized, capsulized religion ready-made, and effortless to consume . . . Salvation made easy? No! Liberal religion (on the other hand) is the most difficult in the world to live up to. Its aims are of the highest order, its demands the most exacting." He goes on to say that liberal religion is self-rewarding. Again and again Unitarian Universalists find their church and faith satisfying.

Is religious liberalism important for the contemporary mind? We think it is. How do people relate to the changes and rootlessness of so much of modern life? Many retreat into the past. Many flounder in uncertainty. Some become purposeless and look upon life as meaningless. Some live for the moment and in the existence of life find their total involvement. Thus Existentialism has been a natural descriptive term for much of the life-experiences during recent decades. Perhaps a better and more expressive term may be borrowed from contemporary merchandising practices which seem to fit the modern temper. "Fast foods" may not be here to stay, but in all probability they will be around for many years, as people queue up for quick burgers, pizza or fritos, and live on instant foods and prepackaged frozen meals. In spite of the loss of nutritional substance, the instant food and quick fix has become for countless multitudes the modern standard. Perhaps it is the demanding scheduling of the day, or the effort to eliminate the pressures of decision-making in personal living in a world where major decisions are seldom required by individuals.

In such an age of stress, we have seen wars, revolts, revolutions, national obliteration, and cruelty beyond comprehension. There have been bloodshed, torture, and death. We have experienced one war of nerves after another. We have seen science saddled by militarism and tyranny and the vaster knowledge of the twentieth century used for greater destruction and oppression. We have passed through a period where our lives echoed the words of Matthew Arnold: "We are living between two worlds, the one dead and the other powerless to be born." Suddenly, with satellites, rockets, and space ships, we know a new day is being born for which we are ill prepared. We have survived earlier periods of concern over flying saucers and the dread of communists; we recall the period of loyalty oaths and the congressional informer. We have faced the astronauts landing on the moon and the moral decay of modern life.

Every age and every day is to some degree an age in transition: sometimes rapid, sometimes slow. It is an illusion that in the past there were days of stability. It is the nature of life that it is changing. A definition of history implies movement and change. Progress and regress have been the lot of mankind. Today, however, we are more conscious of this, because we are more in touch with what happens in distant quarters of the world and are more involved in the happenings in remote areas. As a result, we take these events seriously, for we know how they can affect our lives.

Jesus of Nazareth suggested long ago a recognition of change: "Heaven and earth will pass away, but my words shall never pass away," seemingly suggesting a permanence to his teaching. But he also suggested that there are both permanent and transient values; the transient—the house built on sand—being those which will pass and the permanent or nontransitional—the house built on rock—being the continual values which are adaptable and which grow without withering.

Those who march in his shadow, and carry a symbol in his name are loudly heard proclaiming that the permanent values are theirs. "The old-time religion," the "enduring work," the "Rock of Ages" they chant over and over, as they proclaim the never-changing revelation, maintaining that they have stopped the clock of the ages and hold the values and truths which alone are meaningful in this time or in any time.

We hear their cry: "The absolutes of religion, the unchanging standards, the eternal values are defied by the world, but they alone are sufficient; they alone are true; they alone can save the world." They chant: "The church can restore them; the old values are needed today; the old faith is still the best hope; forsake materialism, renounce naturalism; ignore science; trust revelation; turn to Holy Writ; accept! believe!" This we see to be the challenge of the revival of orthodoxy in our day.

In the conflicting times in which we live, many people hear these cries and are confounded by a choice between a religion which rejects the ideas of the modern day, even while using its techniques, devices, and technical wonders, or of becoming children of the new day at the sacrifice of their religious heritage and values.

This is one of the most tragic choices with which people are confronted. It is tragic because so many people make the choice unaware that these two alternatives are not the only possible solutions to the dilemma of the modern mind.

The changing status of faith indicates that there has always been a choice between an older religion and a newer. There has been a continual struggle. That this has happened is obvious because there is no question that primitive worship was later displaced by the beginnings of priesthood and of ethical religion. The older religion of the Old Testament had engrafted upon it a New Testament; and the mystery cults of the Greco-Roman world, the religions of Mithras and Osiris, were replaced by Christianity. That the religion of the catacombs was different from the religion adopted by Constantine for the Roman Empire is documented by historians. That the religion of the Medieval period was not that of the Roman period is accepted by historians, although church doctrines may claim otherwise. Few of us feel that the religion and faith of our day is unchanged from that of the Dark Ages. That Julian Huxley touched a vital nerve in proposing a continued evolution of religion from supernaturalism to naturalism[5] is seen in the many comments to the contrary. The ancient dies hard, but will die.

There has always been an old-time religion that has had to be displaced in every new and creative age.

Socrates, at the time of the decline of the Athenian republic, sought to direct men's minds to the newer and emerging values which had to be recognized if permanency and social salvation were to be possible. In attempting to bring men's minds to bear on newer values, he gave the appearance of warring on the old ideas and, thereby, fell into disrepute. He became feared as the enemy of the older concepts of truth and was tried, convicted, and sentenced to death for his newer viewpoint. All history pays tribute to the fact that he was right and that the old order could not be saved by destroying those who proclaimed its inadequacies.

In similar manner, Jesus observed, according to the Gospel of St. John: "Ye shall know the truth and the truth shall set you free." He, too, was living in a day when people were searching for the values which would make meaningful a disintegrating culture and aid in its revitalization. What happened is a matter of record, for the Judaic and Roman culture did disintegrate. The Roman attitude was well expressed by Pilate's disdainful query, "What is Truth?"

As we face the days before us we are heartened that people have spoken out in behalf of the progress of truth. Notable and significant leaders have given a new appraisal to age-old questions, forcing fresh insights on religion. Thus the evolution of ideas may lead the way to the evolution of religious systems and, hence, institutions before the sands of time have run down.

We think of Sir Julian Huxley speaking out on behalf of the new naturalism in religion which will replace the older supernaturalism; of the educators and authors who have pointed out how, more than a hundred years after Darwin, older religious systems continue to impede the systematic and ordered presentation of the facts of the biological and natural sciences. We are aware of the sudden discovery that the luxury of the old religious bias against birth control is now a dangerous doctrine which with the growth in world populatin will lead to the destruction of civilization itself. Old sentimentalities, old dogmas, ancient doctrines, must and will be reevaluated in the light of the modern need. As long as the Christian civilization had no strong competitors in the struggle for world power, it seemed an easy and quaint luxury to assume that our old religious mores could be digested, like the carbohydrates, along with the proteins. But with the great advances of Soviet science, of Asiatic economic nationalism, of the regained self-esteem of the African peoples—in a time of the coming-of-age of the non-Christian world—we must move into a cultural orbit that reconsiders its religious heritage. Such great philosophical historians as Sir Arnold Toynbee, once so certain that Christianity was the highest evolution of civilization, began writing about our movement into a "post-Christian era."

This forward movement of society has been recently accelerated by many powerful and vocal impetuses. The organized religious liberal, the Unitarian Universalist, may well rejoice, for what is being emphasized is precisely the position which the Unitarian Universalist has taken for quite some time.

Of all the religions of the Western world, few are so well prepared for the coming new transitional age in religion as Unitarian Universalism. Whatever hope there exists for liberal religious growth lies in this fact, but what is more important is that the hope for our society lies here also. Liberal religion is already existent as a bridge between the old and the new. The saving power of the ancient world was that in the days of the Forty Tyrants there were Socrates and his pupil Plato, and, in turn, his pupil Aristotle. In the days of the congealment of the Roman autocracy there was Jesus of Nazareth to give new direction and liberation to the insights of the Hebrew tradition so that it could suddenly speak to a non-Jewish world.

A transitional society is successful only where there are elements that can relate to both the past and the future. In our day, the religion of Unitarian Universalism relates not only to the Christian heritage and to the other great religious traditions, but to the condition of society, which is being reshaped by science and technology.

In *Educating Our Daughters*, Lynn White, Jr., wrote, "Religion is not, as many seem to think, a way of handling the unknown and irrational which becomes obsolete as things become rational and known; it is adjustment to all the facts, rational or irrational by human standards, known, unknown, and perhaps unknowable. That so many turn to religion in time of trouble and sorrow merely shows that most of us are lazy.

"When our lives are running in smooth grooves we neglect the fundamental problems of meaning and purpose which seem so vivid when we have been jolted."

This is the first great understanding: religion is the adjustment of all the facts and is the relating of facts to each other. Religion does not, as such, deal with superstition. It has appeared to do so, and at times in the remote past people turned to magic, myth, or superstition as seemingly necessary to clarify the relationship of facts. The modern mind should have left this caveman-mind type of thinking back with the weapons of the Bronze Age, but, alas, it had often lingered on.

Lynn White wrote of the turning to religion when one is in sorrow or trouble. The late Dean Skinner, of Tufts University, used to say that in searching for a meaningful religion, "We are concerned with discovering stable foundations for a life that cannot be shaken either by inner stress or outer disaster."

The task of the church is not in finding an armor by which

we are shielded from life, but rather the inner mechanism, the will, spirit, and material by which, in a world of both inner stress and outer disaster, we can stand up calmly and serenely to life. Just as a sailor may walk a relatively straight line on a tossing ship, so we must have as our sea legs an inner equilibrium. Only then can the harassments of life, its tensions, turmoils, and stresses, be managed.

The quest for the values that make this life possible is never ended. Only for many people it may be temporarily halted, as, in a mesmeric trance, they hypnotize themselves into thinking that all their burdens, now cast upon the old-time religion or the Book or the true church, have been lifted from them and they have been redeemed. This, alas, is only a process of self-delusion, and it will end either in frustration or in a loss of reality.

For the religious liberal, for those with a free mind, the quest must be pushed on to examine, to explore, to arrive, and to start out again on the journey to create a livable faith, meeting the many conditions and evolving opportunities of life. Truly, in this sense, we understand the meaning of Jesus that "in my father's house are many mansions." The many aspects of life call for many responses, and there is no static concept that will work for the creative person. We must push on.

But we find the support and help we need in the strength, the vision, and the insights of personal religion. As Dr. Robert Killam put it: "Increasing numbers of men and women are finding that they are able to stand upon their own feet, without external religious authority, who are willing to make the sacrifices that must be made when we leave the religion of our childhood. They must be armed with unusual equipment—doubt and scepticism for theologies, scorn for the empty forms and ritual of religion, respect for their own reason, hatred for every form of injustice and oppression, abhorrence for falsehood wherever they find it (even in established and respectable religions), and a real love of truth.

"In their achievement of a free faith and in the fulfilling of its inescapable responsibilities they will develop their own religious philosophy, and they will work out their own salvation. They will be doing it the hard way, the only way that lies open to those who would be free."

Dr. A. Powell Davies, who for many years was a leading exponent of liberal religion, clearly presented the difficulty of understanding Unitarian Universalism. He wrote that no one can say that our religion does not contain elements of agreement, noting these distinctive clarifications: "Instead of creed, it agrees to follow the living truth and sets its people free to do so.

"Instead of ritual pieties, it asks devotions to the deeds that make the world more righteous and its people just.

"It separates itself from no believers, Christian or otherwise, except as they deny its claim to freedom.

"It asks no wide dominion for its institutions, only a liberty of access for its faith.

"It trusts that, in the years before us, Unitarian freedom will be claimed in all denominations, all communions, and meanwhile, it must humbly do its best to lead the way."

He held it was a truly universal religious experience, encompassing the best of all times and places. Another famous Unitarian Universalist—the late Adlai Stevenson, summarized it this way: "I think that one of our most important tasks is to convince ourselves and others that there is nothing to fear in difference; that difference, in fact, is one of the healthiest and most invigorating of human characteristics without which life would become meaningless. Here lies the power of the liberal way: not in making the whole world Unitarian, but in helping ourselves and others to see some of the possibilities inherent in viewpoints other than one's own; in encouraging the free interchange of ideas; in welcoming fresh approaches to the problems of life; in urging the fullest, most vigorous use of critical self-examination." In such thoughtful expressions, we see the importance of a fresh, contemporary religious outlook. Not only for ourselves, but for all others we call for the courage and freedom to create a modern faith for the modern mind. This is Unitarian Universalism at its best.

Notes

[1] See Marshall, *Church of the Pilgrim Fathers*, Beacon Press, 1950.
[2] See Ernest Cassara, *Hosea Ballou: Challenge to Orthodoxy*, Beacon Press, 1961.
[3] See Earl Morse Wilbur, Vol. II, *History of Unitarianism*, Harvard University Press, 1952; or Wilbur, *Our Unitarian Heritage*, Beacon Press, 1925.
[4] Published in 1926 jointly by Princeton and Oxford Universities, and later reissued by Beacon Press.
[5] Julian Huxley, *Religion Without Revelation*, Harper & Row, 1955.

4

The Religious Liberal Faces Life

A person's religion is not measured by the fervor of one's Sunday devotions, one's frequency at church meetings, or one's pious expressions of faith. A genuine test of faith is how a person stands up in the face of some great grief, some unexpected tragedy, some harrowing experience, or some upsetting crisis. The most devout often stumble, while the presumed backslider measures up. During the tense years of World War II some chaplains reported that religious faith was not measured by chapel attendance so much as by inner fortitude.

Too often the person whose faith relies on the dim religious light of a sanctuary or the soft tones of an organ gently soothing the harried emotions finds it is far removed from the actualities of the highways and byways, the dark street corners, the chill mortuary, or aseptic hospital bed. Often frenzied and harried parents, facing the turbulence of adolescent strivings find this faith inadequate as they struggle with these pressures. The modern adult at home and in business too often finds that the constant demands of "decisions, decisions, decisions" wear down the resistance, so that one loses all sense of perspective, relationship, and serenity, thus acting impulsively without regard to values or primary concerns.

Religious liberalism can be a help. Here is a faith that is not external, but internal. The Unitarian Universalist church makes no other offer than this: to help a person develop the faith that is within. Do not come to a Unitarian Universalist church to find a religion, to learn beliefs, or to be given a faith. Come only when you reach the point where all external faiths are rejected and you are ready to begin with the bedrock of your own being, experience, and character to construct the faith that is meaningful to you. There are two Micahs in the Old Testament, and the religious person must make a choice between them.

The first appears in the charismatic period of the Judges, and his story is recorded in the seventeenth and eighteenth chapters of the book of that name. He enters recorded history having made restitution for 1,100 shekels previously stolen from his own mother, thereby ingratiating himself with her, so that she turns the fortune over to him to have made graven images, molten images, an ephod, teraphim, and other images of divinity cast in precious metal and set with jewels. He thereupon builds a house for his gods and consecrates for himself a priest. In short order Micah has his private chapel, his gods, and his own chaplain. In those days, the lost tribe of the children of Dan were roving the countryside, and a scout returned to the chieftains and reported the private chapel ahead. Accordingly an army of 600 men descended on the chapel, taking the precious images. The priest appointed over them by Micah protested, whereupon the leader said to him, "Hold thy peace. Lay thine hand upon thy mouth and go with us, and be to us a father and a priest: is it better to thee to be a priest to the house of one man, or that thou be the priest unto a tribe and a family of Israel?" And the priest's heart was glad, and he took the precious images and went with them. As they departed Micah came out after them, following and crying, "Ye have taken away my gods which I made, and the priest, and ye are gone away: and what have I more?"

Obviously he had nothing more left, for his religion and his faith were in the external props of religion that could be taken away. This fable of ancient times seems startlingly contemporary, for many people today lose their gods and their priests, and their chapels are barren to them. They too cry, or should, "What more have I left?" A faith in things outside of one can vanish with the dust of the retreating hordes of whatever nature, or of changing circumstances.

Now this Micah and this tribe disappeared from history with their portable external gods that could be made or bought or stolen and taken away. If this were the only Micah in the Bible his name should hardly be recalled today. Yet this is among the most honored names of the Judeo-Christian heritage due to the second Micah, living generations later, the great prophet of ethical conduct and personal integrity. He summed up the religious position succinctly in lines which are familiar to most. He said, "Wherewith shall I come before the Lord, and bow myself before the high God?

Shall I come before him with burnt offerings, with calves a year old? Will the Lord be pleased with thousands of rams or with ten thousands of rivers of oil? Shall I give my firstborn for my transgression, the fruit of my body for the sin of my soul? He hath showed thee, O man, what is good; and what doth the Lord require of thee, but to do justly, and to love mercy, and to walk humbly with thy God?" These three verses from the sixth chapter of the Book of Micah have been called by many liberal religious persons the high point of Old Testament religion because they turn religion from the external forms to the internal faith which propels and guides people. There is nothing more required than to do justly, to love mercy, and to walk humbly. In this sense Micah gives us an adequate definition of religion.

This Micah is honored and respected wherever high religion is known. He calls upon us to turn from the superficiality of religion to the practice of a religion that is from the soul outward, from the mind outward, from the heart outward. One who has learned to do justly, to love mercy, and to walk humbly is equal to the demands of the hour. Ralph Waldo Emerson, the sage of Concord, lived a life in which sorrow, suffering, and disappointment were his lot. The early death of his first wife, the tragic death of his little son, extolled in happier days in poetry as the "hyacinth boy," would have broken the spirit of many others. Still Emerson could take pen in hand and write in his journal, "So that I count these to be low, sleepy, dark ages of the soul, only redeemed by the unceasing affirmation at the bottom of the heart—like the nightingale's song heard at night—that the powers of the soul are commensurate with its needs, all experience to the contrary notwithstanding."

This is the point at which liberal religion comes through: where and when it matters. It is based upon the inward religious experience, so that it has developed and nourished the soul, adequate to its every need. "The powers of the soul are commensurate with its needs, all experience to the contrary notwithstanding." It is the experience of the religious liberal, of Emerson and thousands of Unitarian Universalists, that this is so. Ours is a minority report to general human experience: the powers of the soul are commensurate with its needs, and experience bears this out.

We have previously alluded to William Ellery Channing, the great founder of the American Unitarian movement. His books, sermons, and essays have had a profound influence around the world. Goethe read him. Tolstoy was influenced by the writings of Channing, and Gandhi spoke feelingly of his influence on his own thought. His sermon, "Unitarian Christianity," preached in Baltimore, Maryland, in 1819 is said to have had more copies distributed than any other American sermon. Yet it may well be that nothing he ever wrote was more to the point than a letter he wrote to his young son recruited into the United States Army. In his letter, Channing wrote, "Whatever you may suffer, speak the truth. Be worthy of the entire confidence of your associates. Consider what is right as what must be done. It is not necessary that you should keep your property, or even your life, but it is necessary that you should hold fast your integrity."

These words of a father to his son, a conscript soldier, sum up the liberal religious demands. These are the values that guide us in life. They are more important than all the outward props, and they radiate from within.

There is a modern parable for all to see as we drive along our streets and highways at night. There are communities where there are traffic signs and signals lighted by electricity, and these are fine if there is no power failure or if no city engineer has neglected to throw the switch. These are outside signals over which we have no control. However, on many highways we are guided by directional signals which are lighted by the reflection from our own headlights. We light them up as we come along, and as we pass they fade into darkness again. We carry our own light with us, and so we are never at a loss for our directions. Liberal religion is like the latter. We light up our course by the faith which we bring to bear on the issue. We do not rely upon external light.

Another way of expressing it is to say that liberal religious persons develop their own faith, so that when they face tragedy, crisis, or indecision they are not at a loss for faith, for it is part of them. We have not accepted someone else's faith, remote in time or place or circumstance, memorized and repeated parrot-fashion at church, but we have found the faith in our own experience. We do not grope for external words, look for external power, rely on external miracles, but know it is up to ourselves to survive and to overcome as we hold fast to integrity, knowing full well that, difficult as it may be, "The powers of the soul are commensurate with its needs . . ."

Over and over the religious liberal has the required fortitude to stand up in the face of strife and struggle. Henley spoke as a religious liberal when he penned those valiant words:

> Out of the night that covers me
>   Black as the pit from pole to pole,

I thank whatever gods may be
  For my unconquerable soul.

In the fell clutch of circumstance
  I have not winced nor cried aloud;
Under the bludgeonings of chance
  My head is bloody but unbowed.

Beyond this place of wrath and tears
  Looms but the horror of the shade;
And yet the menace of the years
  Finds, and shall find me, unafraid.

It matters not how strait the gate,
  How charged with punishments the scroll;
I am the master of my fate;
  I am the captain of my soul.

The sense of self-control, of self-containment, and of self-realization is a necessary aspect of meeting crises and tension. The religious liberal feels that self-discipline, self-control, and self-regulation are essential for the handling of situations, whereas popular religion has held that one should lay burdens on the Lord, rely on the "under-lying arms," "safe in the arms of Jesus," and "trust in the Lord." These are the two poles of meeting life, inner or external. A well-known psychiatrist once wrote several books in which he deals with the problems of adolescence. His major theme is that teenage young people cannot stand pressures exerted on them by adults who treat them as children unable to control their own destinies. Dr. Lawrence Frank assures us over and over that young people, seeking to find their own being, role, and place in the scheme of things, need to be allowed enough freedom and growing room to experiment with decision-making, self-pacing, and self-discipline.[1] Allow them to make decisions, right or wrong, and they will grow and be better able to cope with life. They will find their places, find themselves, and find the right solutions more often than their doubting and timid elders think. This does not take a wise parent a dozen years in college, medical school, and residency to discover: many wise parents in dealing with their own youngsters discover this and realize that oftentimes the better direction is non-direction. Moralists and church fathers have been slow to realize that this is so with adults: we do not need a Father-God or Mother-Church to regulate life's decisions, to take away from us all tension, crisis, heartache, or challenge. In fact humanity can thrive on it just as Henley did.

Religious liberalism does not offer the security of transferring our problems to others. On the contrary, it encourages us to carry our own load, knowing that our moral fiber is equal to all demands. This is the great discovery.

So it is with the tensions of life. Religious liberals take them on their own shoulders. Their problem is not how to live without tension, but how to live with it. They can accept the tensions of the moment, because they see that they offer a challenge to creative living. Through stress one may overcome and master the challenges which one is called upon to face. In a religion dedicated to the dignity of humanity it is important to realize that both for one's own sake and that of others, for personal health and social commitment, for individual and family life, tension is to be handled and controlled and must not be allowed to wear one down. It must be met face to face, not avoided. It must be brought out, not turned inward.

Several years ago it was reported that a New York City television program dramatizing the problems of a psychiatric clinic signed off one evening with the announcer inviting the viewers to write if any of them were living under unbearable tension. Most likely the program director was looking for more program material, but he was completely unprepared for the response. In a week's time he was deluged with over 50,000 letters from people who wanted to tell about the tensions they faced. Were they looking for a more concrete form of that "God in the sky" who would take their burdens upon his shoulders and so give them release?

It is interesting that our modern healers of souls—the psychiatrists—do just the opposite of traditional religions. Instead of taking the problems and burdens on their shoulders, they persist in a therapy which forces the sufferers to return week after week until they disclose to themselves and take on their own shoulders through self-recognition and self-expression the problems they have tried to escape. Religion must learn anew from the modern science of healing and stop offering escape. It must call upon people to endure, forbear, and withstand. If the moral fiber is there this can be done, as the art of healing and the science of therapy disclose. Religious liberalism joins hands with modern psychiatry at this point.

There is another curious paradox in facing problems. Religion, our anthropologists and historians tell us, began in the distant past with the need to overcome tensions and cope with life situations. In fact, over and over today people turn to religion for precisely this reason; they face tensions they cannot cope with alone. The curious twist is that traditional religions often increase tensions rather than overcome them. They compound the basis, by guilt, sin, shame, fear, and morbid thoughts. The stress of these feelings is added by orthodoxy to the poor sufferer's burden. We can only pray that a stern God will forgive or a loving God will intervene or that a change of faith, overcoming doubts, will make us worthy of salvation. Then, and only then, will the sinner be cured, the sick made well, and the lame walk. Liberal religion sees not guilt, sin, or moral failure, but rather emotional and social shortcomings calling for a healing therapy.

Dr. Harry Meserve, to whom we have previously referred, wrote of the "prevalent anxiety of our time," which requires that "we be able to live in an anxious world with intelligence, integrity, and courage." He refers to both external social conditions of our complex, overorganized lives. There is, indeed, a very great area of anxiety which grips the lives of people. Years ago I attended a conference in Toronto and heard a partial report from a team of social scientists of the University who were surveying a suburban housing development. It was reported that one busy housewife and clubwoman, catching her breath as she rushed from meeting to meeting, with a quick dash home to change, before heading out again on her busy rounds, paused just long enough to tell the pollster, "When I get up in the morning I go, go, go; and when I come home at night I've been, been, been." How many people live under a similar tension?

There is need in such a life, or such living, for a time to find one's perspective. We submit that the religious liberal in the broader scope of worship and of religion as a way of life has an advantage in helping people find perspective. We develop a sensitivity to the fundamental issues which are at the foundations of life.

One such issue is the sense of purpose and meaning. For what do we live, and to what are we dedicated? What are our commitments? Each person must be able to answer these, in meaningful terms of the output of his energy, thought, and ethics. One of our ministers, Waldemar Argow, summed it up when he wrote "religion is a search for God, or for the highest that man can find and know. It is a feeling of union and oneness and peace with that reality, and a sense that there is some purpose to the great, inscrutable adventure of life on which we are so audaciously embarked." What he is saying is that religion is the quest for purpose and for the fulfillment of meaning through our lives. He is saying that God is the meaning and purpose of life, *i.e.*, that God is a term that means purpose. To the religious liberal, God is not an external force, but meaning itself, purpose itself, life itself. Thus does religion become direct.

Secondly, religion helps meet these anxieties of modern life by reminding us of the great issue of human dignity. "I can and I must reverence human nature," said William Ellery Channing. "In its vast potential lie all the attributes of the godlike we may ever know." The lack of reverence for the godlike leads to much of the crime, violence, carnage, and shortcomings in human action. Many years ago the *Reader's Digest* reported a story of a Jesuit priest who was a famed medical doctor on the faculty of Fordham University. A graduate of Harvard, he took a certain delight in attending the functions of that University, for which he was chided from time to time by some of his confreres. Once when asked, "Why is it that you, a Jesuit serving on the staff and faculty of a Catholic institution, are seen at these secular meetings?," he replied, "It is true that I am a Jesuit, and it is also true that I graduated from the Harvard Medical School. It is further true that at Harvard I studied and associated with people who were unbelievers. Indeed, I had a professor of surgery who was a Unitarian. Each day, as he took his place at the head of the cadaver, which we were to dissect or otherwise study, he would pause and say, 'Gentlemen, before we begin our study, I would ask you to first recall that this corpse was once the temple of the Holy Spirit.' You know, in many years, I've never heard our own professors say as much?" This Jesuit himself probably did, and many others probably do, but the point is well made that the religious liberal is always cognizant that no matter what the condition or circumstance, the sense of the divine image, of innate human dignity, is never lacking. (Hence the relevance of the ecumenical spirit today.) In many ways, we see this as the great underlying issue: reverence for humanity, a proper sense of human dignity. Where this is present, can violence, bigotry, hatred, lust, or carnage triumph? We say no.

The use of thinking as paramount in solving problems is basic with the attitude of the religious liberal. We believe that each person has the responsibility of rational decision laid upon his shoulders, and therefore must think. Albert Schweitzer wrote, "Only through the revival of ethical and religious thinking can the spirit arise which will give to mankind the knowledge and the strength to lead it out of darkness and conflict to light and peace. Liberal Christianity has the great responsibility of bringing to men and maintaining in them the conviction that thought and religion are not incompatible, but belong together. All deep religious thinking becomes thoughtful; all truly profound thinking becomes religious." These words were part of the message from Dr. Schweitzer to the International Association for Liberal Christianity and Religious Freedom, meeting in Bern, Switzerland, in 1947. In his autobiographic account, *Out of My Life and Thought*, he had written earlier: "Faith which refuses to face indisputable facts is but little faith. Truth is always gain, however hard it is to accommodate ourselves to it. To linger in any kind of untruth proves to be a departure from the straight way of faith." He continues in this book, writing in the epilogue, "To make men thinking beings once more, then, means to make them resort to their own way of thinking that they may try to secure that knowledge which they need for living. In the thinking which starts from Reverence for Life there is to be found a renewal of elemental thinking." Dr. Schweitzer had begun this concluding epilogue by writing, "I therefore stand and work in the world as one who aims at making men less shallow and morally better by making them think."

We quote Dr. Schweitzer at some length because this emphasis on thinking as basic to faith is a key to facing life. Religious liberals, among whom Dr. Schweitzer was numbered, face life successfully only when they use their rational powers and assume the human perspective, which is that they are thinking persons. To vary the thought only slightly and the person speaking, the American philosopher, John Dewey, stressed that "man is a problem-solver." The religious liberal does not transfer problems to others, but solves them.

The areas of thought, human dignity, and self-confidence lead naturally into that of individuality. The religious liberal has more assurance in the self and so is freer to resist the pressures of overorganization. James B. Conant, the former Harvard University president and United States ambassador, noted that the turtle gets where it is going by sticking out its neck. People, too, have to stick out their necks, stand up, and be counted and be willing to assess a position. Emerson in *Self-Reliance* wrote, "Whoso would be a man must be a nonconformist." Paul wrote to the Romans, "Be ye not conformed to this world, but be ye transformed by the renewing of your minds that you may prove what is the good and acceptable will of God."

One must be a nonconformist at times to become fully human,

being not conformed to the social milieu, but transforming it if necessary. Another way of saying it is that the well-adjusted person must not be overadjusted. We must not be so well-adjusted that we lose our identity. We must "hold fast our integrity." Religious liberalism leads the individual to be first and always a person.

The religious liberal throughout history has been such a nonconformist. Religious progress has been made by liberals who challenged the conformities of the religious institutionalism of their day. Among the great religious liberals were the Hebrew prophets of righteousness and justice: Amos, Hosea, Micah, and Isaiah. They were prophets precisely because they were out of adjustment with the social conditions of the times in which they lived. They spoke forth out of an outraged sense of moral indignation, seeking to right the social abuses and correct the moral shortcomings of the kingdom which was trampling upon the integrity of the individual as well as of Yahweh, their God.

In another culture and place, Confucius also took his stand. Since his day he has often been called the leader of a religious system that emphasized conformity. Yet his system was one of conforming to a higher ethical code than was acceptable or considered practical, and it was his unhappy lot in his own lifetime to be driven forth from one Chinese country after another in which for brief periods he held office. The political thinker is not welcomed when he becomes the social reformer. Confucius, who lacked all concern over the existence or nature of Deity, merely sought to show how to better order society by breaking with the conventional patterns of tradition and making a fresh start, learning from the mistakes of both contemporaries and elders. Because he would not be acceptable as a political leader, his pupils taught his teachings as applying to a better day to come, and so he became looked upon as a religious leader. His religion was akin to that of the religious liberal who defies the conformities of the present to dream and work for a better tomorrow.

In India also this same concern with overcoming the conventional pattern was to operate. Here a royal prince, Gautama, was taught all things by his father's chamberlains to make him a worldly wise, possessive, and avarice-driven person, who, wanting much, would persevere for its acquisition and hence would become a great king through the invidious drive to accumulate. To avoid any sense of the compassion of human feeling, great effort was made to keep all unhappy experiences and sights out of his knowledge. He was to be made the most selfish and self-centered of persons. But this was not to be. On four occasions he went outside of the palace walls where he saw events that even the king could not control. The first time he saw a person wracked with the suffering of disease and so learned that mankind suffered from illness. The second time he saw a man bent by the weaknesses and infirmities of old age and so learned that life builds to its enfeebled end. The third time he saw a funeral procession and so learned that man dies and that loved ones suffer. Finally, he saw the serene countenance of a yellow-robed monk who held his composure in the midst of the frenzied marketplace and so learned that people can find a peace that passeth understanding and determined that he would know what this was.

He secretly deserted the palace, donning the yellow robe of a monk, and fled to the hills to spend days and weeks in meditation, fasting and seeking after a better way. He had become the least well-adjusted in the kingdom. After tasting the bitterness and futility of life, he came to discover a religious principle through the anguished mind and social discontent of his sensitive personality. Never again could he return to the conforming society represented by the palace, but became a savior to those who would listen and since then has been known as the Buddha.

Jesus of Nazareth likewise was far from an adjusted person in his culture and time. He rose up saying, "Woe unto you, scribes and Pharisees, hypocrites! For ye shut up the kingdom of heaven against men, for ye neither go in yourselves, nor will you permit others to go in. Woe unto you . . . ye blind guides, for ye pay tithe of mint and anise and cumin, and have omitted the weightier matters of the law: justice, mercy and faith!" Here was the religious liberal again striking out against the conformities of society.

He was ill-adjusted to most of the social customs of his time: "Was man made for the Sabbath, or Sabbath for man?" he challenged the religious institution. Let us quote but one more example of his nonconformity, although we are tempted to quote many more. It is written in the seventh chapter of Matthew (verses 21-22) that he was gathering together those who would be his disciples, and "Another of his disciples said unto him, Lord suffer me first to go and bury my father. But Jesus said unto him, Follow me; let the dead bury the dead." Was a stronger rebuke ever given to a prevalent social custom that is almost unquestionable?

High religion, great religious experiences, have often flourished where men have been strong to resist the conformity and the too easy adjustment and acceptance of things as they are. All new religious ventures begin with such nonconformity, and only out of nonconformity has new direction and new movement been brought into religious experience. Every new ethical religion has begun with a liberal religious movement. As Channing noted, however, the followers too often "make an orthodoxy of the liberalism of our youth" so that new religions soon cease to be liberal. It is the genius and mission of Unitarian Universalism to maintain a liberal religious attitude growing out of the Judeo-Christian heritage, which holds open a door of universality with other world faiths, as well as with the secular ideas of the contemporary world.

It is a paradox that we meet life best in facing death. Every combat soldier learns this. Let us accordingly turn our attention to how the religious liberal faces death, which is one of the great inevitabilities of life. It comes not only to every man and woman but to every family. The easiest course is often that of dying. The harder task remains for those who mourn, whose lives are left void of something purposeful, loving, and intimate. When families are faced with the void created by the loss of loved ones, life crashes about them, and they, whose lives were wrapped up in one no longer present, must build a new life often when there seems hardly the will to do so.

Our religion has been filled with a heritage of immortal hope, but that religious heritage has not solved the practical problem of the mourner. There is hope for the dead, but "what is there for the living?" the pleading, plaintive heart often cries out.

Our attitude toward death often shows most clearly our attitude toward life. A person who can face death with strength can face up to life. The religious liberal often makes an amazing discovery: the words life and death are almost synonymous terms, and, indeed, in many instances we can substitute the one word for the other and increase the meaning of that which we face and endure. For example, in Louisa May Alcott's poem, "Transfiguration," change the word death to life, in these lines:

> Mysterious death! who in a single hour
>   Life's gold can so refine,
>   And by thy art divine
> Change mortal weakness to immortal power!

Is it not mysterious life which has suddenly become clarified and heightened for us?

Again, take Milton's stoic stanza from "Samson Agonistes":

Nothing is here for tears, nothing to wail,
Or knock the breast, no weakness, no contempt,
Dispraise, or blame—nothing but well and fair,
And what may quiet us in a death so noble.

Is it not the contemplation of the life so noble which calms and steadies us in this hour? The great poets themselves often realized this, too. Shelley in "Adonais" built to this climax:

The One remains, the many change and pass;
Heaven's light forever shines, Earth's shadows fly;
Life, like a dome of many-colored glass,
Stains the white radiance of eternity.

A lesser poet would have used the word "death."

One of our great parish ministers, Dr. Vivian T. Pomeroy, who served many decades in a New England community, reminisced with these words:

How often have I watched and wondered at the way in which simple persons face some dark and desperate hour. More often than not they are people from whom one has expected no special fortitude. In the ordinary ups and downs of life they have behaved neither too well nor too ill. But stripped of the cushioning of circumstance, thrust astonished and quivering into the heat of some awful battle or into the freezing cold of some lonely sorrow, they suddenly bring forth unsuspected reserves: their God-given rations of the soul.

This sense of strength, growing out of the self-containment of the individual, brings with it a balance (to be well-balanced is, after all, considered desirable) which the Rev. William L. Sullivan caught in these words:

To outgrow the past, but not to extinguish it:
To be progressive, but not raw;
To be free, but not mad;
To be critical, but not sterile;
To be expectant, but not deluded;
To be scientific, but not live in formula that cuts us off from life;
To hear, amidst the clamor, the pure, deep tones of the spirit;
To turn both prosperity and adversity into servants of character;
This is to attain peace; this is to invest the lowliest life with
    magnificence.

These represent the inner resources of religious liberalism—of Unitarian Universalism—which enable many to face the crisis, the tragedy, and the issues of life.

In conclusion, we should note that the requirements for facing life are not only in terms of the crisis element, but in how we use the wholesome and valuable experiences, how we accept the bounty which life has bestowed on us in a world in which others have less. We have already mentioned Dr. Albert Schweitzer, a religious liberal who having achieved much greatness in the fields of theology, philosophy and music before the age of thirty, gave it all up to go to Africa "to help repay the white man's debt to the black," as he sought to make his life his argument. Adlai Stevenson, already quoted, was a Unitarian Universalist who, although a man of means, could have lived out his days in selfish oblivion, but who chose to spend his days in efforts to serve his state, his nation, and humanity. One is humbled at the thought of the many others who have followed suit. Such lives are a mark of the ability to meet the demands of life. In an affluent society, where there is so much to make life easy, one must develop the graceful ability to accept the good and order life accordingly, not succumbing to the weaknesses and temptations along the way. One of our Universalist poets, John Holmes, a Tufts University professor, caught up the ethical participation which touches us all in a poem written after the newspapers carried the reports of the invasion of Czechoslovakia by Nazi Germany, entitled "Evening Meal in the Twentieth Century":

> How is it I can eat bread here and cut meat,
> And in quiet shake salt, speak of the meal,
> Pour water, serve my son's small plate?
> Here now I love well my wife's gold hair combed,
> Her voice, her violin, our books on shelves in another room,
> The tall chest shining darkly in supper-light.
> I have read tonight
> The sudden meaningless foreign violent death
> Of a nation we both loved, hope
> For a country not ours killed. But blacker than print:
> For the million people no hope now. For me
> A new hurt to the old health of the heart once more:
> That sore, that heavy, that dull and I think now incurable Pain:
> Seeing love hated, seeing real death,
> Knowing evil alive I was taught was conquered
> How shall I eat this bread gladly, unless more share
> The day's meals I earn?
> Or offer my wife meat from our fire, our fortune?

It should not have taken me so long to learn.
But how can I speak aloud at my own table tonight
And not curse my own food, not cry out death,
And not frighten my young son?

The response we make to the good life in the midst of the not so good about us tells much. The many students during the 1960s who entered the Civil Rights movement, unable to close their eyes to underprivilege and social injustice, showed that large numbers of people in comfortable circumstances are seeking ways to face life meaningfully as well as with integrity. Others who entered the Peace Corps likewise embodied this principle. Liberal religion helps furnish the inner resources for such commitment and involvement.

Note
[1]Mary and Lawrence Frank, *Your Adolescent At Home And In School*, New York, Viking Press, 1961.

5
The Historical Roots of Unitarian Universalism

In examining the phenomena of religious liberalism, we have seen that Unitarian Universalism is an organized expression of the liberal religious way of life. Without this acquaintance with liberal religion as a broader movement, Unitarian Universalism would be difficult to understand. Now we must pinpoint our discussion and turn our attention to the organized, unique expressions of liberal religion that have flourished through the years as the Unitarian and the Universalist movements until the two met and merged, so that now it is difficult to distinguish between them.

Previous chapters have already dealt with the needs for an inner faith that can be freely expressed in external responses—the gods who "write their names upon our faces"—so that the genuine test of religion is to be found, for us, in the ethical and moral response made by individuals. We have also considered the modern need for a modern faith consistent with contemporary culture. We have implied that Unitarian Universalism, although possessing ancient roots, is basically a religion oriented to the present. Finally, we have pointed out that the liberal religious way makes it possible to face life and death with assurance in our individuality, with strength to withstand conformity, and with an affirmation of the innate dignity in humankind. It is, in substance, a liberal religious way because it turns religion from institutional conformity toward individual integrity and personal responsibility.

How did liberal religion come to its present state? Almost all religions began as reformation movements against previous orthodox institutions only to become new orthodoxies in turn. Has

Unitarian Universalism maintained itself free from any orthodoxy of its own? If it has, how has it done so?

Where did Unitarian Universalism come from? How did it develop? What is its history and genealogy? Who are its great proponents?

It may be said to have begun in the distant past when humans first protested against conformity and the closed mind of the fetishman or tribal witch doctor. We may say that those who called for the purification of ancient oriental religious practices high in the plateaus of the Himalayan Mountains were our ancestors. Akhnaton, the eighteenth dynasty pharaoh who developed an ethical monotheism, was certainly one of the first Unitarian Universalists of history. In the Fertile Crescent of the Near East, other reforming movements, notably that of the Hebrew prophets, who developed a universalizing concept of one God reigning supreme over all peoples, were in the stream of development. The great insights of pagans in Greece, of such philosophers as Socrates and of his pupils—Plato and Aristotle—were contributors to our heritage. However, we must not claim them for ourselves, although they have contributed to the liberalizing spirit of religion, to the dispassionate and open mind, to the quest for new truth that will explain human experience and relate it to the natural environment.

For those living in the Western world, with its Judeo-Christian heritage, Unitarian Universalism begins with Jesus of Nazareth and the preceding social teachings and universalizing vision of the Hebrew prophets. We will discuss Jesus in a later chapter, but here we note again that he was a reformer and a seeker. Within the days following his death, an orthodoxy about him rapidly developed, in part because people sought to find what to believe about him. There was no unity of the Christian faith or Christian doctrine for the first four centuries after Christ, and it took two centuries before broad consensus began to develop, dividing Christianity into schools or, as we say today, into sects.

Even in the days immediately following his death, his immediate followers and Paul found themselves in conflict over the nature of their faith in Jesus. Thus, there was at once a struggle between orthodoxy and liberalism in Christian beginnings. This is seen most dramatically in the struggle between Paul and Peter. Paul did not know Jesus personally and, apparently, lacked a specific knowledge of his sayings, if we can judge by Paul's extant writings. Only in one place does he quote Jesus, and, so far as we know, it is incorrect ("Remember the words of the Lord Jesus who said it is more blessed to give than to receive"), for it is found nowhere else. He also gives an account of the Last Supper, but this varies greatly from the Gospel accounts. Paul felt so sure of his own position that he apparently flew into a rage upon hearing that the other Disciples were welcomed at a church he had founded. He wrote to the church at Corinth, "Let their names be anathema!" Dr. Schweitzer points out that there is a paradox here in that the Disciples who knew everything that could be known about Jesus were restricted by Paul, who knew nothing about Jesus except as "Christ crucified"—that is, after death. With the destruction of Jerusalem, the influence of Peter and the Disciples who were limited to that area was practically wiped out along with their churches. Paul and his influence, spread throughout the Greco-Roman world, continued. Hence, Christianity rapidly developed into a religion about Jesus rather than the religion of Jesus. Not entirely, however, for, with the dispersion of the Jews by the Romans, the influence of those who knew Jesus as a man, a teacher, an ethical and heroic example who courageously stood up for the right was carried throughout the Roman world. Hence, there always remained a dissenting element who saw a human Jesus rather than a deified Christ returned from the dead and ascended into heaven. In this emphasis on the human nature of Jesus, and on his ethical teachings, the elements of Unitarian Universalism are founded. It has not continued throughout history as an organized movement, but has always been a latent, sometimes a vocal force and for the last 400 years an organized branch of Christianity. We might say that Unitarian Universalism has been a lever to liberalize Christianity. Certainly, it began as a liberalizing movement within organized Christianity no matter where it ensues.

A Roman Catholic book already referred to, *Our Separated Brethren*, says, "Denial of the divinity of Christ and of the Trinity seems to be the chief Unitarian position, but the Unitarians oppose not just one or two basic Christian dogmas, but all dogmas. Not only antitrinitarian but antisupernatural, the Unitarian Universalists would be better classified as religious liberals who oppose all dogma and all ecclesiasticism." This is how we may appear from the outside. We hope to clarify our own understanding of our heritage, concepts, and relationships in this and the following chapters.

Tertullian (160-230 A.D.), one of the most notable of the Church Fathers, wrote that in his day, "the common people think of Christ as a man." Constantine the Great (Roman Emperor from 306-337 A.D.) had the inspiration (or, as is commonly said, saw a vision) of *in hoc signo vinces*, "by this sign conquer," and "accepted"

Christianity, proclaiming it the state religion. His vision, as we understand it, was that the crumbling Roman Empire which he was fighting to weld together, needed a new unifying force, a new center of integration or orientation, and in the height of battle he had the inspiration of a new official religion which would accomplish this unification. Imagine his dismay to find it was not a united faith, but a loose conglomeration of churches ruled by local bishops and presbyters. There were separate gospels, different versions of the nature of Christ, and different understandings of the messianic expectation. In time, dismayed by this lack of unity—how could you unify an Empire with a faith that itself was not unified?—he summoned all the bishops of the church to Constantinople to confer and agree on the articles of faith. Thus, in the suburb of Nicea in 325 A.D. the first great council met. It early appeared that they were divided into two great camps: those following Bishop Arius and those surrounding the presbyter Athanasius.

Arius was the holder and champion of the view that God is one, unknowable and separate from every created being. Jesus, the Christ, was a created being and, therefore, not God. He could be worshipped as a secondary being, but not as deity. In regard to the incarnation, Arius allowed that the Logos could assume a body, but not a human soul. Consequently, his view was that Christ was not divine in the fullest sense, but still had more attributes than mere man.

Athanasius, known traditionally as "the Father of Orthodoxy," was a powerful controversialist who challenged specifically the views of Arius and was the principal supporter of the doctrine of the divinity of Christ. He held that Jesus was "very God of very God" and that Jesus was "of one substance" with God.

We cannot go into the great debate, the shifting loyalties, the dynamics of intrigue, and the bitterness of the wrangling that took place. The Council could not agree and after two years, impatient at the delay, the Emperor Constantine appeared and addressed the assembly, ordering them to agree on the divinity of Christ (how could the emperor claim divinity if the Savior's was denied?). Therefore, even though Arius and his followers had gradually secured a slender margin on the basic argument that Christ should not be confused with God, the assembled church dignitaries fell into line and voted as the state required—the beginning of a long, sorry story of church subservience, which in many countries even today weakens and paralyzes the church that dare not resist the state.

The issues continued in the churches, however, and it took a

second Council, that of Constantinople, called by Emperor Theo-
dosius in 381 A.D., to affirm the position adopted in Nicea in 325
A.D. Now the Arians were banished from the Empire and made
their way out among the barbarians. The story of the influence
and extent to which the barbarian invasions of Rome were Uni-
tarian-Trinitarian invasions has never been fully determined, although a few important scholars have felt the influence of Arianism to be a motivating force for the invasions from the East. This
second Council added to the early article regarding the divinity of
Jesus, that of the Holy Spirit, so that in 381 A.D. the trinity became
a fully evolved doctrine of the Church; and Unitarianism, as represented by Arianism, was considered heretical.

Universalism had an earlier battle when Origen, the great
Church Father, heretic, and thinker, brought the full pressure of
a great mind to bear on the troublesome contradictions of evolving
church doctrines.

Origen (185-251 A.D.) has been called "the first Universalist."
This amazing intellectual in the Early Christian Church wrote over
6,000 tracts and volumes. He has been described as "one of the
most appealing characters in history" with a "balanced mind in
which the intellectual did not destroy the spiritual." "From his
youth to his last hour he showed an uncommon fearlessness."
"He had the conscientiousness and patience of the true scientist."
"He had the admirable qualities of a good teacher, and his pupils
worshipped him." "His critical judgment, creative energy, and
catholicity of knowledge are not equalled in any Christian thinker
before Erasmus." He rejected the concept of Hell, believed in the
benevolence of God, who would offer salvation to all mankind;
emphasized the humanity of Jesus; and minimized the importance
of miracles. On this subject he wrote that even though he might
admit that a miraculous power to cure is possible, "I might still
remark. . .that such curative power is neither good nor bad, but
within reach of godless as well as of honest folks. . . .The power
of healing diseases is not evidence of anything specially divine."

Dr. Fred Gladstone Bratton's book, published as a Beacon
paperback, *The Legacy of the Liberal Spirit,* from which we have
quoted, opens with the rise of religious liberalism through this
first Universalist whose positions and opinions were to be quoted
by the Arians. This greatest scholar of the early Church was later
to be declared a heretic, and "since the seventh century he has
received the eternal condemnation of the papacy."

Origen represented the concept of early Unitarian Universalism as it emerged in the Christian tradition, offering a faith based

on reasonable conclusions, anticipating the modern Biblical study through his denial of the literal validity of Scripture. It is a pity he and those who thought like him—the Arians, Pelagians, and Nestorians—were bypassed by the orthodox thinkers. It has remained for us today to organize a vital movement to liberalize Christianity, which he sought to do in the third century before condemnation as a heretic.

The church from the fourth century on was based on orthodoxy and authority rather than liberalism and freedom.

Indeed, many peoples and movements of Christian antiquity contributed to liberal religion and called for a more simplified understanding of Christianity. They were the leaders of a series of progressive movements to liberalize Christianity. Even today in books of theology, Unitarianism is often referred to as Arianism, and Universalism is traced back to Origen.

Space will not allow us to consider them further. We must skip over the growth and continuation of Arianism among the barbarians. We must also omit details of the outcroppings of liberalism in the following centuries in the abortive reformations of local freethinkers within the Catholic Church. We bring our attention next to bear on the Protestant Reformation of the fifteenth century.

Interesting conclusions may be drawn from the free-thinking Erasmus, most ecumenical of all the Reformation leaders and yet one who never broke from the church to join the Protestant movement because of the dangers and weaknesses he beheld therein. We recall only that he showed the error of the Trinitarian belief in this period of religious intensity as being a doctrine without Biblical foundations. We jump over the Anabaptist movement and Zwingli, with all its anti-Trinitarianism, noting its close relationship to Unitarian Universalism, which continues the traditional free church of the martyrs.

We focus our attention upon a fiery and dynamic reformer out of Spain. Michael Servetus (1511-1553) became the leader who planted the Reformation roots of Unitarianism. He led a life of tremendous activity and intellectual accomplishment and personal excitement. His great religious writings included two monumental books: *On the Error of the Trinity* and *The Reconstitution of Christianity*. He was forced to change his name; he had to go into hiding; he had to change his profession; he had to flee from country to country. When he became a doctor, Servetus was aware of the circulation of the blood, a first scientific step forward, although it remained for Harvey to develop and popularize this concept.

In Spain, he had his first chance to read the Bible for himself while a college student. Being a sensitive person, he was appalled that the Spanish Inquisition had bathed so many homes in blood as it sought to root out all non-Christians in a country with large settlements of Moors (Moslems) and Jews. They were spared the sword only if they would publicly confess a belief in the Trinitarian formula of the Catholic Church: "I believe in God the Father, God the Son and God the Holy Ghost." Imagine, therefore, his excitement upon reading the Bible, to find that the Trinity was nowhere a part of its teachings! The Trinitarian formula was not a basic Christian doctrine, according to the Bible! Therefore, he would tell the world! The different faiths could live in peace! The divisive formula was unnecessary! Oh, the assurance of youth! How little it understands the deep roots of entrenchment! He would send it to Calvin and Luther, the new Protestant churches would become Unitarian, and a world of tolerance would become a possibility based on one God, the father of the family of mankind.

Luther and Calvin, however, would have nothing to do with this doctrine. They feared that the Reformation would go too far. They were more interested in establishing churches than in rewriting the doctrines of Christian faith. Indeed, they went to great ends to contain the Reformation religion within a framework of orthodoxy. Their quarrel was not so much with the theology of Rome as with its organization. They joined with Rome in trying to protect the Christian teaching of the centuries, and Calvin actually turned the Unitarian Protestant Reformer, Servetus, over to the Catholic officials. In the end, Servetus went to see Calvin, certain that a meeting of minds was still possible. Calvin had him arrested and tried for heresy. Calvin then sentenced him to death by burning at the stake with his books tied to his waist. Thus did Servetus die on a hill outside Geneva. The people of Geneva were to remember him, and following Calvin's death they erected a great statue, not to Calvin, but to the man he burned alive, the Unitarian Servetus. Castellio, one of Calvin's earlier lieutenants, summed up the protest: "To burn a man is not to prove a doctrine; it is to burn a man!" That protest has never ceased.

Slightly younger than Servetus was Faustus Socinus, who inherited the Unitarian writings of his uncle, a religious liberal of Northern Italy. Socinus, reading his uncle's unpublished works, became imbued with the fire of his uncle's protest and wrote a book entitled *On Christ as Savior*. He makes the point that Christ was savior only because he showed by his own example the way to salvation and that only by example can we be his followers. He denied the doctrine of the Trinity, the deity of Jesus, the personality of the devil, the total depravity of man, and the eternity of punishment. These were the staples of Christian thought—both Catholic and Protestant—in that period, and he had to flee from both Italy and Switzerland, finally coming to Poland. Here he established over 300 Unitarian Churches, becoming the tireless leader of a people's religion. Upon the restoration of the Jesuits, the orthodox factions conspired against him, and he was arrested and tried, his books burned in the public square of Cracow. With a sword held over his head, it was demanded that he publicly recant his writings as the flames devoured them. This he refused to do. Rather than being burned, he was turned over to a mob to throw into the river. He was rescued by two Jesuits, giving illustration again that good men rise above the systems and organizations of which they are members.

Francis David in Transylvania and Hungary proclaimed Unitarianism between 1566–1579. This led to the enactment of the first edict of religious toleration in the history of Europe by a crowned head, King Sigismund of Transylvania, a Unitarian, in 1568. The Unitarian movement in Transylvania and Hungary is still strong.

In England, Unitarianism was long a persecuted religion. The persecution of Arians and later of Socinians were persecutions of those who were Unitarian in theology. Unitarianism, under this name, began in England, we might say, with a remarkable church called The Church of the Strangers in London which was chartered in 1550. In 1599 the Dissenting Church at Gainsborough and then, in 1601, the Pilgrim Church in Scrooby were founded, both with John Robinson, one of the great exponents of liberality and freedom in religion, as their first minister. His followers gained a measure of fame in being the settlers of Plymouth Rock, establishing continuous English-speaking settlements, never to be broken, on the shores of the American continent. The church in Gainsborough became openly Unitarian in 1701, the date the Act of Toleration permitted Unitarians to worship openly (but not yet own property or hold public office), and the Pilgrim church in Plymouth likewise joined with other Unitarians as soon as there were others to join with. Thus, it may be said that Unitarianism was one of the bridges by which the freedom of the English nonconformists was transplanted across the ocean.

In 1615, John Biddle was born in Gloucestershire. Educated

at Oxford, as Robinson had been at Cambridge, he wrote *Twelve Arguments Drawn from Scripture, wherein the Commonly Held Notion Touching the Deity of the Holy Spirit is Clearly Refuted.* He was imprisoned as a heretic. One of his biographers wrote, "This was the beginning of a life passed, with a few short intervals of precarious liberty, almost entirely in dungeons." In 1648 he wrote from his dungeon *A Confession of Faith Touching the Trinity,* in which, like Servetus, whom Calvin burned at the stake in Geneva in 1553, he refuted the Biblical foundations of the Church doctrines. In the year that Biddle published this statement against the Trinity, Parliament passed the "Draconic Ordinances," which made the heresy of denying the Trinity punishable by death. Fortunately, the ordinance was not enforced and was repealed in 1652 by the "Act of Oblivion," and Biddle was released from prison.

He started Bible classes in London, wrote a Children's Catechism, setting forth the Unitarian and rational answer to questions on religion asked by children. This might be considered the beginning of the important emphasis Unitarians have always placed on religious education.

Time would fail us to go into all his arrests, releases, the converts to his liberalism, his writings, and finally his death in a dungeon by starvation.

His greatest convert was a wealthy manufacturer, Thomas Firmin, who gave lavishly to charity, founded factories to employ the destitute of the great London Fire of 1666, establishing the first example of a work-relief program rather than a dole, which became the ideal that both British and American cultures were to follow. John Wesley, as an old man, on reading the life of Firmin, wrote, "I was exceedingly touched with it, having long settled in my mind that the entertaining, wrong notions of the Trinity were inconsistent with true piety. But I cannot argue against matter of fact. I dare not deny that Mr. Firmin was a pious man, although his notions of the Trinity were quite erroneous."

Thus, we have from the first, the type of testament that has come to Unitarians, outcasts doctrinally from the church, but often saints by their character, their humanitarianism, and their works. The social concern of Unitarianism has always been a cardinal tenet of their faith, from John Biddle's time until the present.

In the meantime, another new development was beginning in England. A student of Wesley, John Relly, began preaching a variation of the Wesleyan doctrine in London. His views were set forth in a number of books, most notably *Union,* published in

1759. In this book he opposed the Calvinistic doctrine of salvation of the elect—that is, that salvation is only for those elected for salvation from the foundations of the world—stating that God would eventually save all mankind. His conviction of universal salvation, based on the Wesleyan doctrine of Grace and supported by a courageous willingness to defy conventional Protestant orthodoxy attracted a large following to Relly. John Murray (1741–1815) was the son of a father who was wrapped up in what John called "the doctrine of the gloomy Reformer." Murray is the first of the liberal religious leaders we shall study whose life spanned both sides of the Atlantic. Relly, his inspiration and teacher, however, was a London preacher. He had been influenced by George Whitefield (1714–1770), the great English evangelist who succeeded the Wesleys as leader of the Methodist movement. Whitefield was, perhaps, the most powerful religious figure in England in his day and toured the American colonies seven times. He departed from the Calvinistic Methodism of the great leader, laying greater stress on the Grace of God and the Love of God. John Murray first learned of the perfidious doctrines of the restoration of all men through his fiancée, and it disturbed him that he could not persuade her of the error of her thought. At this time, while active with the Whitefield movement, one of the other leaders, a man by the name of Mason, prepared a rebuttal to Relly's *Union* and asked John Murray to read and comment on it. Murray read it, was persuaded by the attack on Relly, thought that Relly was more correct than were the Calvinists, Whitefield, or Mason. Consequently, he went to hear Relly preach and became active in his anti-Calvinist movement. Thus, Murray became one of the active members of Relly's Universalism in London. We will pick up his story in America shortly, for here his great influence was felt.

John Milton, a leader in the Puritan Commonwealth with Cromwell, became a Unitarian, and in his *Areopagitica* wrote one of the great credos for the freedom of religious publishing. John Locke, author of *The Essay Concerning Human Understanding*, smuggled both his and Sir Isaac Newton's documents on Unitarianism into France to have them published there because of the penalties for Unitarian publishing in England.

Newton, discoverer of the law of gravitation, was the first of a line of great English scientists who expressed liberal religious views. Among those who came after him were Joseph Priestley, the discoverer of oxygen, and Charles Darwin, discoverer of the theory of evolution.

Priestley saw his house, library, laboratory, and church burned to the ground in Birmingham and came to America.

Many literary people were Unitarians in England. Charles Dickens wrote *A Christmas Carol,* bringing a new and mature spirit of humanity into the celebration of the Christmas season. His novels on social conditions in England aroused a protest that was important in making England a leader in a social progress and reform. Samuel Coleridge, "The Rising Star of Unitarianism," refuted the Biblical inspiration in *Confessions of an Inquiring Spirit.* It was not published until 1840, although he shared the manuscript with friends in his own lifetime.

Florence Nightingale, whose organization of the nursing corps in the Crimean War led to the development of the nursing profession and brought a new dignity and moral grandeur to women, was a devout Unitarian throughout her life. As a young woman, she attended the Unitarian Chapel at Lea. Later she worshipped at Essex Street Chapel, London. At 80 years, she supported a fund to raise money for new Unitarian chapels.

Theophilus Lindsey, in founding the Essex Street Chapel, the first openly organized Unitarian church in London, began a movement that was henceforth publicly recognized. His petition, signed by 250 clergymen, while a member of the Established Church, to have Parliament repeal the requirement for subscribing to the Thirty-nine Articles was rejected. He alone resigned for being unable to subscribe in spite of his bishop's plea to "stay and do good works, forgetting this nonsense over creeds." By the time of his death in 1808, he saw more than 20 Unitarian churches founded in England by his followers. Later on many Nonsubscribing Presbyterian Churches became Unitarian. They did not subscribe to the Westminster Confession of Faith.

We now come to those whose influence was felt on both sides of the Atlantic. There are three who stand out who originated in Europe and moved to the North American continent. These three are: George de Benneville, John Murray, and Joseph Priestley.

George de Benneville (1703–1793) was a French Huguenot by birth who grew into an aristocratic young man attached to the English court, spending time on a diplomatic mission in Africa. He was later given a heresy trial by the Huguenots, and then after an illness he went forth to preach. In the process, he secured his medical education in Belgium. His preaching ministry was to carry him to various parts of France, Germany, and Holland. Condemned to death, he was reprieved at the last moment and came to America. Here he settled in Germantown and Oley, Pennsylvania, and published the first Universalist textbook known to be published on these shores. This was *The Everlasting Gospel*, published in 1750. De Benneville influenced men who became great leaders of the Pennsylvania Universalism, which grew out of the liberal wing of the Baptist denomination. Among persons influenced by him were Dr. Elhanan Winchester and Dr. Benjamin Rush. Active in the American Revolution, his influence was to touch a later pioneer Universalist theologian, Hosea Ballou. De Benneville was not of the same school or temperament as John Murray, generally regarded as the founder of American Universalism. De Benneville's universality and message may be summed up in a single sentence: "My happiness will be incomplete while one creature remains miserable."[1] He wrote, "Since the beginning of Christianity, the unhappy situation in the world has been that the priesthood has been greatly divided and widely separated in their opinion. . .What can be the reason for so many disagreements? The only reason is that the essential truth is so divided and torn into so many pieces that it is often lost in the strife. One party has truth; another also has some truth, but each thinks it has the whole truth and, therefore, tries to reject that of the other, imagining it is error."[2]

Such quotations as these appeal to the modern religious liberal who reads de Benneville since they show the remarkable broad-mindedness of his outlook, despite the lack of scientific and cultural developments necessary to lead him to a wholly modern position. He, nonetheless, marked a route along which Western thought was to travel in the development of religious liberalism.

John Murray was born in Alton, Hampshire, England in 1741 and died in 1815 in Massachusetts. Growing up in a strict Calvinist family in England, he was a victim of the utter morbidity of religious orthodoxy. Of his father's relentless teachings of Calvinism, Murray wrote:

> Hence my soul frequently experienced the extreme of agony. . . . Hence religion became a subject of terror. I was not ten years old when I began to suffer; the discovery of my sufferings gave my fond father much pleasure; he cherished hope of me when he found me suffering from my fears, and much indeed was I tortured by the severe unbending discipline of my father, and the terrifying apprehensions of what I had to expect from the God who created me."[3]

Such were the terrible experiences in those days of Calvinistic upbringing. Speaking of "the terrifying apprehensions of the future and never-ending misery" he continued with this description of the God of Calvinism:

> "I would no more offend either my father or *his* God; I dared not say *my* God, for I had heard my father declare, that for any individual, *not* the elect of God, to say *of* God, or *to* God, 'Our Father,' was nothing better than blasphemy: when most devout, I was prevented from deriving consolation from my pious breathings, by a persuasion that I was a reprobate, predestined to eternal damnation.[4]

With such a religious indoctrination, we can well imagine that John Murray as a young man found a great release and uplift to discover a preacher who denied the estrangement and unworthiness of Man. Relly taught and preached, not the cruelty of a God who was an oriental tyrant, but the loving God who sought the Union of all his children with him, a religion based on harmony rather than fear, and proclaiming the universal salvation and joy of the divine family of the human race. His biographer, following Murray's own account (published in 1851 under the title *The Life of Murray,* mostly written by himself, with an Appendix, Boston, Abel Tompkins, 38 and 40 Cornhill) tells us:

> But Murray (developed) . . . faith in the doctrines of Relly . . . So great was the discovery he thus made for himself, that the whole current of his life was changed. The saddening gloom of a false theology, no longer 'ate, as doth a canker' at the very center of all his enjoyment. God became, to him, the Father of all, and the whole human race were brothers. The yawning gulf of never-ending agony no longer stood ready for its prey; but bright and beautiful, above all human ill, shone the sun of perfect love for all the children of God's creation, and that sun, as he believed, would finally warm all hearts, enlighten all minds, and draw all souls to heaven in perfect righteousness and in perfect bliss.[5]

One of the great compensations of modern Unitarian Universalists, we may note parenthetically at this point, is the knowledge that comes to parents when they realize that their children grow without the terrors that stalk by night or the fears that haunt by day, such as were known by John Murray. Since so many modern Unitarian Universalists are come-outers of orthodox religious traditions and themselves knew what Murray experienced, it is a matter of elation and jubilation to realize that our children through this sane, rational, well-balanced religion can grow freely, without fear. They are free of the old superstitious nagging suspicion that a mean and spying God is checking up on every small detail, storing it up like some accusing parent, to use against us at the day of judgment. So many of those who grew out of the orthodox traditions remember how the faiths of childhood affected our lives, our outlooks, and our acceptance of life and natural order: how we were kept awake at night by the fear of an avenging God, or of the terror of the devil and hellfire damnation. The dread of death has tortured many a child.

Dr. Andrews Norton of Harvard University wrote in 1819: "As though all religion were the same! It is as though one were to go to the apothecary and take any medicine from the shelves, content with it being called medicine." John Murray nearly two centuries ago discovered this great difference and launched a new movement which we today may inherit and cultivate.

All was not to be easy for John Murray. He had married, and both his wife and young child died. Deeply sorrowing and in great depression, he decided to leave England and bury himself in the American wilderness. He would never preach again. He sailed for the United States, and after a series of mishaps the ship put in and was grounded at Sandy Hook on the Delaware in Cranberry Inlet, New Jersey. Having to wait for the tides and wind, he went ashore and eventually was required to spend several days there. He met up with a wealthy farmer, Thomas Potter, who had built a church where he welcomed visiting preachers. It turned out he had read Relly's *Union* and was eager to find a preacher who agreed with these sentiments. Through the uncertain and undesired developments of the week-end, it ended up with John Murray committed to preach on Sunday, and, with great recalcitrance, he entered the pulpit again. Thus, at which is now Murray Grove, New Jersey, the first American Universalist sermon of John Murray was preached.

From New Jersey to Philadelphia to New York and back and forth he was to preach—at first always against his personal desire and better judgment. He did not want to preach at this time. His depression was not yet overcome, but in bringing himself to preach the glad tidings of Universal salvation and the hope for the final harmony of all souls with God, he talked himself into a more hopeful and promising frame of mind. A doughty old war horse and a valiant crusader, he was the toughest of fighters with indomitable courage and great strength of will. Once he came to recognize that he was to be "a preacher in spite of his own wishes," he entered into the activity with a stalwartness that attracted others to him, and he soon became a natural leader among the more freethinking and liberally inclined clergy.

It is reported by his biographers that he was not a philosophical thinker or systematic organizer of a theological system, but he had the ability to construct a powerful sermon, straight to the point, mincing no words, and making crystal clear where he stood and what he considered the false teaching of the theology of doom. His condemnation of it gladdened the heart of many who looked for a religion of hope rather than of fear and of love rather than of damnation. He aroused bitter criticism from the older schools of religious thought which believed that only hellfire and fear could compel men to be good. They believed that people were driven to goodness, not enticed to it. Consequently, they called Murray a libertarian, a heretic, a pied piper of irreligion, a Deist, a menace. They saw clearly that he would undermine their churches and faiths, and indeed he would, but only to clear the rubble to raise a more stately mansion of the soul.

He gave this account of his dealings with the other clergy: "The combined efforts of the clergy in Philadelphia barred against me the door of every house of public worship in the city. Bachelor's Hall was in Kensington. But at Bachelor's Hall the people attended, and a few were enabled to believe the good word of their God. There was in the city a minister of the Seventh-day Baptist persuasion; for a season he appeared attached to me, but soon became very virulent in his opposition. He told me he passed on foot nine miles, upon the return of every Saturday, to preach. I asked him how many his congregation contained. 'About a hundred.' 'How many of this hundred do you suppose are elected to everlasting life?' 'I cannot tell.' 'Do you believe fifty are elected?' 'Oh no, not twenty.' 'Ten perhaps?' 'There may be ten.' 'Do you think the non-elect can take any step to extricate themselves from the tremendous situation in which the decrees of Heaven have placed them?' 'O no, they might as well attempt to pull the stars from the firmament of heaven.' 'And do you think your preaching can assist them?' 'Certainly not; every sermon they hear will sink them deeper and deeper in damnation.' 'And so, then, you walk nine miles every Saturday to sink ninety persons out of the hundred deeper and deeper in never-ending misery!'"[6]

Later he traveled to New England and became a preacher there, being heard in Oxford, Gloucester, and Boston, Massachusetts. Before settling down, he ran into many experiences which show the hostility with which the orthodox greeted him while others enthusiastically supported his preaching. He wrote: "Many religious people were violent in their opposition; they insisted that I merited the severest punishment; that the old discipline for heretics ought to be put in force; and I was thus furnished with abundant reason to bless God for the religious liberty of the country of my adoption, else racks and tortures would have been put in operation against me, nor would these holy men, moved by the spirit, have stopped short of my destruction. Yet was the charge of heresy never proved against me. I was never silenced either by reason or scripture. I had called upon men everywhere, clergymen or laymen, to step forward and convict me of error, promising immediately upon conviction to relinquish the obnoxious tenet, whatever it might chance to be, and to adopt that better way, which would, in such an event, become luminous before me."[7]

Murray relates one exciting incident of his dealings with Rev. Mr. Croswell of Boston, who determined to stop Murray's preaching. After an exchange of letters, Murray explained the development: "This letter enraged him, and he sent it back declaring he would have nothing to do with me. But, on the following Sunday evening when I repaired, as usual, to the meetinghouse to preach, Mr. Croswell was upon the stairs of the pulpit, with a number of his violent adherents, for the purpose of barring me out. Making no resistance, I requested the gentleman be heard with patient attention; and silence being obtained, Mr. Croswell entered the pulpit and declaimed for a long time, with great bitterness; accusing me of preaching damnable doctrines, though he had never heard me preach, but so he had been informed; asserting that I was one of Relly's followers, and Relly believed all mankind would be saved; and Relly was a blasphemer, and denied the atonement; and I was a Deist, and it was dangerous to allow me to speak; for I said once, in his hearing, that God loved the devil's children; and then, raising his voice, he vociferated, 'It is a lie, a lie, a lie, it is a damnable lie.' Thus he went on, alternately crying out against me and against Mr. Relly, damning my preaching, and his writings, and exhorting the people to avoid me etc. etc."[8]

Yet this man called a heretic and Deist and infidel, had still more trying days in Boston. He describes a later meeting in Boston: "My next evening lecture was uninterrupted; but on the succeeding Sunday evening, the throng was so prodigious, that it was with much difficulty I reached the pulpit; and when entered, I was nearly suffocated, by the strong effluvia, arising from the asafoetida[9] with which the tools of the adversary had wet the pulpit and the pulpit cloth, plentifully sprinkling the whole house with the same noxious drug. For some moments I was so much overpowered as to induce an apprehension that it would be impossible I should proceed; but the God of my life was sufficiently abundant for me. The demons of confusion were, however, not quite satisfied; many stones were violently thrown into the windows; yet no one received any other injury than the alarm which was created. At length, a large ragged stone, weighing about a pound and a half, was forcibly thrown in at the window behind my back; it missed me. Had it sped as it was aimed, it must have killed me. Lifting it up, and waving it in the view of the people, I observed: 'This argument is solid, and weighty, but it is neither rational nor convincing.' Exclamations from various parts of the house were echoed, and re-echoed: 'Pray, sir, leave the pulpit, your life is at hazard.' 'Be it so,' I returned; 'the debt of nature must be paid, and I am as ready and as willing to discharge it now as I shall be fifty years hence. Yet, for your consolation, suffer me to say, I am immortal, while he who called me into existence has any business for me to perform; and when he has executed those purposes for which he designed me, he will graciously sign my passport to realms of blessedness. With your good leave, then, I pursue my subjects, and while I have a "Thus saith the Lord" for every point of doctrine which I advance, not all the stones in Boston, except they stop my breath, shall shut my mouth, or arrest my testimony.'"[10]

Murray settled in Gloucester in 1779 as the minister of the Independent Christian Church, which won an epic law case establishing the right of members of an independent church as free from the requirement to be taxed for the support of the state church. Thus, he and his congregation by going to court won the first major legal victory on the road to the establishment of the American principle of the separation of church and state.

With the advent of the American Revolution, Murray signed up as a chaplain and was appointed in May, 1775, to service in the First Rhode Island Regiment, stationed in Roxbury, assigned to "the army of Observation" under General Nathaniel Greene. The First Regiment was under Colonel James H. Varnum, later a general. Other chaplains complained about Murray's heresy and asked for his removal. The matter was eventually referred to General George Washington himself, who issued the following statement:

"General Orders, Sept. 17, 1775. The Rev. Mr. John Murray is appointed Chaplain to the Rhode Island Regiments, and is entitled to respect as such."[11]

Cole and Skinner in their account of the situation quote the *History of Essex County* (Massachusetts), by John Prince as further stating, "Washington answered criticism by having Murray transferred from the chaplaincy of a regiment to that of a brigade, which change was a promotion. And he officiated thereafter as the chaplain of three combined regiments of Rhode Island troops. History furnished no more signal instance of a rebuke of bigoted intolerance."

Thus, whatever his service or calling, it seemed that John Murray was always a stormy center of hotly contested issues. His was not a towering intellect, but he was an articulate voice and clear-headed thinker, and, as such, he organized the first Universalist General Conventions and became properly regarded as the father of the Universalist movement, although others were to be the systemizers of its thought and the leaders in developing a theology of the goodness of God and confidence in the human venture that motivated him.

The third great religious liberal whose life's effort spanned both sides of the Atlantic was Joseph Priestley (1733-1804). Priestley, unlike Murray, was a systematic thinker and was the learned man rather than the controversialist. However, he was a courageous spokesman for his understanding of the truth, which led to greater controversy than he cared to court. Samuel Coleridge in *Table Talk* wrote, "I think Priestley must be considered the author of the modern Unitarianism," and a biographer (Professor Basil Willey, who was King Edward VII Professor of English Literature at Cambridge University from 1923–1963) added, "and this is broadly true, if, by emphasizing the word 'modern,' we understand Coleridge to have intended to distinguish Unitarianism as an English nonconformist sect from the Unitarianism of Socinus, or of Christ and the Apostles (who, according to Priestley, were the first Unitarians)."[12]

Priestley is presented by Prof. Willey as "the chief apostle of modern Unitarianism" as well as the man who welded together the two main currents of English life and thought of the eighteenth century: the mechanical philosophy and the traditional spirit of Protestant Dissent. He was a major figure in the English Enlightenment and moved freely among the great towering figures not only of English, but of European thought. Priestley was the most distinguished English scientist of that time, and the high regard in which he was held is noted in the current use of his name in his adopted country of the United States of America, where he and his friend Benjamin Franklin (who lured him to these shores) are regarded as the first great American scientists. It is not surprising, then, that the newly established National Presidential science award given each year at the White House is named for

Joseph Priestley. As a chemist, he is distinguished foremost for the discovery of oxygen, as well as nitric and nitrous oxides and the absorption of carbon dioxide by chlorophyll in sunlight. He was made a Fellow of the Royal Society for his volume, *History of Electricity,* "and became the honored friend and acquaintance of many of the most eminent scientists and philosophers of the time, both in England and France, consorting in London with men like Franklin, Pringle, and Price; in Paris with Lavoisier, Morellet, Turgot, and the Encyclopedists; or at Birmingham with Erasmus, Darwin, Day, Edgeworth, and the other members of the Lunar Society." However, we are told "religion was the core of his life," and unlike the other Deists, he placed interest in religion before that of Nature.

He was actively engaged as a minister of religion throughout almost all of his life, whether teaching, doing research, writing, collecting the famous assortment of scientific instruments that made his laboratory so celebrated before it was destroyed and burned by the mob incited to hysteria against him. "Priestley's incessant transitions between religion and philosophy, and his diffuse productivity as a writer, suggest, what is indeed the fact, that his mind was comprehensive rather than profound" (p. 170). Here we find one of the great comprehensive minds, not only of the Enlightenment, but of all English letters. He approached the truly universal concept of a person capable and, indeed, superior in every field of human endeavor. "But through this very versatility his work becomes interesting as a compendium of contemporary notions, and it would be hard to find a better representative of what was admirable in the mind and spirit of the late eighteenth century" (Ibid).

His credo may well be summed up, Professor Willey tells us, in this passage from Priestley's book, *History of the Corruptions of Christianity,* Vol. 4, p. 4: "The morning is opening upon us, and we cannot doubt but that the light will increase, and extend itself more and more unto the perfect day. Happy are they who contribute to diffuse the pure light of this everlasting gospel." This optimism was true not only of religious enlightenment, but in all fields. "For him all truth had religious value, and he worked at his philosophical instruments in the same spirit."

A seemingly strange occurrence was that in England he constantly attacked Christianity, while in France he defended it. Herein we see the religious liberal mind operating. In his native land, the established religion was a perversion of Christianity as he understood it as it represented the accumulated "corruptions" which needed clearing so that the pure Christian spirit could emerge. However, in France, he found the militant opposition to Christianity to be so strong as to indicate an opposite position from which the mind was closed to the essence of the liberalizing spirit of religion he beheld. Priestley was concerned over "genuine and rational" Christianity.

As a materialist, he labored to show the incorrectness of the concept of the soul and carried his arguments out by denying natural immortality. He was able to destroy the Cartesian dualism accepted by so many, and he presented "the curious spectacle" of a clergyman who "proceeds boldly to deny the existence of a separate immaterial 'soul' and to accept all (or all but one) of the implications of this denial." Willey raises the question: "Why, one may ask, should this Christian philosopher have been so zealous to destroy the soul, hitherto the cornerstone of the religious fabric? Once again we must remember that Priestley's characteristic method of defending 'Christianity' was to expose and remove its 'corruptions,' which for him included nearly everything considered by the orthodox to be of its very essence." The notion of the soul as a substance distinct from the body, he continues, was "part of the system of heathenism, and was from thence introduced into Christianity which has derived the greater part of its corruptions from this source. . . . This thought, which . . . he developed more fully in his later writings on the history of Christian corruptions, furnishes the main clue to his advocacy of materialism . . . which would enable him to rescue Christianity from all the accretions which, as a Unitarian, he wished to be rid of, and especially the doctrine of the preexistence of Christ the demiurge" (pp. 175-176).

Like the Deists and other representatives of the Enlightenment, he accepted the twin concepts of Necessity and Freedom, which appear to be contradictions. To accept Necessity meant to accept the scientific view of the universe—cause and effect; it meant to accept the unalterable laws of Nature as against superstition and supernaturalism. It, therefore, seemed indispensable for all who held "enlightened and just view of Nature" to be Necessitarians. "Necessity makes for morality where Calvinism undermines it." "Under Calvinism, he says in effect, you cannot urge anyone to turn from his wickedness and live: under Necessity you can and must. Why? Because men's conduct follows necessarily from their motives . . ." (p. 179). He draws from this doctrine also concepts of perfectibility.

By Priestley's time "Deism was professed by isolated freethinkers, while the Unitarian congregation, having evolved by imperceptible stages from the older forms of dissent, retained a strong group consciousness as a religious fellowship." We are told that "The Unitarianism of the last quarter of the eighteenth century, indeed, came very close to Deism of the earlier decades; it differed mainly in origin and organization" (p. 183). Both, however, are the heirs and the products of the Enlightenment. Dr. Willey sums up by noting, "The Unitarianism of Priestley and Lindsey must seem cold to those who seek in religion for colour, and symbol, and ecstasy, but in its combination of 'moon-light'—illumination with religious conviction it remains one of the most characteristic and not the least admirable, of the products of the English eighteenth century" (p. 183).

Dr. Priestley was seemingly at the pinnacle of fame and respect when his world suddenly tumbled about him. A great thinker, a scientist, a universal man of comprehensive scope, he espoused fearlessly and with articulate clarity every rational, freedom-producing, intelligent cause he found worthy. He had not counted in his enlightened age on the hysteria and dread of change that can transform the populace into a fearful and violent mob. Following the unrest stirring in England after the French Revolution, a reaction set in. On the anniversary of the French Revolution, July 14, 1791, a mob set upon his house, his laboratory, with his famous library, and his church, burning all to the ground. He barely escaped with his life. Previously he had been encouraged by Benjamin Franklin to come to America. On April 7, 1794 he began a new life in Pennsylvania. He preached in Northumberland and in Philadelphia organized the first Unitarian Church to bear that name on these shores, although both Unitarianism and Universalism were already being preached. Here he became the friend of the great—Thomas Jefferson, Benjamin Rush, Benjamin Waterhouse and many others. Franklin had died in 1790 and Francis Hopkinson, to whom Franklin bequeathed his scientific experiments and apparatus, had died in 1791. A new life of usefulness for his elder years resulted, nonetheless, and he contributed to the scientific, cultural, educational, and religious life of the new nation.

He reached a different level of people than did Murray; his arguments were different, but his hopeful optimism was the same. He was more scientific and better grounded in comprehensive knowledge than was de Benneville, None of these three alone could have created the many-faceted advance of religious liberalism, but each one of them made a contribution that influenced its development. These three towering individuals brought to this continent the major strains of religious liberalism, of the conviction that it was wise and proper to resist institutional religious orthodoxy. Thus out of their private thought and witnesses they set the stage for the organized movements.

Notes

[1] Albert D. Bell, *The Life and Times of Dr. George de Benneville*, Boston, 1953, Universalist Church of America, page 65.

[2] *Ibid.*, page 66.

[3] S. C. Hewitt, *A Brief Sketch of the Mortal Life of John Murray*, 1852, Boston, Bela Marsh, 25 Cornhill, pages 50–51.

[4] *Ibid.*, page 52.

[5] *Ibid.*, pp. 58–59.

[6] *Ibid.*, pp. 85–86.

[7] *Ibid.*, pp. 99–100.

[8] *Ibid.*, pp. 91–92.

[9] A fetid oil of an Oriental gum, with an odor similar to that of garlic, superstitiously used to drive away evil spirits.

[10] *Ibid.*, pp. 98–99.

[11] From the original *Order Book* in Washington, D.C. (see p. 125 and end notes, *Hell's Ramparts Fell, the Biography of John Murray*, Cole and Skinner, 1941, Boston, Universalist Publishing House.)

[12] Basil Willey, *The Eighteenth Century Background*, 1961, Boston, Beacon Press, p. 181. (Numerous following quotes are from Chapter X, pp. 168–204, "Joseph Priestley and the Socinian Moonlight.")

6

An Organized Movement in America

In America there were early outcroppings of religious liberalism that were forerunners of Unitarian Universalist teachings. Before there was an organized movement of Universalists or of Unitarians, there were churches that took theological stands, mediating religious questions within their own membership, so that they developed covenants and agreements that marked them as Unitarian or Universalist. Ministers were called or dropped from these churches according to their agreement with majority votes of church or parish.

It would not be completely fair to say that the first church organized in New England—the Pilgrim church of Plymouth, Massachusetts in 1620—was Unitarian from its inception; however, one cannot deny some degree of Unitarian influence. The church "became" Unitarian when it called the Rev. Nathaniel Kendall as minister in 1801 and revised the Calvinistic covenant of 1786 reasserting the strong liberal, Arian, Arminian, and Unitarian Universalist influences that operated in this old congregational establishment. In 1656 the Plymouth church was chastised by the Massachusetts Puritan Divines for its lack of "a pious orthodox ministry . . . so that the flood of error and principles of anarchy . . . will not long be kept out . . . to the crying down of ministry and ministers . . ." Earlier the Plymouth Church had petitioned the Massachusetts Bay General Court (1645) to grant "full and free tolerance of religion to all men that will preserve the civil peace and submit unto the government" so that there be "no limitation or exception against Turk, Jew, Papist, Arian, Socinian, Nicolaitan, Familist, or any other."

That this was in the tradition of the Pilgrim Fathers' church may be noted in the farewell address in 1620 of the Pilgrim Pastor, Rev. John Robinson, who said according to Winslow:

> He took occasion also miserably to bewail the state and condition of the Reformed Churches who were come to a period in their religion and would go no further than the instruments of their reformation. As for example: the Lutherans they could not be drawn to go beyond what Luther saw: for whatever part of God's will he had further imparted or revealed to Calvin, they would rather die than embrace it. And so also, saith he, you see the Calvinists they stick where he left them—a misery much to be lamented.

The most quoted line from that sermon sums up the belief in progressive revelation of advancing truth held by the religious liberal: "The Lord hath more truth and light yet to break forth from out his holy word. . . . It is not possible that full perfection or knowledge should break forth at once." Accordingly, we see that religious liberalism was as old as the Mayflower voyage to these shores, although it fed into the Unitarian Universalist movement only after it was later organized elsewhere. Following the rise of an independent Universalist movement, a schism took place in the first Parish in Plymouth. Standing atop Cole's Hill, where the Pilgrims looked out over the famed Rock, and where they later buried their dead beneath the corn, the Rev. James H. Bugbee, the Universalist pastor at the dedication service of the new church in 1822, defiantly proclaimed to those who asked why they withdrew from the Pilgrim church, "It is to maintain the faith of our forefathers who voyaged here in the Mayflower. The faith we proclaim is the faith of the founding fathers who sailed here in 1620." Thus in 1822 the Universalists boldly proclaimed in Plymouth that their faith was the Mayflower faith. In a more mellow age we say today that the Mayflower faith was a shared faith not only of Unitarian Universalist and Congregationalist, but of all who seek freedom for themselves and others.

Great colonial Divines (as the established clergy of the colonial theocracy were called) numbered Unitarians and Universalists among their membership, serving churches which were part of the establishment in the Puritan colonies. Most notable are such men as Charles Chauncy (1704–1787) and Jonathan Mayhew (1720–1766) of Boston. Ebenezer Gay (1696–1787) of Hingham is often called the first recognized Unitarian minister in New England. Controversies surrounded many others apparently holding Universalist Unitarian (Arminian or Arian) views, including Benjamin Kent (1708–1788), Robert Breck (1713–1784), and Samuel Osborn (1685–1774).[1]

To understand Unitarian Universalist beginnings doctrinally, we need to understand its Calvinistic heritage. It is probable that with the exception of Plymouth Colony, the New England colonies were largely settled by Calvinists, although the Puritans slightly modified the continental version. In Calvinism, election, by which the freedom of God was maintained, created a God who was free from human coercion, that is, the individual could not force salvation. In their opinion, God could condemn the most moral and save the most depraved, and perhaps would do so merely to maintain his independence. However, a rational approach to this theology indicated that God had some basis of decision, and that somehow he could and would save those elected, and they in turn could have this assurance. But how? The New England Puritan modified Calvinism by offering a process through which a covenant of God was established. In a lesser degree it was reflected in its own way by the Church Covenant.

God demonstrated a covenant for salvation through the religious experience we call conversion. The founders of New England Puritanism had grown up in England during a period of intense religious excitement, and this excitement induced (we might suppose) a conversion experience. Consequently, this became the means by which one recognized election; the converted were the Saints and the unconverted were the Sinners. To join a colonial church, which meant the right to be a citizen—to vote or hold public office—required a conversion. These colonies (excepting Plymouth and later Rhode Island) were theocracies. The Puritan founders presupposed a commonwealth of the Saved. However, the second and third generations had men and women of sound doctrine, exemplary lives, but who were not citizens because they did not experience conversion. The colonies were in danger of disenfranchised pluralities, and many of the disenfranchised were from "good families" or "first families." (This explains the compromised halfway covenants).

In this situation, Arminianism entered as an easy and natural way of explaining that good people who lived moral lives were among the saved and were entitled to church membership and equality in other respects. One is a free moral agent who can accept or reject God's grace through rational as well as emotional experiences. Out of this gradual step developed the great movement that in three generations was to undermine the Calvinist household of New England, so that churches and parishes were to be voting on whether or not to hold the line or modify it. Regardless of the majority vote, indications are that sizable groups representing both the Arminian and the Calvinist point of view were to be found in nearly every parish. Rigidity of doctrine was crumbling. Arminianism developed into Arianism and then into Socinianism, and, finally, a full-fledged Universalism and Unitarianism emerged. Unitarianism emerged first and most conspicuously from the Calvinistic First Parishes of the Congregational order, whereas Universalism emerged from the Methodist and Baptist churches.

After the Great Awakening (1735–1745) revival the cleavage between liberal and orthodox was complete. Jonathan Edwards and George Whitefield had made their evangelistic inroads everywhere, and the gradualism of evolving patterns was disrupted. A stouter stand by the orthodox was to call for a stouter resistance by the liberals. It may be supposed that Arminianism was most clearly the Universalist concern with the goodness and grace of God, who would save and elect all worthy of it. Thus Arminianism brought the concept of Universalism into the emerging pattern of colonial liberalism. However, the First Parishes, with their educated clergy, sought for the deeper subtleties and systematic connections, which were not only implied by the evolving thought, but which in turn resulted in other modifications of doctrine. Hence, as one Roman Catholic writer has suggested, beginning with rejection of one doctrine, the Arian went on to the necessary rejection of other doctrines. This process took place during the second century of the colonial establishment, so that Puritanism yielded to Arminianism, which yielded to Arianism, then Unitarianism, and in our day to Unitarian Universalism.

On the other hand, the Methodist and Baptist churches of the colonial period were not guided by the same sophisticated clergy as were the Puritan parishes, with a few notable exceptions, such as Roger Williams, who served the Pilgrims in Plymouth and Puritans in Salem in his early career before becoming Baptist. Most Baptists and Methodists were concerned with a more straightforward moral interpretation of the Gospel and were involved in a struggle for sustenance and were against the established religion. They accordingly were not concerned with the systematic ramification, and where the liberalizing process went on it was sufficient to reject Calvinism not through reformation or evolution, but simply by a direct assault upon it. This resulted in inverting the Calvinist argument that Salvation was from God to humanity and insisting it was from humanity to God—determined by one's faith and moral conduct. Hence, erstwhile Methodist and Baptist liberals were satisfied with the Universalist position, and here Murray, de Benneville, and Ballou found their major supporters. By the second generation of Universalist preachers—that of Hosea Ballou (1771–1852) Universalism had need for a more systematic presentation, and evolved into a Unitarian Universalism even before Unitarianism did.

An illustration of this evolution is preserved in an account of the time when the older John Murray was preaching regularly in Boston, but asked the younger preacher, Hosea Ballou, to occupy his pulpit for two successive Sundays. Mrs. Murray attended the services, and was so aghast at the increased liberalism of Ballou, and worried that strangers would not return to hear her husband, that she asked an usher to interrupt the service to announce, "The doctrine heard from this pulpit today is not the usual one preached here." Dutifully the usher stood up and read the note at the conclusion of the sermon. Hosea Ballou, still in the pulpit, stood silent throughout the announcement, prosaically and imperturbably, and then said, "The brethren will be pleased to note what the gentleman has said. We will now proceed with the singing of the last hymn."

An even more startling event is to be found in the records of the Pilgrim Ministerial Association of Plymouth, Massachusetts. This group for some years was under the control of the Calvinist clergy of the area. The author once served as moderator and on studying the old records found what appeared to be an eerie entry. Imagine the bizarre scene, as Puritan ministers, in quaint garb, gathered about the grave of the dead Unitarian Universalist minister, on the hallowed Burial Hill in Plymouth to read the following lines. The entry and reading follows as it is given in the Record Book of the Association:

> 1833: Lines written on the occasion of orthodox ministers gathering in Plymouth to renew their faith and read over and around the grave of the Universalist, Rev. James H. Bugbee:

> Sleeper, awake, and say how camest thou here
> 'Tis hallowed ground, and around thee everywhere, Puritans
>   sleep.
> Art thou a Puritan? For fear of Sin,
> For love of worship pure, didst ever thou endure a
>   Cross or lose a Home?
> A preacher thou, but Herald, didst thou ever say one word
> One burning word about the Curse of God, or Second Death?

When in thy grave they let thee down,
And placed thee close beside the mouldring bones of
   honored men long dead;
Why didst thou not, though lifeless, feel their touch,
And springing Live?
O stay not here; this spot is Sacred to the Pilgrim's rest,
Stranger and foe to all that they loved best—Fly
   hence for Fear!

Go to some cavern deep, where Christian deeds are not,
Nor Christian name
Where Sin and Holiness and Love and Hate are all
   the same—
There steal thy sleep.
Or shouldst thou stay, prove once thyself a Preacher bold:
Proclaim the Truth as it was told of old, as well thou mayest.

Stay Vandals, Thou'rt done enough
Enough to give yourselves a lasting name
Enough to blot the Puritans' fair name, then why not cease?
You've sold for gold the land on which they trod
You've undermined the house they built for God.
Its cornerstone is gone, Jesus is dead except in name.

God of all grace, redeem this rock, this cornerstone
Return and shower upon us the Spirit of thy Grace.

                                                  Finis.

The first clearly organized Unitarian Universalist Church was
that of John Murray in Gloucester, Massachusetts, formed in 1779
under the name of the Independent Christian Church, an
avowedly Universalist Church. In 1785 Kings Chapel in Boston,
the first Church of England congregation in New England,
adopted Unitarian principles in revising the prayer book. Then in
1796, Joseph Priestley established the first Unitarian Church in
America to use openly that designation and to bear that name.
This was the First Unitarian Church of Philadelphia, Pennsylvania.
Of course, by this time many ministers, congregations, and individuals were already calling themselves Universalists or Unitarians, and sometimes others were accusing them of being such.

Free thought in American life began in earnest with the publication in 1784 of Ethan Allen's *Reason the Only Oracle of Man*. The
Library of Congress still prints on its index card the words of

Timothy Dwight "This is the first publication in the United States openly directed against the Christian religion." Ernest Cassara documents the influence of this book on the early Universalist leader, Hosea Ballou. Ethan Allen is known to all American school children as the Revolutionary War hero of the Green Mountain Boys. Allen certainly was a Unitarian Universalist, as his logic indicated: "We will premise the three persons in the supposed Trinity are either finite or infinite; for there cannot in the scale of being be a third sort of being between these two. . ." Then he goes on to show that any such concept is unintelligible. He was called a Deist and an Infidel by the great bulk of orthodox Christians, but Cassara reports that Allen's book was passed from hand to hand by Universalists who found in it support for their Universalism.[2]

The next great step came with the publication of Thomas Paine's *Age of Reason*. When Paine was imprisoned at Luxembourg prison on December 28, 1793, he handed the manuscript of *The Age of Reason* to his friend, Joel Barlow. His aim was to separate essential religion from theology and magic "lest in the general wreck of superstition, of false systems of government and false theologies, we lost sight of morality, of humanity, and of the theology that is true." Thus, he was seeking to save pure religion, not abolish it, as his detractors were to claim. Why, then, the cry against him? He smashed the symbols of superstitious faith, establishing himself as a Unitarian Universalist. He wrote: "I believe in one God, and no more, and I believe in happiness beyond this life. I believe that religious duties consist in doing justice, loving mercy, and endeavoring to make my fellow creatures happy."[3] Yet almost universal designation of Paine as an atheist is still heard. It was superstitious, supernatural religion he opposed, however, and he stood in the line of freethinkers who progressively led to the liberalization of Christianity.

Elihu Palmer lacked the wartime fame of Allen and Paine, but he was the most effective organizer of Deism and free thought in America. His numerous societies served as tangible examples to orthodox preachers that free thought and Deism were not merely English and French phenomena, but were "a weed" in their own backyards.

In the interaction of the free thought movements and the intellectual concerns within the churches of Revolutionary America, a strange leaven was working, which brought forth Universalism and Unitarianism as separate movements. Marty, in *The Infidel* reported that Timothy Dwight in his book, *The Triumph of*

Infidelity (1788) in "twenty-seven of the forty pages . . . deal(s) with the American scene, but twenty-five of these Dwight devoted to attacks on (Charles) Chauncy, the early Universalists, and theological liberalism."[4] Charles Chauncy of Boston and theological liberalism were the incipient Unitarian precursors that came to definite organizational status in the following generation. The English Evangelist, William Wilberforce, in 1797,[5] traced the course "from nominal orthodoxy to absolute infidelity, Unitarianism is indeed, a sort of halfway house . . ." This characterization of Unitarianism as "the halfway house to infidelity" according to Marty, was "a millstone around the neck of Unitarians during their emergence as an American denomination in the early nineteenth century . . ."[6]

It forced the Unitarians to defend themselves against charges of infidelity, even while they were involved as a movement to liberalize Christianity and create a free religion.

Thomas Jefferson, the great liberal, wrote to Dr. Benjamin Waterhouse, the Universalist: "I trust there is not a young man now living who will not die a Unitarian." One cannot help asking why Jefferson's expectation was not fulfilled.

We would answer: because it allowed itself to be caught in a trap. It became tabbed as a type of Protestantism, and as such had to defend itself in terms of generally accepted concepts of Protestantism. As Professor Sidney Mead of Claremont College, former President of the Meadville Theological School points out, this led to nineteenth-century Unitarianism being caught in a whole stream of negations. Unitarianism simply cannot be explained in terms of Protestant beliefs in a positive way. It varies from Protestantism on almost every point, and thus the Unitarian Universalist must say over and over "we do not believe" in terms of Protestant beliefs. Look at the points which Unitarianism, if it were Protestant, would have to explain: The Bible as the foundation of faith; the miracles as the proof of faith; the Deity of Christ (not to mention the Trinity); the concepts of salvation, bodily resurrection, the virgin birth, and so on. Unitarianism cannot completely affirm any one of the general principles of Protestantism.

The Unitarian knew this, of course, but objected to the charge of infidelity, so he tried to cling to his origins and protested that these were the beliefs of orthodox Protestantism, that he was a liberal Protestant. But the fact is that to all others, orthodox Protestantism is the total concept of Protestantism. This is a psychological trap in which Unitarianism became caught, so that it was unable to present its faith in positive terms of what it believed about life, truth, religious knowledge, and the relationship of person to person and to nature.

Unitarianism is the great affirmation of faith in the modern world, but in trying to defend its right to remain within the category of Protestantism it lost its opportunity to explain itself in its own fresh, vital, affirmative terms.

Channing, that great early "apostle of Unitarianism," concerned with clarifying the distinctions between the emerging Unitarianism and the orthodoxy of the colonial churches out of which it came, referred to "Unitarian Christianity." Even he could not remain so limited when he tried to express the affirmative nature of the new faith, for he said many things like this: "This is the bond of the Universal Church. No man can be excommunicated from it but by death of goodness in his own breast."

In the following generation Ralph Waldo Emerson, a Unitarian minister, turned to the study of the Hindu scriptures and the Eastern mystics, and he introduced their thoughts to American letters. He sought to find the larger relationship of the liberal spirit which was represented by Unitarianism. By the 1850s, Emerson had fully launched the emerging Unitarian movement upon the quest for its larger inclusiveness in the family of world religions.

The older organized Universalist groups also were involved in such struggles, and for them it was climaxed in the controversies surrounding Abner Kneeland, fiery Universalist minister and free thought leader, who was tried for blasphemy in 1833–1834 and sentenced to sixty days in prison. A petition for pardon was signed by 168 persons, headed by William Ellery Channing, showing that Unitarians did not stand aloof from the more daring liberalism of the Universalists. Kneeland advocated land reform, abolition of slavery, public education, and birth control long before these issues became of popular concern. His rationalistic approach to religion, his deep ethical and social concerns found tangible expressions when he established his social community in Iowa, "Salubria," typical of the social "communitarian" groups, such as those founded by Robert Owen in Indiana, Wright in Tennessee, Ballou in Hopedale, Massachusetts, and Parker and Alcott at Brook Farm—the most famous of them all.

As we have previously indicated, the evolution of Universalism beyond Murray was at the hands of an amazing scholar, without benefit of much formal schooling, but himself a schoolteacher while still in his teens. Hosea Ballou was born in the small town of Richmond, New Hampshire, in 1771, the year following the landing on these shores of John Murray. Born the son of a Baptist minister, Ballou grew amid the rigid teachings of a stern Calvinist father, suffering the same gloom and despair as did Murray. However, succor came for Ballou first in terms of the book by Ethan Allen, *Reason The Only Oracle of Man*. This amazing book, banned almost everywhere, was the first undeniable work of Deism published in America and was openly opposed by all orthodox clergymen. Ballou as a young man broke with his father's religious views and, rejecting vicarious atonement and eternal punishment, moved on to Universalism and before he was thirty had moved from Trinitarian beliefs to Unitarian. He rejected the concept that some are to be saved and others damned by God and found it impossible to believe the prevalent concept of God's hating this depraved world. Love, not wrath, became for him the fundamental tenet of faith and the basis of doctrine. Once this is accepted, no other doctrine of orthodoxy follows automatically. All doctrines need reexamination. A wholly new theology was needed in an enlightened age by enlightened men, and Ballou proposed to offer one. His volume, *A Treatise on Atonement*, published in 1805, was the first systematic American study of liberal theology. Written eight years before Channing's great utterance on *Unitarian Christianity*, this was the first American effort to carry the rational implications of Universalism and Arianism to their logical conclusions, so that a consistent Unitarian Universalism could be developed. God was one, not three; God was loving, not vindictive; God was the creator of a harmonious world, not a depraved world; God created the rational mind to interpret not only scriptures but all other areas of knowledge. Other concepts could also be drawn: we are not defeated creatures, but the heirs of all the ages, empowered by the creator to build a fairer and better world and hence, capable of doing so. Religion was turned from fear to hope, from Oriental despotism to humanism and the mind was set free.

Abner Kneeland was a lifetime friend of Hosea Ballou and typified the practical implementer, who takes the theory and message of religious faith and applies it to society—not merely in the ideal community of "rustic utopias" but in its application to the social issues and reforms needed in society—political, social, and intellectual. Theodore Parker did the same thing for the Unitarianism of Channing in the Unitarian movement.

Few Americans have been the equal of William Ellery Channing (1780–1842). He is regarded by many as one of the few authentic religious geniuses of America. When he died all the church bells of the Catholic Diocese of Boston were tolled in mourning—a truly signal honor for the acknowledged leader of a liberal movement which avowedly undermined the foundations of religious orthodoxy. World travelers returned home to report that wherever one traveled in England, Germany, and France, scholars asked about the latest views of Dr. Channing. In later generations Tagore and Gandhi in India and Tolstoy in Russia acknowledged debts to William Ellery Channing.

It is probably true that as many historians have said, Dr. Channing added no new concepts to the systematic theology of Hosea Ballou; however, in the erudition with which he presented it, the scope of his application, and the wide-ranging development of his sympathies he added new and larger dimensions to the religious liberal movement. Channing's rhetoric was as distinguished as that of any other writer in America and equal to the great contemporary English essayists, such as Matthew Arnold, John Ruskin, and Carlyle. Consequently his thoughts are expressed in a universal idiom, and we see the relevancy which makes his writing fresh, vital, and valid today. Channing, in other words, is still highly quotable, and his words are appropriate even today.

He was a man of distinguished antecedents. He was the grandson of William Ellery, a signer of the Declaration of Independence; George Washington was an overnight guest in the Channing home in Newport, Rhode Island; he knew Chief Justice John Marshall from his two years in Richmond; and the great of Massachusetts—the Adamses, Daniel Webster, Josiah Quincy, and Charles Sumner—were his friends. It is no accident, therefore, that he was the conscience for a new society and a new culture that would arise in America. "We want a Reformation, we want a literature"; he wrote, "and our chief hopes for an improved literature rest on an improved religion—a new action and development of the religious principle in this country."

While a student at Harvard College, Channing had a moment of insight while studying under the willows along the banks of the Charles River. Reflecting upon the derogatory views of human nature then dominant in theology, of the French sceptics and the Calvinist doctrine of the utter depravity of humanity, of the accepted concept of the moral weakness of mankind, he knew the same gloom and despondent outlook that brought depression to John Murray. On this spring day in 1796, however, as pensively he kept going back to the affirmative concepts of the Roman Stoics and the enlightened views of the Age of Reason, light broke through for him.

It seemed to him in retrospect that he had passed through a second birth at this moment and an insight bringing inward peace enlightening his mind. The insight was the sublime idea of man's natural and moral freedom, his heritage of divine powers, his infinite spiritual perfectibility. From this day hence he possessed a counter argument to the dark and gloomy forebodings of Calvinism, which attempted to scare people into the churches and into heaven. From this day hence both Calvinism "and the Lucretian materialism of the foes of the Infamy in France" were to Channing the true blasphemy. This was nine years before Ballou (already approaching the height of his powers) wrote *A Treatise on Atonement*, but Channing was still a student. Channing received his degree from Harvard that spring and accepted a position in Richmond, Virginia, as a tutor, where he was free much of the time for reading, studying, and reflection by himself in the schoolroom. He read almost all the available literature in the libraries and homes open to him and returned, broken in health, but a learned and well-read man two years later to resume studies at Harvard for the ministry. He graduated in 1803, and entered into the ministry of the only pulpit he ever served, that of the Federal Street Church, Boston. In 1812 he preached his first great antiwar sermon, which was to mark him as the founding spirit for the first peace society organized in Massachusetts. Pacifist, abolitionist, internationalist, believer in human dignity and the rights of all people, he became the universal scholar whose conscience sharpened the sensitivity of America. Emerson said later that in his day at Harvard, Dr. Channing stood out as the great shining light on the intellectual landscape, and many were to bear a similar witness.

When the Universalist Abner Kneeland was convicted of blasphemy by the Massachusetts Superior Court, Dr. Channing organized the repeal petition; when Theodore Parker was under attack by the other Unitarian clergy for his new, more radical ideas, Dr. Channing invited Parker to sit with him at the meeting; when he was invited to address students at Harvard in 1830, his mind tingling over the recent news of European political uprisings which promised democratic self-government opportunities, he excoriated the student body for its apathy. "I see the young men of Harvard are quite sedate and unconcerned over the new revolutions in Europe. I was in Harvard in the days of the first French Revolution," he cried with eyes aflame, "and at every turn of events we lighted bonfires and marched in torchlight parades at each new outburst of freedom." Told this was a childish response, he shouted, "We were always young for liberty!" His life showed this to be so. His last public appearance was to speak out on behalf of West Indian independence at Lennox in 1842.

As a systematic thinker, his thoughts, drawn from the clear insight under the willows, deal with the concepts of moral freedom and the natural inheritance of divine nature. These developments were shown in his application. He dealt with such broad concepts as the moral dignity of human nature, one's kinship to God, the religious life as both internal and external, a universal human family, the evils of war as betraying human dignity and respect, and the moral law that applies to nations and politics. He stressed the numerous applications of religious principles to social affairs; secular and religious education; anti-slavery, social reforms, citizenship; the elevation of the laboring masses, the church universal, and democratic demands for excellence and progress.

His most important utterance in the field of religious reform was the famous Baltimore sermon, *Unitarian Christianity,* preached at the ordination of Jared Sparks in 1819. Here, in a two-hour sermon, he systematically developed religion as based on reason, on the use of reason as sufficient to interpret scripture, in the reading of scripture as one reads all books, on the moral concept of a divine spark in life, and the humanity of Jesus as inferior to God as divinity, showing then that the ancient theological systems no longer were essential. In place he offered a platform for the liberal reform of Christianity, which he called Unitarian Christianity, but which Universalists were quick to point out was the Unitarian Universalism of Hosea Ballou.

The aftermath of the Baltimore sermon was a widespread discussion in the churches. Timothy Dwight and Jedidiah Morse took this occasion to reiterate that the liberalism in the congregational churches was really a Unitarianism, and they and others called for a separation of parishes and the exclusion of the liberal Unitarians from the church conferences. Thereafter, doctrinal tests were administered to the ministers as they arrived, and the liberals found themselves being turned away. So many were denied fellowship in the vicinity of Boston that a new Berry Street Conference met, composed of the disenfranchised Unitarians. This was the forerunner of the American Unitarian Association, which the conference voted to establish in 1825, with William Ellery Channing as first president. As he was in poor health, it was understood he could not undertake the administrative role, but his prestige attracted prominent support to the infant organization which became the eventual guardian of Unitarianism. Other groups of a wider nature were subsequently formed: the National Conference of Unitarian Churches (later the General Conference), and the Western Unitarian Conference. Unitarianism as well as Universalism was now organized as a denomination.

Theodore Parker brought to the group the new insights of the European scholarship, notably that of German philosophy, biblical criticism ("The Higher Criticism"), and theological inquiry, and a new catholicity and broader discipline of study was introduced, breaking the limitation of the Puritan religious experience. Emerson, minister of the Second Church in Boston, began the study of Eastern religions, bringing an awareness of the validity and value of the non-Christian religious experience. Transcendentalism, the broader concept of the religious experience, broke the final bonds of the colonial religious establishment, and the opportunity existed for a broader and more dynamic religious movement than had ever appeared before. This was frightening to many who did not see Unitarianism as more than a sensible adjustment or moderate evolution of religious thought. They were happily entrenched in free churches which interfered little with their cultural and intellectual lives, but were still comfortably ensconced in the proven ways of Federal Society with its genteel traditions. They continued the Puritan tradition by holding an anniversary celebration in May for the establishment of the Massachusetts Bay Colony. This became the annual meeting of the new anti-Calvinist (hence anti-Puritan) American Unitarian Association. The irony of the continuation of the anniversary meeting escaped them. The early weekly Unitarian journal, the *Christian Examiner* (founded one year before the Association), in which Dr. Channing and Theodore Parker published so many of their works, typified the concern for the liberals: the examination of all things religious and the questioning of all theological doctrine. A more conservative paper, the *Christian Register*, replaced the old *Examiner* after 1830 as the sole Unitarian publication, and the movement to simply register opinion rather than examine it may be inferred. The old guard seemed to be gaining control of the young movement. The Unitarians erected their headquarters (strange name for a nonmilitant ecclesiastical organization) on Beacon Street and relished Oliver Wendell Holmes's eventual characterization of it as the "Little Old Lady of Beacon Street."

There was inevitably a struggle between the conservative Unitarians and the more liberal. It centered in part around Ralph Waldo Emerson's resignation as minister of the Second Church after two years during which he refused to celebrate communion, calling it the vestige of an out-grown past. It centered again in the theological controversy surrounding Theodore Parker and the new continental influences for a broader intellectual foundation to liberal religion which stemmed from his European scholarship; and it centered about the social concerns and issues of those great reformers who helped determine the nature of the church: Julia Ward Howe, Dorothea Dix and the reform of mental and penal institutions; Joseph Tuckerman and the creation of social welfare; Thomas Mott Osborne and prison reform; Dr. Samuel Gridley Howe and work with immigrants, the blind, and the feeble-minded; Henry Bergh and the Society for the Prevention of Cruelty to Animals and the Society for the Prevention of Cruelty to Children. There were many others, not the least of whom as the century progressed were the feminists, Susan B. Anthony, Elizabeth Cady Stanton, and Mary A. Livermore. In education there was Horace Mann, Ezra Cornell, Leland Stanford, Peter Cooper, John Lowell, Jr., and Charles W. Eliot. Thomas Starr King, "who saved California for the Union"; James Freeman Clarke, who saw the more progressive religion of the future, and Edward Everett Hale of *Man Without a Country* fame, were to become the great symbols of a fresh approach for Unitarianism. Nevertheless the movement came close to being fractured in the first generation of its existence.

In the following generation the religious liberals—Universalists, Unitarians, free thought societies, Transcendentalists, evolutionists, etc.—found themselves drawing new battlelines to clarify the issues left unresolved by an honest facing of the implications of liberalism in religion.

The story is highlighted by Stow Persons in *Free Religion*.[7] The struggle for the separation of church and state seemed completed and, in consequence, the American phenomenon of voluntary denominationalism had sprung up, bringing a new vitality to churches. Abolition had seemingly brought a great crusade for human freedom to conclusion, and the churches basked in the illusion of a successful social accomplishment. The Unitarians were split over the issue of Christian Unitarianism versus Transcendentalism. The Universalists were busy with the problems of structuring state and national conventions that were compatible with the ideals of their democratic faith, free of authoritarian restrictions. "Calvinism rushes to be Unitarianism, and Unitarianism rushes to be Naturalism," Emerson wrote in his journal (Vol. X., page 9). The rush to naturalism marked the liberal religious development of the last third of the nineteenth century.

A few days after Lee's surrender ending the Civil War, a memorable and important meeting was held at All Souls Church, New York. A national convention of Unitarian Churches was called to consider the proper modes for the development of a national liberal Christian faith. Out of this meeting came the National Conference of Unitarian Churches, which continued into the 1920s as a major denominational channel for deliberation and action. However, its start was far from auspicious because of the struggle between what Persons calls "Unitarian orthodoxy" and free religion. Those Unitarian clergymen whom the majority called "young radicals," watched with dismay the All Souls meeting adopt a purpose that included affirming the "positive work of the gospel of Jesus Christ." The young radicals said they had come to witness the organization of the liberal church of America and instead saw it scuttled while being launched. The noted clergyman, Octavius Brooks Frothingham, went uptown and persuaded his Third Unitarian Church to become the Independent Liberal Church, and Francis Ellingwood Abbott journeyed back to Dover, New Hampshire, to lead his church into becoming for one glorious decade one of the most important and articulate liberal churches of the land.

The National Unitarian Conference had seemingly organized Unitarianism as a semi-orthodox movement in 1866. In consequence, the young radicals (including many not so young), felt they were now orphans. A power structure seemingly thwarted their efforts to make Unitarianism the free religious movement they believed it to be. Consequently, they began to meet separately.

In October, 1866, eight radical Unitarians, both ministers and laypeople, met at the home of Cyrus A. Bartol on Chestnut Street, Boston. They were compatible with the neighboring Boston Radical Club, and between these two groups a fuse was lighted to explode the seemingly calm exterior of the Unitarian movement. Bartol "was ripe for revolt." Samuel Longfellow feared "the inevitable consequences of ecclesiastical organization." He said that free religion could only be promoted by "free institutions, the free church and its preacher, the free magazine, and the free lecture platform." Sidney H. Morse, editor of the influential journal, *The Radical*, concurred with him and was to be an influential leader in the new movement of free religion as a radical religious movement.

Many were determined that some sort of free religious movement outside of Unitarianism must be organized, and these men, together with Abbott, Towne, Potter, and Henry W. Brown, proceeded to take steps. Octavius B. Frothingham was approached and consented to chair a meeting for the organization of a free religious movement, giving them the necessary status for a public meeting called for May 30, 1867, in Boston. Sponsors of the meeting were approximately thirty persons, Unitarians, Universalists, "two or three Quakers" and "several members of Parker's old Twenty-Eighth Congregational Society." Speakers at the several-day conference represented "left wing Unitarianism, progressive Universalism, the Quakers, progressive Quakers, free religionists, liberal Jews, and 'come-outers'" as well as others including such unlikely soul-mates as Spiritualists, with the concluding address to be made by the greatest liberal of them all, Ralph Waldo Emerson.

The Free Religious Association began with great hopes, but floundered from its inception. It was impossible to set forth a platform of agreement for the broad collection of points of view included. More seriously, it could not even agree on a program of action, and so never effectively demonstrated its vitality. It did, however, alert the Unitarian majority to the danger that religious liberalism would be diffused through other movements if the old guard made what Channing had called "an orthodoxy of the liberalism of our youth."

The last quarter of the nineteenth century was largely a struggle between organized Unitarianism and Universalism against the free religious movement with its affiliated radical clubs, liberal leagues, free-thought societies, which vied for dual allegiance of Unitarians, Universalists, and other come-outers.

Throughout this period the great counter-attack to "make the United States a Christian nation" by the proposed Constitutional Amendment "to recognize the Lord Jesus Christ," was symptomatic of the resurgence of Christian orthodoxy. This always could be relied upon to marshal the forces of free religion, which were united in opposing state-churchism. Other issues divided rather than united the free religionists. One such issue was the Comstock Laws pertaining to the shipment of obscene materials through the mails, which raised the specter of censorship. Even when the laws were applied against the publication of free-religion journals, the liberals could not unite, for some felt the greater evil of obscenity required censorship. This theoretical juggling that paralyzed the forces of free religion constantly forced out of the movement genuine religious liberals who were called "actionists."

In desperation, the greatest actionist of the day, Felix Adler, a member of the association, was invited to become president and served from 1879–1882. When he resigned he carried the Ethical Culture groups with him into an independent organization. With Adler's resignation, following the failure to adopt his program, the last effective opportunity for making the Free Religious Association a meaningful movement disappeared. When it organized the World Parliament of Religions in Chicago in 1898, it was giving, in effect, the death gasp of the Free Religious Association, although it lingered on into the twentieth century.

In the meantime, the National Conference of Unitarians and the American Unitarian Association had revised their bylaws and purposes to make the Unitarian movement undisputedly a free religious movement. From the formation of the Free Religious Association in 1867 until the reabsorption of the bulk of its membership around the turn of the century, the role of the free religionist in the Unitarian movement had completely reversed. In 1867 he was a hopeless minority surrounded by a majority of "Unitarian Christians." At the turn of the century, the free religionists were the avowed majority of the Unitarian movement, as witness its programs, statements, purposes, and directions. Consequently, it is not surprising that today it is the Unitarian Christians who organize separately, as a century ago it was the free religionists who did. Both groups have always been part of our movement, however, and shall undoubtedly continue to be. Both are historically germane, and it may well be that the vitality of religious liberalism requires the cross-fertilization or interaction of these two groups. Certainly, Unitarianism and Universalism have continued to be more vital with these tensions than the Free Religious Association ever became without them.

The Universalists were a freer religious movement than the more structured Unitarians during the nineteenth century; consequently they never needed the Free Religious Association to the extent that the Unitarians did. As a result, while Universalists were always active in it, it was more as individual religious liberals. To Universalists the Free Religious Association was not as necessary as it was to the Unitarians who used it to combat the ecclesiastical policies of their denomination. The Free Religious Association was designed and built by Unitarians who never intended to withdraw, but meant to exert pressure toward changes in the denominational structure. The freer structure of the Universalist state conventions and the general convention (which continued down into the 1930s) made possible continuous pressure internally to keep Universalism growing and developing as a free religious movement.

Nonetheless, there are great achievements to be credited to the Free Religious Association. Its involvements quickly indicate the nature of the vital influence it had on both Unitarian and Universalist organizations. It became the articulate champion of naturalism in religion, of efforts toward a "scientific theology," on acceptance of evolution and rapport with modern natural science, and embraced the theories of Darwin, Huxley, and Spencer. It found the agnosticism of Huxley acceptable and was the first champion of humanism and "the religion of humanity."

It proclaimed a religion of democracy, with its faith in persons and its confidence in the triumph of reason and rationalism. Freedom became its byword, and it sought the means for achieving "the good society," through not only the "rustic utopias," but socialism or the class struggle, on the one hand, or pure democracy and the perfectibility of the individual, on the other hand. It gave lip service to social reform and urged individuals to furnish leadership. (Although the Free Religious Association never succeeded in organizing a social action program, it was charged that the bulk of the Free Religious Association leadership felt no need for it because their respective Unitarian and Universalist societies were already furnishing leadership in social reform.)

It moved rapidly from the liberalization of Christianity to a concern with all the world's religions, and the comparative study of religions became an essential element of free religion. It is not without significance that the only effective and endurable action program ever agreed upon by the Free Religious Association was the organization of the World Parliament of Religions in 1898.

The final solution by which the free religionists were welcomed back into the National Conference of Unitarian Churches (after 1911 the General Conference) came with Rev. William Channing Gannett's resolution, adopted overwhelmingly: "All names that divide 'religion' are to us of little consequence compared with religion itself. Whoever loves Truth and lives the one or lives the other better than ourselves is our teacher, whatever church or age he belongs to." With this new attitude, it was clear that Unitarianism and free religion had now healed the breach.

The Universalists were also moving toward the fuller recognition of their role in free religion, as well as the oneness of their cause with the Unitarians. Indeed, they recognized it long before the Unitarians apparently did. The great Hosea Ballou in a sermon at the time of the Unitarian controversy in which he took for his text, "Nevertheless I have something against thee" (Rev. 2:4), dealt with this phenomenon. When the Unitarians were seceding from Congregationalist churches, the Universalists were already active, fighting the identical battle of ideas. They looked to the Unitarians for support, common cause, sympathy, and an alliance, as well as for reinforcement. One historian, John Coleman Adams,[8] declares flatly that six years before Channing's Baltimore sermon there were only two Trinitarian ministers left in the Universalist ranks—all the others being Unitarian. The Universalists, hard pressed by the Baptists and Methodists, needed support, fellowship, and encouragement. The Unitarians gave them none. Accordingly, Ballou charged that the Unitarian fight was already being waged by the Universalists, and that, so far as ideas went, these two groups were very close together. He asked why they could not become one organically as well as intellectually and spiritually and then charged that the Unitarians were unwilling to be identified with them, noting they were more friendly to other groups than to the Universalists.

It took a long time for the Unitarians and Universalists to grow close to one another. Individuals moved in the orbit of both denominations: Rev. James H. Bugbee became minister of the Plymouth, Massachusetts, Universalist Church in 1822 and concurrently served as minister of the First Unitarian Society after 1831. When Thomas Starr King, son of a Universalist minister and himself a Universalist minister in Charlestown, Massachusetts, moved to the Hollis Street Unitarian Church in Boston in 1848 he assured his former parish he was not changing the faith he professed and which they affirmed, because Unitarians and Universalists held the same faith, merely altering the idiom slightly. His famous remark was made at this time: "The Universalist thinks God is too good to damn him while the Unitarian thinks he is too good for God to damn."

Throughout the long period of the nineteenth century the Universalists were as busy as the Unitarians in good works and the clarification of faith. The Universalists founded a number of colleges: St. Lawrence University in Canton, New York; Tufts

University in Medford, Massachusetts; Lombard College in Illinois (now continued as a part of the Meadville Theological School, Chicago, as is Ryder College). Buchtel College evolved into Akron University, Akron, Ohio. Old Universalist seminaries continue as Goddard College, Plainfield, Vermont; Dean Junior College, Franklin, Massachusetts; and Westbrook College, Portland, Maine. One of the world's greatest technical colleges grew out of a Universalist founded institution: Throop Institute, becoming the California Institute of Technology, Pasadena, California. None of these schools are under direct denominational control. In fact, in founding Tufts University, the Universalist General Convention passed a strong resolution stating it was not their intention to found another sectarian college, pointing out there were already too many such. "We propose to found an institution where any parent may send his son to study without fear of proselytizing." The college charter was the first in America to specify there would never be any theological tests for faculty, students, or trustees, nor would any such test be required for admission or graduation. This presented the freedom of the Universalists as much as anything could. Universalism was the first denomination to go on record as being opposed to slavery; and the greatest of all abolitionists, William Lloyd Garrison, was a member and grew up in a family active in a Universalist church. Clara Barton, founder of the Red Cross, was a Universalist from Oxford, Massachusetts; and the first peace movement launched in the United States was the work of the Universalists.

Universalists prided themselves on being a noncredal church, and yet sought constantly to systematize their common beliefs through a "profession of faith." The first was adopted in Philadelphia in 1790, followed by a revision in 1803 (the Winchester Profession), and in Boston in 1899. The final revision was that of 1935 in Washington. Throughout this process, the Universalists were always jealous guardians of a famous "liberty clause" which ended their professions with the provision "neither these words nor any other shall be required as a test of membership. . . ."

As we review the history of the Unitarian Universalist movement, we note the tensions and interactions of divergence and nonconformity within each group, as well as between the two groups. There was a choice of Unitarian groups, such as the Association in Boston, the Western Conference centered in Chicago, and the General Conference centered in New York. The differences were ideological rather than geographical, however, and through-out their history they were poles between which the loyalties and orientations of churches, ministers, and lay members fluctuated. Similar distinctions existed within local churches oftentimes, and the camps divided wherever Unitarians gathered. In like manner the Universalists, with their state conventions and general con-vention, also divided not only geographically but ideologically. Various journals of opinion represented contending positions in their denomination. For both groups the words "a unity of spirit amid a diversity of convictions" were meaningful. Hosea Ballou summed it up beautifully when he said, "If we agree in brotherly love, there is no disagreement can do us any injury, but if we do not, no other agreement can do us any good." We have pointed out that today we can say "a church not for those who think alike, but for those who alike think."

Consequently, with a spectrum of liberal belief in both de-nominations, many have looked at the other and found there were groups within it that they were closer to than some in their own denomination and sought a basis of great cooperation or unity. The first vote on record seems to have been in 1865 when the American Unitarian Association voted on two propositions offi-cially presented to the anniversary meetings in Boston. One was a simple proposal to merge with the Universalists. This was tabled, the arguments generally being that the mode of organization of the two was not conducive to immediate merger. The second was a motion to bring together in an interdenominational body the more liberal denominations such as the Christians (Campbellites), Methodists, Universalists, and Congregationalists. The impracti-cality of proceeding seemed to foredoom this to a later time. However, the Campbellites, a frontier liberal movement out of the Baptists, seemingly coming closer to Unitarian Universalists at that time, resulted in a program for a joint frontier theological school, which was established in Meadville, Pennsylvania. The Campbell-ites moved from liberal to conservative orientation, however.

The Free Religious Association was organized two years later, as we have noted, and it seemed to meet the need for an umbrella organization for liberals from a larger circle.

The next important merger proposal was a result of the World Parliament of Religions, and led to a motion in 1899 to appoint commissions of five members from the Unitarian and Universalist denominations, to "seek coordination, not a consolidation; unity, not union." There followed attempts to strengthen this effort, and in 1908 when the National Federation of Religious Liberals was formed, it included not only Universalists, Unitarians, Friends, but the Central Conference of American Rabbis (*i.e.*, Reform Rabbis). Later union talks were entered into by the Unitarians and Universalists with the Congregationalists, but the Universalists in 1923 voted that union with Unitarians was to be preferred to a Congregational union at this time.

The Free Church of America was established in 1933, following an earlier vote of 1931 to explore the possibilities of a liberal equivalent of the Federal Council of Churches. Although open to individual parishes of other denominations, not many joined. It never became effective, although it continued until 1938.

In the meantime the youth groups of the Universalist and Unitarian denominations were enthusiastically in favor of the merger and were stopped only by the counsel of adult church leaders who said that it was impractical to merge the youth while the adults were not merged. It was accordingly not until 1953 that the youth merger took place, although for a generation the youth of both denominations believed in and worked for it. Likewise, other common ventures were undertaken. In 1935, after years of editorial work, a joint commission of Unitarians and Universalists brought out the first joint hymn book of the two denominations, *The Hymns of the Spirit*. Thus Unitarians and Universalists now began using the same materials in their worship. About this time also the Unitarian religious education curriculum committee invited the Universalists to send representatives, and the Beacon curriculum of religious education came into being, serving both denominations. Thus, in practical ways, from childhood education, through youth activities and worshipping experience on the adult level, the Unitarian Universalist denominations moved to practical unity long before a formal church merger was accomplished.

A resolution was presented to the General Conference of the American Unitarian Association, meeting in Washington, D.C., on October 16, 1947, calling for the establishment of a "Commission on Church Union," which was passed unanimously. This resolution reads as follows:

> WHEREAS: The American Unitarian Association and the Universalist Church of America are broadly similar in purpose, scope and aims; and

> WHEREAS: Both ecclesiastical organizations and their constituent fellowships come under the common heading of Liberal Religious Fellowships; and

WHEREAS: In times past, plans of merger and common organization have been discussed; and

WHEREAS: Section 4 of Article I of the Bylaws of the American Unitarian Association lists among the purposes of the Association: "And to encourage sympathy and cooperation among religious liberals at home and abroad"; and

WHEREAS: A larger fellowship of religious liberals is deemed desirable to speak with concerted voice, and act with uniformity in the name of all religious liberals;

BE IT THEREFORE RESOLVED: That the American Unitarian Association, assembled in General Conference, recommends to the Board of Directors the creation of a commission on church union which shall be empowered to meet regularly with any duly authorized committee or commission of the Universalist Church of America to explore the field of church unity, and prepare a report for the next General Conference of the American Unitarian Association; to study separately the feasibility of such action; to report to the Board of Directors and to the fellowship as a whole as it sees fit from time to time; and to be prepared to recommend to the next General Conference the feasibility of the continuation of such commission; and

BE IT FURTHER RESOLVED: That this commission be authorized to study the basis of union with other liberal religious groups; and

BE IT FURTHER RESOLVED: That this commission be composed as follows: seven members appointed by the Moderator upon consultation with the respective presidents of the General Alliance of Unitarian and Other Liberal Christian Women, the Unitarian Laymen's League, the American Unitarian Youth, the Universalist-Unitarian Joint Advisory Committee, the alumni associations of Unitarian clergymen representing the Harvard Divinity School, the Meadville Theological School, and the Tufts College School of Religion; one member appointed by the Moderator upon consultation with the president of the Unitarian Ministerial Union, this member to act as convener; and three additional members appointed by the Board of Directors of the American Unitarian Association; and that during the next two-year period this commission have power to fill vacancies in its own membership; and

BE IT FURTHER RESOLVED: That all appointments be made at the earliest convenience, and that the commission be considered operative upon the election of the first six members, and hold its first meeting prior to January 15, 1948; and

BE IT FINALLY RESOLVED: That an invitation shall go to the General Convention of the Universalist Church of America at the earliest convenience, to appoint a similar commission.

A joint commission was appointed, which proposed a "federal union" rather than an organic union, and successive steps were taken along this line, resulting first in the establishment of the Council of Liberal Churches in 1953 at a joint session of the two denominations in Andover, Massachusetts. Two years later a joint merger commission was elected which, under able leadership, brought forward a plan for consolidation which was presented to both denominations in Syracuse, New York, in October, 1959. This led to the final consummation in Boston on May 11, 1961. Since 1953, however, both denominations had held their biennial meetings together, so that practical union ensured the creation of a merged Unitarian Universalist Association long before the accomplished fact.

During the twentieth century the Unitarian Universalist movement has constantly reached out to create international arrangements with established fellow religious liberals in other countries, to pioneer in new contacts, and to actively involve itself in efforts for international religious cooperation.

In doing so it utilized the facilities of the International Association for Religious Freedom (I.A.R.F.), founded in Boston in 1900. Its offices were located in The Hague, where it remained until 1974, when its offices were re-established in Frankfurt, West Germany. The I.A.R.F. brings together the American and Canadian Unitarian Universalists with those of Great Britain, Western and Central European countries, as well as with non-Christian groups, such as the Brahmo-Samaj of Calcutta, India, and several modern and liberal Hindu, Muslim, and Buddhist groups in Asia and Japan, as it seeks to enlarge the fellowship of a world-wide religious liberal community.

In 1923 the Rev. Norbert Čapek, a Czechoslovakian Baptist pastor who fled Prague during World War I, returned to establish in the newly independent Czech nation the Czechoslovakian Unitarian Association. Norbert Čapek was a singularly gifted, charismatic religious personality whose earlier defense against the charges of heresy had led to an outspoken espousal of the role of religious rationalism, democratic idealism and cultural optimism. This new society thrived and numbered in the thousands when the Nazis invaded Czechoslovakia in 1939. The Czechoslovakian National Church, one million strong, followers of John Huss, co-operated and extended friendly fellowship to the Unitarians. Čapek's outspoken opposition to tyranny, thought control, and book burnings, and his defense of the Jews, led to his arrest in 1940. He was tried by the Nazis and sentenced to death in the gas chamber for expressing "ideas too dangerous to the Reich to be allowed to live." He died in the concentration camp at Dachau in 1942. He was the first genuine Unitarian martyr of the modern era. His work was continued by the Rev. Karl Haspl, a protégé who had prepared for the ministry in the Unitarian Pacific School for the Ministry in Berkeley, California. Dr. Haspl married Dr. Čapek's daughter, and together they held the Czech Unitarian movement together during the Nazi occupation and later, that of the Soviet Union. Facing difficulties, the association of churches continued throughout the 1970s under the leadership of Dr. Dusan Kafka and Mrs. Haspl. It now appears that the seed of a dynamic fellowship may survive if government bureaucracy does not intervene.

In the meantime the flower communion service originated by Čapek is widely used in Unitarian churches the world over, and the flaming chalice symbol developed by a Czech refugee, Hans Deutsch, has been adopted as a Unitarian symbol in many countries.

The British were able through the devotion of Margaret Barr and others to create a Unitarian church movement in the Kasai Hills of India, which continues on under independent leadership.[9]

Other tenuous movements to establish Unitarian Universalism with American support have taken place. The efforts of Jabez Sutherland in India,[10] McChord Crothers in Japan ("We come not to convert, but to confer."), of Harry Carey in Tokyo for the Universalists, and of Louis Cornish's efforts in the Philippines, all had only modest success for a season. The indigenous growth of Unitarian societies out of the national cultures of people, as in Czechoslovakia, has been matched in Lagos, Nigeria, and may be seen in the post-missionary churches of Ghana and elsewhere in Africa, where native people combine their own insights with Christian, Moslem, and native religious traditions to create an independent liberal faith.

Closer cooperation with the most ancient Unitarian churches in Hungary and Romania strengthens their churches and ours. Newer contacts with ancient Socinian and Arian groups in Poland are now possible. Servitites in Spain (who do not consider their body to be "religious") may open more doors for a wider fellowship of Unitarian Universalists with other liberal faiths. Such faiths include Christians, non-Christians, humanists, naturalistic theists and democratic persons—a truly universal church.

The current chapter of free religion is not yet written. The major advance in our day has been the fusion of Unitarianism and

Universalism. Modern Unitarian Universalism likewise is in evolution, and we confidently expect that it is the heir to the free thought movement and free religion and will create in our day a new entity—Unitarian Universalism—that goes beyond the history of its component parts.

Notes

[1]C. Conrad Wright, *The Beginnings of Unitarianism in America*, 1955, Boston, Beacon Press, Chapter 1.

[2]Ernest Cassara, *Hosea Ballou: Challenge to Orthodoxy*, Boston, Beacon Press, 1961, Chapter 5.

[3]Bratton, *Legacy of the Liberal Spirit*, pp. 133–134.

[4]Martin E. Marty, *The Infidel, Free Thought and American Religion*, Living Age Books, 1961.

[5]William Wilberforce, *A Practical View of the Prevailing Religion Systems*, London, 1797, p. 309.

[6]Marty, *op. cit.*, p. 88.

[7]Stow Persons, *Free Religion*, Boston, Beacon Press, 1963.

[8]See Adams' short biography of Ballou in *Pioneers of Religious Liberty in America*.

[9]See Lavan, Spencer, *Unitarians and India*, 1978, Boston, Skinner House, page 149 ff.

[10]*Ibid.* Nos. 143 ff.

7

What Do Unitarian Universalists Believe?

In one of the classic moments of religious history, Confucius and Lao Tze came face to face in the Imperial Library in the city of Lo-Yang, 500 years before the birth of Jesus. For a brief moment sparks flew and harsh words were exchanged between these two seers, both venerated in their day and both destined to be the founders of great faiths. Confucius believed that in studying social and political affairs and diligently searching history for its clues, the way of a better life could be revealed. Lao Tze believed that one should dissociate himself from worldly matters and contemplate the divine way, the Tao. "One should contemplate the meaning of death, and the way of the divine," Lao Tze in effect said to the social student, to which Confucius responded in words that are memorable: "How can one know anything about death when we know so little about life? They who would teach of the gods are often ignorant of human ways."

Thus in dynamic contrasts Confucius sets forth the problem of believing, or of knowing, in terms that many liberals comprehend.

One is reminded of such contrasts within a single life, as one thinks of that characterization of Tom Paine by Theodore Roosevelt, who referred to the great patriot writer of the American Revolution as "that dirty little atheist."

On the other hand, when, in fact, we turn to Thomas Paine's *The Age of Reason*, we find he was not an atheist at all, in spite of being reputed to be. He wrote:

I believe in one God and no more; and I hope for happiness beyond this life.

I believe in the equality of man; and I believe that religious duties consist in doing justice, loving mercy, and endeavoring to make our fellow creatures happy.

But lest it should be supposed that I believe many other things in addition to these, I shall, in the progress of this work, declare the things I do not believe, and my reasons for not believing them.

I do not believe in the creed professed by the Jewish church, by the Roman church, by the Greek church, by the Turkish church, by the Protestant church, nor by any church that I know of. My own mind is my church.

I do not mean by this declaration to condemn those who believe otherwise; they have the same right to their belief as I have to mine. But it is necessary to the happiness of man, that he be mentally faithful to himself. Infidelity does not consist in believing or in disbelieving; it consists in professing to believe what he does not believe.

It is impossible to calculate the moral mischief, if I may so express it, that mental lying has produced in society. When a man has so far corrupted and prostituted the chastity of his mind, as to subscribe his professional belief to things he does not believe, he has prepared himself for the commission of every other crime.

Liberal religious thinkers tend to see the dangers inherent in ill-founded and self-deceptive beliefs that are simply meaningless phrases repetitiously recited from one generation to another. In like manner, this dual nature of religion is illustrated by these words of Jesus:

"You, hypocrites, you read the signs of the stars and of the sky, and know not the signs of the times." . . . "To you it is given to know the secrets of the kingdom of heaven, but to them it has not been given . . . . Seeing they do not see, and hearing they do not hear, nor do they understand." Again, "For this people's heart is grown dull, and their ears are heavy of hearing, and their eyes they have closed, lest they should perceive with their eyes, and hear with their ears, and understand with their heart." Mere words, hollow symbols and signs without relevance to today, immobilize the creative religious spirit. The profoundly religious person knows this.

In consequence, many religious liberals approach the problem of believing with hesitancy, and even with doubt. Can one believe free of dogmatism, without ritualistic ramifications? A long tradition makes it difficult to answer "Yes."

We see the error of the easily accepted beliefs of others. We see the pitfalls. We know the history of belief which often seems to us merely a means of sterilizing creative thought; and we know that uncritical faith too often is an abortion to the intellect.

We recall the words of Dr. Harry Emerson Fosdick:

> Better believe in no God than to believe in a cruel God, a tribal God, a sectarian God. Belief in God is one of the most dangerous beliefs a man can cherish. If the God he believes in is small and mean, the more intensely he holds his belief and cultivates it the small and meaner he will be. Men have believed in a cruel God who will send a large part of the human race to an endless hell, and by this belief all their own cruelty was confirmed. They got the idea that the torture chambers of earth were but replicas of the great torture chamber of God. It behooves us to take care what kind of God we believe in. Some of the people who do not believe in God at all are more merciful, truth-loving, and just than are some who do.

A former curriculum editor of the Beacon series in religious education, Edith Hunter, writes:

> Many of us religious liberals have not given sufficient thought to what we believe. We recite no dogmatic creed. We have no finished faith, once revealed and now neatly packaged and sealed.
>
> Are we in danger then of going to the opposite extreme—of being hopelessly vague about what we believe?
>
> Perhaps we should realize that our need is not to 'find something to believe'—but rather to discover what our lives indicate that we believe right now. This is the place to start.
>
> What did we enjoy most in the day just passed? How did we spend our time? How do we wish we might have spent it? How do we feel about ourselves at the end of the day? Do we like the kind of person we are? What do we worry about? What are we afraid of? What do we hope for? Whose lives did our lives touch during the day? Was it for better or worse? How do we feel about our parents, spouse, children, neighbors, the school, the town? Are we aware of the natural universe? Do the arts influence us and feed our spirits?
>
> To bring our attitudes, our convictions, our practices, out into the open and to look at them systematically is to find out what we actually believe.

Here, we see opening the new vista of belief, not in static terms of abstractions, but of God in the image of that which holds value for us as given by Dr. Fosdick and as given by Mrs. Hunter—the meaningful values out of our everyday lives.

A. Powell Davies said, "Most of what we learn we learn from living; and for the larger part, that means from other people. Nor does it mean only such people as we like."

William James agrees in philosophical terms that this is so, when he writes: "Our nonintellectual nature does influence our convictions." He sets up the criterion that there is a genuine option offered us on many propositions in which we cannot resolve the matter of belief, knowing, or acceptance, in purely intellectual terms. Then he says the emotional nature must resolve the matter. Thus there is the combination of intellect, our voluntary will, social experience, and the emotional reaction involved in the development of the area of faith or knowledge. This is the experience and meanings others are getting at. "We must know the truth, and we must avoid error"—these are our first and great commandments for religious liberals: to know the truth and to avoid error. This is what Tom Paine had in mind in listing the errors he would not accept while trying to set forth his testament.

James is known as the great radical empiricist and pragmatist. Yet he noted, in the essay referred to, that we are all absolutists in a sense, because we must accept things on no adequate basis as though they were gospel truth. It may be on a matter of prestige or of culture or of utility or of subjective comfort, but for reasons we know not we will accept them. We must recognize that we do accept them on this basis, but we must not forget that it is a weakness to accept them as absolutes and so keep the door of faith open to finding the valid reasons for believing. It is in this essay that he recalls the school boy who said, "Faith is when you believe something you know ain't true."

For the intellectual and religious liberal, there is the prophetic risk which sets the person of belief apart so one willingly runs the risk of taking the world religiously.

When our ministers talk about the faith in God found in common things and people, without even the use of the word, they are talking about taking the world religiously without known *a priori* data, without the need for static concepts of believing. Then belief is expressed through the heart, not the intellect. This is the creation of faith in terms of nature, children, or the "simple things," of Edith Hunter. It is the reason that one of the greatest voices of modern liberal churchmanship, Dr. Fosdick, can say that it is better to believe in no God than in a petty God. To take the world religiously is the true basis of faith and belief.

In our day, we know there are many who take the world too seriously and often do so in such an indiscriminate manner they end with a good case of neuroticism. To take the world seriously is one thing; to separate religion into a church practice and the holding of views one could not possibly live by or apply in daily life is another. This will lead to a sick approach rather than a healthy view of the world. Some of religion in our day is this compartmentalized religion: to believe when in church on Sunday and to live as though it didn't matter the rest of the week.

But to live religiously is the prophetic risk for the Unitarian Universalist. It means to live as though there are values in life, that we will create through experience the arena for expressing those values. It means we have a faith that shines through life. This is to take the world religiously and to respond to it on every level in terms of integrity.

By living religiously we will constantly grow in experience and fellowship, that is, we will be growing with our actions and deeds. Our ideas and our principles lead to the courage to act. Once this becomes a part of us it no longer seems courageous.

So much for the general area of believing and the pitfalls and dangers of beliefs. It is easy for us to recognize that there is a static aspect to beliefs that can halt the progressive development of faith. It is precisely because of this that Unitarian Universalists have gloried in being noncredal and have nearly made a fetish of freedom from dogma. Yet it is important for us to clarify the faith of Unitarian Universalism and to find the consensus we hold without sacrificing the freedom of the individual.

Theodore Sorensen, a layman in our church who became a special assistant to the late President John F. Kennedy, spoke before a Unitarian church group and was reported as summing up the fundamental faith of the Unitarian Universalist Church in these words:

> Its faith is expressed in its purpose and spirit rather than in a creed or set of beliefs, which the individual is free to shape for himself. Our central purpose may be summed up as follows:
>
> To seek and welcome the truths of life, old and new, since the past must always prove itself anew, and a living religion must change as thought advances and must be free to grow.
>
> To respect in each other, and in all persons, the authority of the individual conscience, and the freedom of the mind, since the human spirit is guided most truly from within.
>
> To discover and advance the world-unifying faith revealed in the deeper insights of all religions, and derived from the wisdom of all cultures.
>
> To utilize for man's advancing life all available knowledge from every field of human endeavor and exploration into the unknown.
>
> To uphold respect for all persons, and the equal rights of all

human beings to share in the benefits of civilized life and to contribute to the common life.

Mr. Sorensen's words are valuable because they stress purpose and spirit rather than creed or doctrine, and his summation
of our purpose in terms of strong verbal actions—to seek and
welcome, to respect, to discover, to utilize, and to uphold—suggests the dynamic nature of believing for the religious liberal.

I ponder the question from time to time, "What is it we try to
do in our churches and fellowships?" We are not the same as other
churches joining together for the glory of God and invoking His
Holy Name. Some critics say that we are not really a church, and
some of our members would be happier if we were not called one.
Yet we are more than a debating society or a service club or a
forum.

We are trying to maintain a religious establishment for the
unestablished, to build an organization for the anti-organizational
person, to maintain a church for free spirits and free thinkers.

Its importance is not for us alone, but vital to the warp and
the weft of our society. We are involved in a gigantic struggle to
determine the very nature of civilization, and we represent a philosophy of life and a way of living which we consider important
if a free society is to continue, maintaining the humane qualities
which were advanced by the Enlightenment, the American Revolution and the industrial—that is to say, the individual revolutions.

The great English philosopher Alfred North Whitehead expressed something of this world view or outlook that has taken
hold of us when he wrote:

> In each age of the world distinguished by high activity there
> will be found at its culmination, and among the agencies leading to
> that culmination, some profound cosmological outlook, implicitly
> accepted, impressing its own type upon the current springs of
> action. This ultimate cosmology is only partly expressed, and the
> details of such expression issue into derivative specialized questions
> . . . which conceal a general agreement upon first principles almost
> too obvious to need expression, and almost too general to be capable
> of expression. In each period there is a general form of the forms
> of thought; and, like the air we breathe, such a form is so translu-
> cent, and so pervading, and so seemingly necessary, that only by
> extreme effort can we become aware of it.[1]

It is this sense of a world view—of a cosmological outlook—that in the first instance leads us to undertake the struggle to maintain our Unitarian Universalist church and fellowship program. Our position—our purposes—are the high activities that help in bringing our imperfect culture closer to the ideal.

If our form of thought, our spirit of individuality in expression, our freewheeling, noninstitutionalized, nonconformist spirit is ever banished or liquidated in our society, then the democratic hope will be lost. The open society, with its opportunities for growth and development, is based on individual religious freedom. It is our undying conviction that all lesser tyrannies are only possible because there is an open window in society that allows and ensures, in consequence, the practice of freedom: freedom of belief, freedom of conviction, freedom of expression, freedom of ideas, and freedom of action. Religious orthodoxy would become an intolerable yoke around the shoulders of the American public if it were not for the free religious institution that stands in the way of the full extent of efforts to regiment society and control the mind of the citizen and believer alike. McCarthyism, thought control, the censor, the coercion through establishment of a state religion and a common propaganda line, alike, are kept in check because across the length and breadth of this land there are Unitarian and Universalist churches, backed and supported by ethical societies, Jewish temple, and to our relief and gratitude sometimes the support of fearless Christians in orthodox churches, who take just so much and then dare to speak out. We suspect our example often gives encouragement to the courageous in other churches, and they in turn inspire us anew.

Many persons believe that the Unitarian and Universalist movements are new. This is not so, for, as we have seen, there were Unitarian Universalists at the time of the Council of Nicea (Arius) and in the time of the Reformation (Servetus and Socinus), and of course we know the modern movement was actually born in the Enlightenment. We recall also that John Murray, the founder of American Universalism, was decried (improperly) as a Deist, and when other chaplains petitioned General Washington to remove him as a heretic from service as a chaplain in the Continental Army, General Washington (who was himself a Deist) responded by promoting John Murray to be the Regimental supervising chaplain over the very men who had complained of his heresy!

It is little wonder that so outstanding a scholar of the American mind in the early life of this nation as Professor Perry Miller of

Harvard University wrote of the American Founders a few years ago in the book section of *The New York Times*, "They were of a 'liberality' of spirit which must forever and properly remain a scandal to the rank and file of professing American Christians."[2] This liberal tradition of the Founding Fathers is continued in the Unitarian Universalist church, and, as we have seen, many of them were, in fact, members of this faith.

Our concern is not merely with Unitarian Universalism as an American phenomenon, but as a world faith.

A contemporary English thinker, Arnold Toynbee, one of the best-known historical philosophers of our times, whose monumental *Study of History* must be considered by every historian, wrote a few years ago, "In the new age on which we are now entering, the standard type of community, in my expectation, is going to be not the territorial national state, but the world encompassing religious community. It is in fact going to be the type of community that has been represented already, for some 2,400 years past, by the Jewish Diaspora."

He reaches back into the age of the nomad, linking our modern industrial worker with the earlier nomad who was as rootless as us today, who too often live in a rootless culture—a new industrial diaspora. States will continue to be necessary for mending and minding, he tells us, but the allegiance of people in the days ahead will be to their religious community: "Ubiquitous, but non-monopolistic religious associations will, I believe, be the standard type of community in our Atomic Age."

In such a world as we see developing around us, there is increased need for us to develop the Unitarian Universalist faith because it is our best safeguard for the arena of freedom in our world. A world without intellectual and spiritual freedom will become a stagnant, suffocating world.

Religion is still more than this. It has another factor. Whitehead, with his incisive ability to see through the welter of conflicting and confusing issues, wrote, in *Religion in the Making*, "Religion is the art and theory of the internal life."

The Unitarian Universalist church has as a basic principle that of helping one develop this art and theory of the internal life. We have a technique and a discipline in our churches and fellowships that differ in degree if not in kind from almost all other religious groups. Religion must be primary and firsthand, not something adopted from others. We have a saying in our denomination: "Don't come to a Unitarian Universalist church to be given a religion; come to develop *your own religion*." A religion given you by a church, a pastor, a book, or a school may be memorized, recited, parrot-fashion, like the Lord's Prayer; but when the chips are down in some great crisis those book words are not what come to mind.

This is what our unstructured type of church, our individual experimentation, our effort to articulate and make individually meaningful our church life points toward. Another way to put it is that just as a person brings with him to church the religion he will practice, so his religion is only practiced after he leaves the church and goes back into the marketplace, the streets, his home, and school. Religion is not divided into compartments.

Someone has made the knowing remark that you do not need a doctor's degree to be a Unitarian Universalist, but that it helps. This jest arises from the fact that Unitarian Universalists are people who are expected to use their own minds and to arrive at their own rational conclusion. Here are people going to a church where, as we have already said, everyone does not think alike but all alike think.

Affirming one's place in nature and looking upon this world as our true home and, therefore, the first concern of religion, we accept the findings of science. Even though our roots go back into the prescientific past, Unitarian Universalists have welcomed the partnership with science because it offers us a method and a procedure for approaching truth which is better than the old worn methods of the prescientific era. This does not mean we have substituted a new authority, however, for it is the scientific method, not the results of any one period, that we accept. Naturally this leads us to consider carefully the explanations, theories, and hypotheses of science.

We believe that religious expressions should be in accord with modern knowledge, and we see modern science as better equipped to help us with explanations than is theology. More conservative religious thinking says, "But science is not able to give final answers." This is true, but the Unitarian Universalist believes that tentative answers are on the right track. Such answers contain the conditions for correcting their own errors and, thus, are to be preferred to absolute answers that in the end are absolutely wrong, because they cannot adjust to new knowledge as man's intellectual horizon broadens.

Accordingly, Unitarian Universalism is not a superstitious religion. It is a well-rounded faith, grounded in the natural order and based on common sense.

Someone has said that when Unitarian Universalists pray, it

is to "at the most, one God." By this, it was suggested that we do not turn in our worship, or our prayers, to the type of superstitious personal God that sets aside the laws of the universe to aid a single individual. God does not place a pot of gold at the foot of the bed or a bicycle in the playroom, nor does he smite our enemy dead and send his rain on us and not on others. Those who believe in this type of personal string-puller in the clouds cannot understand our worship, with its warmth and inspiration, which is not an insult to the intelligence but a constant challenge to the mind. Someone accused us, or perhaps chided us, by saying Unitarian Universalists pray "to whom it may concern." Instead of becoming defensive, we laugh at such descriptive phrases. Our experience may be quite different from that of the great majority of churches in this regard, for our naturalistic and humanistic emphasis defines God as a less personal, less arbitrary being whose power is not what he does for us, but how we respond to it. Unitarian Universalists were a generation ahead of other churches with a nontheistic theology which we have called humanism.

Worship for us is a quite different thing from what it is for many groups. Some of the frequent questions that come to my desk in the Church of the Larger Fellowship ask: "But are we really a 'church'?", "Is it fair to call our meditation 'prayer'?", "Do we not mean something different by 'religion' than do others?", "Have we a right to call ourselves 'Christians'?", and even "Should we not use some word other than 'God' for the spirit or the force we mean, because God implies an anthropomorphic being?"

All of these questions can be answered by any minister or member, although we will often answer them differently, and we suspect the same person will give different answers at different times to the same question and be completely honest each time he or she answers.

Our religious experience is as genuine and meaningful for us in its unique way as that of orthodox worshippers is for them, although neither would be comfortable in the other's type of worship.

Unitarian Universalists find a beauty in thoughtfulness, a sense of exaltation in facing a challenge, and our security rests upon those things which make sense to the mind. Thus, our worship experience becomes a warm and moving experience for us, and we leave the church personally exhilarated and stimulated. We will have followed some definite thoughts (both in sermons and services) leading to an inner spiritual development, as well as stimulating us with contemporary concerns as diverse as the world population growth, the international situation, or some challenge to human dignity. We may touch on the problems of censorship of books, archeological discoveries throwing new light on Biblical history, a new book of current vogue, a philosophical concern, or a challenge to the popular religious myths of our time. There will also be rational examination of many religious positions. Over a period of weeks a broad sampling of religious, scholarly, social, and personal concerns will be dealt with.

We will have worshipped with words reminiscent of ancient liturgy, but filled with modern passages from contemporary thought, uplifting or provocative prose or poetry, in the aesthetic setting of an old New England meeting house, a modern Frank Lloyd Wright design, or a substantial medieval Gothic adaptation. Color, warmth, and flexibility will no doubt have been brought into the service by modern hymns, music and readings, and humanized by the flexibility and disdain of cant that mark our worship leaders, whether they represent the ministry or lay leadership.

Both Unitarianism and Universalism for the most part grew out of Puritanical backgrounds in the English-speaking world and so have traveled a long road in developing emotional and aesthetic expressions. Our contribution to hymnology has been great. So many of the great modern hymns set to stirring music are by Unitarian Universalist writers. We mention John Haynes Holmes, the minister, and John Holmes the poet; Jacob Trapp, Vincent Silliman, and Kenneth Patton as mid-century hymn writers. An earlier generation produced the poetry and hymnology of Whittier, Longfellow, Hosmer, Lowell, and Samuel Johnson.

At the present time, there are creative persons such as Robert Shaw, Christopher Moore, Arthur Foote, and others whose work in anthems and church music shows fresh interpretations. Von Ogden Vogt's two epic books, *Art and Religion* and *The Primacy of Worship*, along with Clarence R. Skinner's *Worship and the Well Ordered Life*, or the many volumes of Kenneth Patton (most notably *A Religion for One World*), point to new, creative, fresh approaches to the worship experience. The UUA Worship Arts Clearing House materials, issued cooperatively by the Unitarian Universalist Musicians' Network and the Department of Ministerial and Congregational Services, bring together many innovative and creative ideas for upgrading and encouraging more experimental religious expressions in local churches.

Individual churches have been seeking fresh, creative resources to assist in the expression of the religious spirit. When one church, such as the First Unitarian Church of Los Angeles, California, prepared an exciting and highly regarded new hymnbook called *Songs of the Free Spirit*, it soon found itself in a book publishing business, as many others wanted to buy it for their congregations. A denominational commission on hymnology suggested the degenderizing of popular hymns, and as an example, created a small booklet, *Hymns in New Forms*, which was offered tentatively to those who wanted to see how hymns would sound if degenderized. It instantly became so popular that the printing presses had to run overtime producing enough copies to meet congregational demands. Today, this demonstration booklet will be found in many of our churches, and frequently used in the selection of hymns. It indicates that the proposed new hymnbook will follow the pattern of degenderized hymns and updated wording for traditional hymns to express contemporary values. Some of our churches have experimented in the past with loose-leaf hymnbooks. While it had been suggested that the revised hymnal be published in loose-leaf form, it is probable that this is an idea whose time has not yet come. In spite of this, the symbolism of a changing format of worship and regular updating of worship materials is becoming more firmly established, if not through loose-leaf binders, then through the frequency of the issuance of new hymnbooks in this century.

Traditionally worship arts of an experimental nature have been promoted in Unitarian Universalist quarters by the Religious Arts Guild which has now been replaced by the Worship Arts Clearing House and Musicians' Network through a new Worship Resources Office. The UUA General Assembly in 1986 appointed a new Hymnbook Resources Commission to begin work preparing a new hymnal for congregational worship, including both hymns and worship resources for the fourth time in this century. A traditional *Hymn and Tune Book* was issued in 1914; more modern *Hymns of the Spirit, with Services* was published in 1937; in 1964 a more contemporary *Hymns for the Celebration of Life* was adopted. Now, with the accelerated thinking regarding gender, religious paternalism, religious expression in general, there are many reasons for revising, altering and updating thinking concerning worship and religious expression. Leo Collins, former president of the Musicians' Network, recently stated, "When we are done we may have the most remarkable hymnbook of any church, including hymns in pop styles, jazz, blues, folk, traditional, contemporary, dissonance, harmonies, aleatoric instrumentation—the works. We will have publish a book which says 'here is what we are—all of what we are.'"[3] It will be a book, he said, that will offer songs in which both texts and tunes are new; then, new words to existing melodies; also, new tunes for existing words, and finally, songs which are expressed in folk, jazz and popular musical idioms. Of course it will include an appropriate share of the great stirring, moving hymns of the ages as sung in the liberal churches. It will be expressive of the experimental, creative mood and spirit of liberal religion searching, seeking and affirming the joys of human fulfillment.

Churches such as the Los Angeles Church, which published *Songs of A Free Spirit*, are publishing their own worship materials. Others are following the plan of the Waltham, Massachusetts, Unitarian Universalist Church, which pioneered loose-leaf worship books, where services, hymns, music, and readings may be constantly changed. Many churches, like the Arlington Street Church in Boston or the First Parish Unitarian of Harvard, Massachusetts, have recently scheduled meetings of a worship seminar or workshop which plans experimental services. These influence the entire church, so that there is a constant air of expectancy which finds many variations to enrich the total worship and emotional experience.

In some churches, pulpit dramas, performed by casts from the congregations, have taken the place of sermons in recent years, and in other churches, chancel plays are a regular feature. Still more daring in its departures is the practice in some well-established churches, where the traditional white box pews have been taken up and remodeled into new shapes to create modern and pleasing churches in the round. Here startling new adventures in religious expression take place. More and more the creative and aesthetic element is developing so that we may forecast a trend away from a Puritanical heritage toward something new, experimental, flexible in our worship services. We have mentioned the two extremes of Puritanism and the experimental workshops and worship in the round, but most of our churches and fellowships lie somewhere in between.

This is our English-speaking Unitarian Universalist experience, but in Hungary, Transylvania, Romania, and to a lesser extent in Czechoslovakia, Unitarianism has a rich cultural tradition filled with aesthetic expressions from which we might draw. There Unitarianism has produced art, literature, music, folksongs, and dances, which are expressions of the freedom of liberal religion and has maintained for more than four centuries a growing Unitarian culture. The English-speaking Unitarians and Universalists are just beginning to discover this rich cultural legacy created by the Unitarian way of life, and it should be adapted more and more to our uses.

With this growing development of a new awareness of aesthetic forms to fit the needs of liberal and liberating religion will come also the development of new symbolisms, but there is not a movement among us, such as is evident in many other churches, for the overemphasizing of symbolism and myth. In fact, the free mind, creative and experimental as it is, is a bit wary of mythology. It is too often a cloak to cover up what one does mean or a legend to say something that one does not believe. Accordingly, even while we recognize the valid uses of myth and that it has been dynamic in the past to release new forces or to assist people to express their emotions and feelings not otherwise articulated, we must candidly admit that in this area we have not been overly active. This I ascribe to the fear that myth is a device for not saying what we mean. Integrity in word and thought is, of course, paramount with most Unitarian Universalists, as with others.

Accordingly, not merely faith, but practice; not merely thought, but worship are utilized for the enhancement and expression of the modern beliefs of Unitarian Universalism. The old charge that Unitarian Universalism was a cold, lifeless rationalization of religion, lacking emotional content and an aesthetic appeal no longer applies. Modern movements, drawing upon the broader universal background, and the increasing depth with which life is understood as emotional as well as intellectual and subconscious as well as votive, promise to lead religious liberalism into new fields of expressive and participative religion, fit for the free mind and the whole person.

Now that we clearly understand this greater flexibility in the approach to believing, we can discuss specific beliefs. Let us first review some major beliefs which make up the intellectual milieu of Unitarian Universalism. We will then discuss in greater detail the major areas against which beliefs are judged in the Judeo-Christian heritage: prayer, the Bible, God, and Jesus.

The author was associated with a noted Jesuit priest, president of a college, when both served as chaplains in the United States armed forces, and during this time some interesting conversations took place. On one occasion, Father Long said, "A Roman Catholic can understand a Unitarian because he has the only other logically consistent system of theology to the Roman. If one grants the original premise on which Unitarianism rests—that of naturalism—everything else follows logically, just as if one grants the Roman Catholic original premise of supernaturalism, then everything we teach logically follows." He felt that the other Protestant denominations, resting on supernatural premises, were inconsistent because they emphasized merely a tangent of faith, without following it through, as is done in the ordered system of the scholastic mind of a Catholic theologian. One step leads them to another, until they are led from a supernatural God, to a supernatural Son, to a supernatural Church, which is the guardian of the supernatural in the natural world, and so on through their oral and written traditions and the whole range of dogma and doctrine of Catholicism. To an ordered mind this makes sense, granting the original assumption of the primacy of the supernatural world. For the Unitarian Universalist, however, reality is found in this world, in the natural world, and hence our steps lead us to natural, rational, scientific, and common-sense assumptions and deductions. In fact we reason inductively rather than deductively in our system of understanding the world.

The first great point of Unitarian Universalist belief, therefore, may be stated as our acceptance of the natural world as the chief arena of living if not the sole area of life. In addition, this leads us to discount basic assumptions of orthodoxy. The afterlife and immortality become secondary considerations. It is this life lived on this side of the great divide that is important. This natural world being the chief environment for living, there is no need for miracles to prove the intercession of the supernatural powers in the natural world. Events and purposes are understood by us, because they are part of the natural order; and we are confident that whatever explanations may be found will be natural ones. Revelation is hence not necessary, for the Scriptures and the teachings of the prophets and apostles stand on their own merit, along with all other sources of knowledge and authority.

Some persons, taking the first tentative step of doubt which leads away from orthodoxy, say, "But why do you have to go all the way to the other extreme?" We reply, as you can now understand, "Because this is the only other logical system of faith." You predicate the natural and you build on that, as do the Unitarian Universalists; or you predicate the supernatural and build on that, accepting the supernatural without deviation (for how can mortal man evaluate immortal faith?), which means all of it, including the supernatural Church, which, according to revealed scripture, is Christ's vicar on earth. Incidentally, this system of logical construction has led some important marriage counselors to suggest that "mixed credal marriages" are most happily resolved when the choice made is between Catholicism and Unitarian Universalism.

In the natural order, homo sapiens stand at the apex of the evolutionary ladder, and with innate dignity and sublime powers of reason, our depth of emotional and psychological nature, the magnificence of our moral perspective, we are able to make decisions, to plan for the morrow, to feel the depth of sympathy and compassion that brings human love and kindness into being; and so we may structure life as it could be and as it should be. This is the religious quest. It requires a sense of fellowship, of continuity with kindred spirits and the background of the human endeavor; and so turns to the larger community of thought and faith for sustenance and reassurance. Humans are problem-solvers, creators; we hold the future in our hands and minds. We cannot escape our responsibility, cannot defer or turn aside, except at the moral peril of failure. This is the great religious imperative. It calls upon people to be strong, but strength is found and supported not by character alone, but by our common involvement one in another.

The dangers of such thought lie in a narrow circumference of what we mean by human fellowship or community, and our involvement one in another. Consequently, we need a broader perspective of religion that takes in not only the present day, but the lessons of the past and the projections of the future. There are three relationships in which we must be involved: the relationship to oneself, the relationship to others, and the relationship to causes and purposes that are greater than oneself and one's own group and that involve one in worthy ends touching eternal values. These eternal values are not supernatural in a strict sense, however, but are the natural orientations, the focus of experience and existence, the focus around which life must evolve if the universal, humane, just, and compassionate world of life is to develop.

When we say humanity we should be conscious, like Albert Schweitzer, that all life possesses that sense of fellow-feeling that does not truncate our loyalties and involvements.

Joseph Priestley anticipated Schweitzer in regard to our relationship to other than human life. He dealt in one discussion with the Christian concept of immortality of the soul, showing the inconsistencies drawn from pagan sources. He then noted that Christian doctrine denied immortality to animals. According to doctrine, "man would be saved," whereas animals would be doomed or cease existence altogether. In view of the suffering people inflict on animals in this life, Priestley observed that if there were a just God he would condemn humanity to death or nothingness and save animals for a world of bliss and happiness, so righting the balance of this life in an afterlife!

Once we start to draw lines of exclusion, the exclusions can multiply in a geometric ratio: first we eliminate animal life from fellow-feeling, then life on other planets, then life of other races, then life of other countries, then life of other religions, then life of other ideologies, then life of nonfriends, then life of all outside our family (blood is thicker than water), until humanity, egostistical, self-satisfied, selfish, is all that remains! Once we eliminate a sense of total life-involvement, which Schweitzer calls Reverence for Life, we have begun the ethical retreat. Actually, this larger identification has been absent for ages, and in our day the positive ethic needed is to reverse the pattern. We need to reach out from human life to family, to friends, to nonfriends, to those who differ from us, whether in ideology, nationality, or race; to life on other planets; to all life of whatever source and judge and respect all that lives. We need to develop the sound rational basis of selectivity and judgments as Dr. Schweitzer tried to do. All modern science is actually on this side, although the articulation of it may be an ethical and religious concern.

There is a great chain of life from which none can be separated. It is what Channing called the universal church, from which no one can be separated except by the death of goodness in one's own breast. Even this is doubtful today, for one thing we have learned is that most sin and crime is not malignant choice, but mental and psychological shortcomings built into life through frustrations, failures, and pressures applied thoughtlessly in the past. There is no longer in a strict scientific sense any such thing as a good or bad person, but only people warped or developed by circumstances, who have had the intelligence and character (or strength or will) to cope and master, or else, be unable to cope, having become pitiable, frustrated creatures who strike out like a bewildered, frightened child. Accordingly, sophisticated modern knowledge makes it increasingly difficult to accept the old-fashioned moral judgments of churches.

These considerations are all part of the Unitarian Universalist understanding of the need to come to terms with a rational universe in which we live and move and have our being. Everything is, or could be, understandable, and all can, or may, fit together if intelligence rather than blind emotions guides our decisions, observations, and judgments. Science is our great ally, as is history, as are psychology and psychiatry, as is modern medicine, and as is the thoughtful and compassionate person. Hence education, free inquiry, democracy, which seek for intelligent actions to create a superior social life for humanity, are the handmaidens of faith.

They must not be controlled by any religion, for "the tyranny over the mind" which has always resulted from the liaison of ecclesiastical power with temporal must be avoided. Individuality is still an important ingredient for the good life. In fact, many religious liberals are uncertain how the good life can be developed when efforts to enforce conformity and controls are turned over to governments. The purpose of much social legislation is good, but there must always be a careful discrimination between individuality and social controls. The greatest good for the greatest number must not run roughshod over minorities. In fact, the test of a democracy may well be not what is accomplished for the majority but how, in majority rule, the rights of minorities are safeguarded. Great opportunities for individuals, after all, have been the seedbed of the advancement of civilization and culture. The maintenance of the integrity of the individual, of the dignity of each life, of the supreme worth of every human personality must not be sacrificed before the mass society or the welfare state. Religious liberals see both sides of the coin, knowing that the integrity of the individual requires the assault on poverty and discrimination, on the one hand, and, on the other, the creation of conditions of freedom that allow and encourage the growth of individual initiative and opportunity.

Finally, the Unitarian Universalist approach to life requires a serious consideration to the means of eliminating warfare and the development of the just and durable peace if "men shall beat their swords into plowshares and their spears into pruning hooks . . . neither shall they learn war any more" as Micah forecast 3,000 years ago. Unitarian Universalists tend to agree wholeheartedly with Dr. Schweitzer that the major indictment against the Christian Church is that in 2,000 years it has failed to create conditions of peace, even though Christianity has been a dominant religion in the civilized world during this period. While the Unitarian Universalist movement is not essentially a personal pacifist movement, it is committed to the principle of influencing the civilizations, cultures, and states of the world to place human rights and respect for the individual above other considerations and, thus, to eliminate war and militarism as an instrument of national policy. Unitarian Universalists have been staunch supporters in the past of the efforts toward this end, such as the League of Nations and the Federal Union plan, and now are overwhelmingly committed to the support of and reliance upon the United Nations as the medium for international cooperation.

Freed of all concepts of the depravity of humanity, or original sin, which sinks us into a human morass from which we cannot extricate ourselves without necessary reliance upon outside mediators, saviors, saints, atonements, etc., to solve the human dilemma, Unitarian Universalists see the major religious role enacted by humanity to be that of taking the offensive against all shortcomings and failures. Only we can solve these problems. The world has no moral values. These are provided by people. The natural order is neutral, even though vital. We are the moral agents and must bring to bear the values and the problem-solving to correct the old faults and make a living paradise of the earth. Our confidence is that we can do this.

In summary, we may note that Unitarian Universalism is not a negative religion because it accepts the present life and natural world. It looks upon traditional Christianity as negative, because it rejects this world for an afterlife and is self-defeating in relying upon divine intervention for solving problems that can only be solved by the application of human will.

We affirm a rational universe, a positive life-relationship, the dignity and worth of the individual, the necessity for service and social action, the validity of religious fellowship, and a religion expressed in ethico-moral terms. All this follows from accepting our natural role as standing without apology in this natural environment, as rational creatures confronting the demands to build a good life for the earth's people. Only with intelligence and consideration (which we traditionally call love) can we succeed; and if we have courage, energy, and perseverance, we will.

Another way of summarizing is to note, as did A. Powell Davies, that a Unitarian Universalist "regards creeds as negative; they say 'no' to new truth." This is so because the mind can only honestly affirm what actually persuades it, and this is often in conflict with the creeds. The creeds are the accepted truths of a past age, but not necessarily the verified truth of our age. The truth for today may not be the truth of tomorrow: tomorrow morning's newspapers have not yet been printed, and new discoveries, research, thoughtfulness may change our knowledge. The guardians of the creeds try to shut the door to new truth. Dr. Charles Edwards Park, for forty years minister to the First Church in Boston, Massachusetts, noted "The point of all this is that in its main features Christian theology is the work of ill-balanced, and nervously over-wrought men, laboring at times of passionate feeling and under great emotional pressure, and influenced by just the forces that should be kept out of the picture when matters of this nature are under consideration; and that the mood of broad-minded observation, calm study, sensitiveness to true intuitions, and reasonableness in speculation—in other words the mood one would consider indispensable for the best and most constructive theological industry—is not to be found in either Paul, Athanasius, Augustine, or Calvin, but in their opponents.[3]

What Park is saying is that the creeds of Christendom are the product of anxious men in retreat from the world instead of confidently meeting it on its own terms. Accordingly, our confidence must be in the world; not in those who built fences to shut out the world from intrusion into the world of faith.

Notes
[1] A. N. Whitehead, *Adventures of Ideas*, New York, 1933, pp. 13, 14.
[2] Review of Norman Cousins's *In God We Trust*, N.Y., Harper & Row, 1958.
[3] "Music in the Air" by Michael Finley. *The WORLD*, June, 1987, p. 13.

8

What Do Unitarian Universalists Believe About Prayer, the Bible, God, and Jesus?

These questions are often asked by those not understanding our approach to religion. It is to be expected that these questions will be asked, because among Christians, the manner in which these questions are answered indicates one's degree of orthodoxy. We have already shown that for the religious liberal there is a danger that in answering according to prescribed Protestant formulas one may present a negative approach to faith, and this is precisely what Unitarians and Universalists have often done. However, with the presentation outlined in the preceding pages, it is now possible to clarify the viewpoint concerning these Christian concepts that we hold without jeopardizing our affirmative faith.

The way one prays indicates to some extent the way one looks at the universe, telling us more about basic faith of people than is generally realized. Accordingly, the role of prayer for a Unitarian Universalist is important. At the mid-century White House conference on youth and child work it was tentatively suggested that a working definition of religion on which all faiths might agree would be helpful. Among the experts present were clergymen of four American faiths—a Catholic, a Rabbi, a Protestant clergyman, and a religious liberal. The religious liberal was Rev. Raymond B. Johnson, then director of the department of the ministry of the American Unitarian Association. Each of the four clergymen brought in a statement, and eventually it was agreed that no common working definition was possible that would combine all. However, the statement of our former ministry department head is worthy of recollection, as it stresses what most Unitarian Universalists would hold as a working philosophy of our approach to faith. He wrote:

> I observe the universe in which I find myself and discover in it an orderly procedure based on natural laws. I further examine the way it works for all living creatures and particularly note the development of man. It is religion when:
>
> 1. I conclude that the scheme of things makes sense, that it shows convincing evidence of purpose;
> 2. I realize the obligation upon me to contribute myself to the forwarding of this purpose;
> 3. I study myself and recognize my limitations and my potentialities, and especially the presence of a spiritual force within me;
> 4. I discover that associating myself with the spiritual force in the universe adds to my own power to make a contribution to it. I prefer not to say 'God' because there are so many varying definitions which could make for disagreement. Theists like myself can supply it in their minds.
>
> My religion is my orientation of me in the universe. Religion answers the questions: Where am I? What am I? Why am I?

Such an approach to faith will help clarify why and what and where and whence is prayer. Prayer deals with how we relate to the universe; with the question of our potentialities and how we answer the questions where, what and why. A medieval monk by the name of Theophilus noted that prayer was talking to God and meditation was listening to God. Unitarian Universalists do too much talking, it sometimes seems, among themselves, but the art of meditation, of listening, is an essential virtue and necessity. Indeed, many of our churches have periods of meditations rather than prayers in the service. In an age that puts great stress on communication, the form of communication called prayer should call for attention. It is the direct means by which we relate ourselves through directed thought with a cause and relationship larger than our human fellowship, and it is very important.

We all need to see that life is not limited to the here and now, but that there is a boundless dimension touching life, stretching far beyond us in time and space, and extending our lives to connections beyond the limits of our skin and this bit of protoplasm which makes up our bodies. Many Unitarian Universalists believe that there is a mystic element, call it what we will. However, as we have already mentioned, it is not the personal thanksgiving for good beyond our own merit; and we bow in penitence for our shortcomings, as we recognize in the words of the ancient prayer, "We have done those things we ought not to have done and have left undone those things we ought to have done."

Many prayers, of course, are not in words. There is an old hymn sometimes sung which says "Prayer is the soul's sincere desire, uttered or unexpressed." Emerson expressed the heritage of St. Benedict when he wrote, "All honest work is prayer." Everything constructive we do is prayer. *Aspirati laborare.* Richard Llewellyn, in the novel *How Greeen Was My Valley*, gives us this definition in a memorable scene, in which the boy, Hew, injured and sick, needs the encouragement of the Welsh minister, Mr. Gruffydd, who knows there is a question of whether or not the boy will ever walk again:

> "Men who are born to dig coal," Mr Gruffydd said to me, "need strength and courage. But they have no need of spirit, any more than the mole or the blind worm. Keep up your spirit, Hew, for that is the heritage of a thousand generations of the great ones of the earth. As your father cleans his lamp to have good light, so keep clean your spirit."
>
> "And how shall it be kept clean, Mr. Gruffydd?" I asked him.
>
> "By prayer, my son," he said, "not mumbling, or shouting, or wallowing like a hog in religious sentiments. Prayer is only another name for good clean, direct thinking. When you pray, think well what you are saying, and make your thought into things that are solid. In that manner, your prayer will have strength, and that strength will become a part of you, mind, body, and spirit. Do you still want to see the first daffodil out up in the mountain, my son?"
>
> "Indeed I do, Mr. Gruffydd," I said.
>
> "Pray, my son," he said, and left.

Another example is given by Sinclair Lewis in his novel about a scientist, *Arrowsmith*. Arrowsmith finally has the chance he has always dreamed about, which is to dedicate his knowledge and skill to pure research. In his new laboratory for the first time, he pauses for a moment and mumbles this prayer:

"God, Give me unclouded eyes and freedom from haste.

"God give me a quiet and relentless anger against all pretense and all pretentious work and all works left slack and unfinished.

"God, give me a restlessness whereby I may neither sleep nor accept praise till my observed results equal my calculated results, or in pious glee I discover and assault my error.

"God, give me strength not to trust in God."

"This is the prayer of the scientist" Sinclair Lewis adds, and we, too, find it fraught with significance for the modern mind.

Do Unitarian Universalists pray? Indeed they do, although not always in expected ways: We have illustrated some here, thoroughly consistent with the beliefs of Unitarian Universalism. It may be by listening or talking, working or thinking, but it is there. Sometimes the purpose of a prayer is for our own good more than others, and sometimes we pray to be heard by ourselves rather than God, but like religious people everywhere we take hold of a larger dimension than that which ends with self, and when we do we are at prayer.

These examples and accounts all help show the nonparochial aspect of the religious liberal's approach to the question of prayer, something much more than the formalized pious words of traditional faiths, but at the same time something far less than a structured ritualistic methodology with supernatural ramifications. In fact, we sometimes ask, "Who prays in prayer?" Is it he who prays the words, or he who feels the deepest meanings, who yearns the most and seeks most ardently? "All the world reposes in beauty to him who preserves equipoise in his life," wrote Thoreau; and, of course, just as beauty lies in the eyes of the beholder, so repose lies in the heart of tranquility. Kipling gives us some lines that are worth recalling:

> My brother kneels, so saith Kabir,
> To stone and brass in heathen-wise,
> But in my brother's voice I hear
> My own unanswered agonies
> His God is as his fate assign,
> His prayer is all the world's—and mine.

To us the universality of prayer binds all together. With the heathen we, too, are united, and in his voice we hear our own unanswered agonies. Angela Morgan knew this and also expressed it in poetry in another time and place. She wrote during World War I:

> Last night I tossed and could not sleep
> When sodden heavens weep and weep,
> As they have wept for many a day,
> One lies awake to fear and pray,

and after she tosses, turns, and prays, thinking of the horror of war, she comes to the realization that she alone is not concerned, and in truth:

> All night long I toss and cannot sleep;
> When shattered heavens weep and weep,
> As they have wept for many days,
> I know at last 'tis God who prays.

It may be our neighbor, even the pagan, or it may be God or it may be all mankind that somehow gets caught up in the spirit of prayer. It may be we who are in repose or in agony, or it may be others. Somehow or other we enter into a universal experience when we join in prayer, an experience difficult to comprehend and explain, but nevertheless meaningful if freed of the old supernatural limitations.

Robert Frost, with the prosaic comments which make his poetry so delightful, once wrote,

> I turned to speak to God
> About the world's despair
> But to make matters worse;
> I found God wasn't there.

This is often the experience of the religious liberal who does not understand the type of God that presumably is on the other end of the telephone line. A god of this type cannot answer a religious liberal's prayer, because that is not the type of prayer we have in mind, as Robert Frost very well knew. He continued his poem:

> God turned to me
> (Don't anybody laugh)
> God found I wasn't there—
> At least not over half.

Our question is, you see, not who prays in prayer, but are we there, have we found ourselves, and are we whole people when we try to enter a whole relationship with life itself? There is much we do not know about prayer, but we do know enough to see that prayer helps us enter into life relationships, to find perspective, to delve deeply into our lives, and to meditate in a meaningful fashion. If we would be whole people, we need this help in our lives, which is found in a devotional experience.

A major question for the Unitarian Universalist is, "Is the Bible all-important?" and our answer is no, for a variety of reasons. We have already discussed the question of the Bible, or of scriptures in the earlier chapters, as it has a bearing on the developing tendencies of liberal religion. Let us here express a basic point of view.

The Bible is, of course, important to Unitarian Universalists. In the translation of the Bible into the common languages of Europe the door was opened for free inquiry into its pages, and it no longer remained a privileged document of the clergy written in their special tongue, Latin. Consequently with the translation of the Bible came the opening up of universal knowledge concerning its contents, so that people could see for themselves what it actually said. It is no accident that the translation of the Bible coincided with the Reformation. Erasmus in his new translation of the New Testament made the discovery that the Trinity was not a Biblical doctrine, but was superimposed. Consequently he added a footnote to the passages in question, pointing this out. This annotation is the basis of the statement sometimes made that Erasmus was a Unitarian. Zwingli and the German Free Church movement followed Erasmus' teaching in this regard and remained a non-Trinitarian church until a later generation was coerced by Charles V to accede to the Trinitarian doctrine under threat of heresy. As we have already noted, Servetus, a Spanish university student, upon reading the Bible discovered its non-Trinitarian nature; and so began the first great remarkable protest of Unitarian rejection. In England, John Wycliffe translated the first English Bible, and he likewise discovered that the Trinity was non-Biblical and so omitted it, leading to charges that he was a Unitarian. His Bible was banned in many quarters. Accordingly it was not until the King James version of 1611 that the King James translation made a commonly acceptable English Bible available. In the meanitime we note that the Bible has been important in clearing the air and making known the basic Unitarian Universalist thesis that some insistent Christian doctrines, such as the Trinity, are not Biblical and, indeed, that the Bible has had spurious verses added to it to prove doctrine from scripture! We begin a discussion of the Bible by recognizing a debt to the Bible, its translators, and its scholars.

There is a second debt we owe to the Bible. Here is a great treasure of much that is uplifting and noble in religious expression. It contains an accumulation of material rich in faith and ancient culture from Babylonian, Egyptian, and Canaanite sources, as well as Hebrew. In addition there are literary or devotional jewels, such as the 23rd Psalm. "The Lord is my shepherd, I shall not want . . . ," and other psalms such as, "Blessed is the man that walketh not in the counsel of the ungodly. . . ." Here one reads, "I will lift up mine eyes unto the hills; from whence cometh my help . . . ," and "When I consider the heavens, the work of thy hands . . ." and other moving passages of the aspiring soul. Here are the great commandments: love of God and love of man. Here are the Beatitudes and the Golden Rule. Here also is Paul's rule, "Whatsoever things are true, whatsoever things are pure, whatsoever things are honest. . . ." In the Bible one finds Micah's yardstick: "What doth the Lord require of thee, but to do justly, to love mercy and to walk humbly with thy God. . . ." The moral courage of the prophets, the frustration and triumph of the peoples, and the evolving panorama of history are portrayed here. There are mountain peaks of religious literature here, but unfortunately they are few.

There is another value to the Bible: it is a source book of Near Eastern history (Middle Eastern in modern history). It becomes, indeed, a field book for working archaeologists exploring the Near East for clues to the history of that era. The Bible has a remarkable historical memory, although much of it has been re-written, mutilated, and was recorded in written form generations after the events happened, so that it has its share of error. The author of this book has been in the Middle East on archaeological expeditions, has studied the subject, and is concerned with the correcting of previous errors and the fresh discovery of the record of the peoples of that cradle of civilization and birthplace of faiths. The Bible, interpreted by archaeology and paleography, is an important endeavor, and it is essential that Unitarian Universalists take increased concern in this area. It was gratifying to have the Unitarian Church of All Souls in New York City purchase for study and preservation the Dead Sea Scroll of the Book of Deuteronomy, which contains the oldest known wording, and is in fact the oldest known copy of the Decalogue, or Ten Commandments. This scroll is now on file at the Palestinian Museum, Jerusalem. Unitarian Universalist scholarship, furthermore, is able to bring a free mind to bear upon subjects restricted for the most part to the confessional churches or the closed mind of orthodoxy. Several years ago, my former professor, G. Ernest Wright, editor of the *Biblical Archeologist*, was forced to ask the editorial question: "Does the archeologist aim to prove the Bible is true?" Dr. Wright was dealing with specific charges, but the mere fact of the charges—brought forward in this instance by a Hebrew scholar, Professor J. J. Finkelstein—is enough to indicate the need for more liberal religious scholarship in this field. The only identifiable Unitarian Universalist archaeologist that I could find who has actively participated in excavations was Professor Rolland E. Wolfe of Cleveland, Ohio, who has excavated most recently the ancient site of Bethel. Denominationally we should be supporting and encouraging such scientific research.

What will come from such studies? We cannot say in advance. If we could, then we would be brought under suspicion of having a closed mind of our own. However, there is much evidence that partial knowledge today interferes with adequate understanding of the Biblical record.

Likewise, faulty translations create confusions. The noted poet T. S. Eliot in the spring of 1964 called the New English Bible "vulgar, trivial, and pedantic." This was an unfortunate characterization. Here was a modern effort to translate the Bible (only the New Testament was then in print) into the language of today, utilizing the archaeological, historical, and paleographical data of modern scholarship to correct the ancient texts. The English scholars were more daring than a team of American scholars, for they determined to abandon the Elizabethan English of the King James version in favor of modern English. There is a literary pharisaism that says that the King James English is more poetic than any other. It is the work of a time when there was a cadence and majesty to the King's English, which many believe to be lacking in modern times. It was the period of Shakespeare, Marlowe, and Bacon, and some suggest these might even have helped translate the King James version in 1611. The American Revised Standard version followed a different pattern than did the English. The Americans utilized modern scholarship, but tried to keep the cadence and a language reminiscent of the King James.

The King James and Revised Standard versions speak of a "virgin" in the Annunciation account of Luke 1:27, whereas in another modern version, the Phillips translation, we read "young woman," and the New English version translates it as "girl." Even the American version is more straightforward than would be expected, considering the sponsorship of the translation. It changes the traditional wording of the King James, which tells how Joseph sought "to put away his wife," whereas the Revised Standard Version says, "he sought to divorce her." Such clarifications are helpful, but do not ease the need for careful reading of the Bible rather than indiscriminate use of it as a tool for religious instruction.

In fact the Bible requires careful selection to make it a valuable book for religious aspirations. We should remember that much of the Bible deals with the happenings in the remote past of a primitive culture and so presents episodes that reflect primitive and bloodcurdling ethics. Reading it without preparation, one finds passages which may appear indelicate. Bible schools are organzied for the young to study the Bible, and many parents wistfully look upon the Bible as something their children should study, which may indicate how little the Bible is actually read by adults. The Bible should be studied, but by adults or college students, not by children. We will give two illustrations. One of the most beautiful psalms is No. 137. Here is a short psalm written during the Babylonian exile (it is not true that David wrote the psalms, as he lived in approximately 1,000 B.C., whereas the psalm, as you will see, had to be written during the Babylonian captivity, which began about 587 B.C.).

This psalm for the first six verses, is one of the most lovely and tenderly reminiscent sorrowing passages we know:

> By the rivers of Babylon, there we sat down, yea, we wept, when we remembered Zion
> We hanged our harps upon the willows in the midst thereof
> For there they that carried us away captive required of us a song; and they that wasted us required of us mirth, saying sing us one of the songs of Zion.
> How shall we sing the Lord's song in a strange land?
> If I forget thee, O Jerusalem, let my right hand forget her cunning.
> If I do not remember thee, let my tongue cleave to the roof of my mouth; if I prefer not Jerusalem above my chief joy.

Here for six verses we have the tender homesickness of the captives carried to a strange land, sorrowing for home. They speak to us out of the saddened heart for the bondaged people of every age and day. Suddenly, however, the mood changes, and the will to do violence is revealed. The final three stanzas of this psalm read:

> Remember, O Lord, the children of Edom in the day of Jerusalem; who said, Raze it, even to the foundations thereof.
> O daughter of Babylon, who are to be destroyed: happy shall he be, that rewardeth thee as thou has served us.
> Happy shall he be, that taketh and dasheth thy little ones against the stones.

With these verses the mood and ethical standard has shifted. We are back at the primeval beginnings, at the animal level of existence, back with the crude old code of "an eye for an eye and a tooth for a tooth." Happy indeed, shall he be who dashes the little ones upon the stones! Shall we in our day teach infanticide? The murder and destruction of children? No, the civilized man, the religious man, the religious liberal cannot use such teachings. Little wonder, as Dr. Schweitzer pointed out, that the Christian church in 2,000 years has failed to develop an ethical will for peace.

One other passage, if this is not yet strong enough. It is indelicate, yet we do not apologize for forcing it on your attention, for it is part of that dear old book of religious orthodoxy which so many wish to have their children taught to read. We refer in this instance to the 34th chapter of Genesis. One of the greatest of the Old Testament heroes is Jacob, and we call your attention to an event out of his career. The episode takes place when Jacob's family had moved into the land of the Schechemites and purchased land, pitching their tents there. Schechem, the prince, seeing Dinah, the daughter of Leah and Jacob, fell in love with her, slept with her, and wished to make her his wife. The prince with his father went to Jacob to ask for her hand, offering anything desired (verses 11 and 12). "And Schechem said unto her father, and unto her brethren, 'Let me find grace in your eyes, and what you shall say unto me I will give. Ask me never so much dowry and gift, and I will give according as ye shall say unto me: but give me the damsel for wife.'" Fair enough, it would seem but the passage continues (verses 13 ff.): "And the sons of Jacob answered Schechem and Hamor his father deceitfully, . . . and they said unto them, "We cannot do this thing, to give our sister to one that is uncircumcised, for that were a reproach to us. But this will consent unto you: If ye be as we be, that every male of you be circumcised; then we will give our daughters unto you, and we will take your daughters to us, and we will dwell with you, and we will become one people.'"

A fair offer, and it looked like the beginning not only of intertribal matchmaking but of a successful peace parley. To save time, let us skip over the intermediary details.

The Schechemites agree, (verse 24 ff.): "And every male was circumcised, all that went out of the gate of his city. And it came to pass on the third day, when they were sore, that two of the sons of Jacob, Simeon and Levi, Dinah's brethren, took each man his sword, and came upon the city boldly, and slew all the males . . . The sons of Jacob came upon the slain, and spoiled the city, because they had defiled their sister. They took their sheep, and their oxen . . . And all their wealth, and all their little ones, and ·their wives took them captive, and spoiled even all that was in the house."

Jacob was troubled when it was over, as well he should be, and as his sons also should have been. But can one imagine a more barbarous situation? To practice deceit such as this, as an instrument of revenge, covetousness, acquisitiveness, or strategy was beneath the contempt of any civilized people who ever lived. There is no more barbarous account in all the annals of human history of a scheme to weaken a people than this, nor one so ruthlessly carried out. Should such an account be kept alive and venerated as religious literature? The religious liberal thinks not.

This passage is not an isolated one. The Bible abounds in gory incidents. We shall skip over the accounts of abnormal sexuality found through accounts of uncouth conduct and unworthy ethics presented in the Bible. The religious liberal cannot look upon the Bible as a sacred book, but merely as a source book from which we can selectively draw.

"Unitarian Universalists believe in, at the most, one God," is an old joke. The story has been told, not without its point, that a group of Unitarian Universalists were on their way to Heaven and stopped to hold a discussion on whether there really was a Heaven. There tends to be a certain impatience with the tenuous aspect of Unitarian Universalist belief regarding God in orthodox quarters. They "know for a certainty" certain unquestionable beliefs. We cannot know such things with certainty. We grope, we consider, we weigh in an intellectual balance, yet throughout it all we aspire, we dream, we are uplifted, and find the type of faith which leads us to affirm Paul's testament, "I have run the good race, I have fought the good fight, I have finished the course."

Consequently, Unitarian Universalists tend to be, whether they like the word or not, agnostics. We simply do not know for a certainty. We are not anti-God, and few of us would call ourselves atheists, although since we are a non-credal church there is nothing to rule out an atheist being a Unitarian Universalist. One meaning of the designation "Unitarian," however, is a believer in one God. In contrast to theism, many call themselves humanists. A humanist is simply one who defines religion and the religious quest in terms of human duties, responsibilities, and aspirations, instead of God's expectations and demands. Some never use the term God and resist the concept or its implications. Others see the problem as basically a semantic one, a question of terms and the meanings of words. Since to many people God means a supernatural being with human attributes, such as passions and emotions, many humanists and Unitarian Universalists avoid using the term God for fear of misunderstandings.

This is a puzzling discovery to some. Our culture has a great commonplace cliché which says, "You can *believe* anything you wish so long as you *believe* in God." It says, "Religion is belief in God, therefore all religion is good." People who accept this are unaware that great historic religions, among which stand Confucianism and Buddhism, do not believe in God. The Hindu, with his many deities, and the pagan Greeks, with their numerous heroic gods, did not fit the oversimplified description of religion as belief in God.

The tribal God of the Old Testament, the Lord God of Hosts who went into battle breathing fire and smoke with his obedient warriors, is not the God of countless clergy and civilized people in numerous churches of the Christian or Hebrew tradition today. The simple God, who, like a bountiful father, turns a kind ear to the request of his children and grants requests—"Yes, you can have a bicycle; no, you cannot have a red coat; yes, if you are good you can drive a sports car when you grow up."—this type of loving, doting father is not an acceptable deity, even for children. The oriental monarch of Calvinism, who condemns the just and saves the wicked to prove his own unaccountability to his subjects and whose lack of compassion and justice makes his subjects cringe in terror, is not an accepted image of the divine. Thus when you ask Unitarian Universalists if they believe in God, the answer given may very well be "which God?" by which is meant "which concept of God?" Up to this point we have been talking about concepts of God, not about God.

One might admit to believing a concept of God who is the creative force in the universe, to the first cause of the philosophers, or to the center or orientation of the psychologists. During the 1963 commission meetings on the "Free Church in a Changing World," one of the commissions dealt with theology and the frontiers of learning. In discussing the diversity of beliefs concerning God held by Unitarian Universalists, it summarized by grouping the various poles of belief into six categories. They are:

1. *Christian liberalism.* By using reason and ethics to reinterpret Christianity, its abilities to promote moral values are emphasized.

Jesus of Nazareth is both the motivation and guide in serving humanity and in achieving personality fulfillment. Christian doctrines of God, sometimes reinterpreted in terms of contemporary understandings of myths and symbols, provide a central focus.

2. *Deism.* Although the term is in disuse today, many liberals remain basically true to the position. They stress the order that is discovered by science. Not only is the physical universe marked by order, but there is also a moral universe. The highest life is to learn and follow its laws. Nature provides the best basis for a theology.

3. *Mystical religion.* Many liberals have focused upon attaining direct intuitions of oneness and relatedness with nature and/or the divine. The Universe is characterized by a unity that many may experience directly by cultivating the proper sensitivities. Such experiences, for the mystic, are of greater value than any subsequent intellectual formations.

4. *Religious humanism.* Humanity will find the resources and enough additional support within the natural universe to create a better life in a better society. This will be achieved if people turn from concentration on a future life and God to this life. In the social and natural sciences, together with the arts and the humanities, are to be found our most helpful guides in living wisely and creatively and in the realization of a sense of at-homeness in the universe.

5. *Naturalistic theism.* The world that the sciences are discovering is marked by evolutionary processes, only in part controlled by people. Our highest good lies in discovering and serving this creativity. The God of creativity operates within nature under specifiable conditions and, thus, is not marred by the mysteriousness of a supernatural God. Preserving and destructive forces are also recognized as involved in the creative process.

6. *Existentialism.* Existentialism protests philosophical orientations that ignore the living individual, as well as the technological developments which treat people as objects to be manipulated. People in their loneliness and estrangement are required to make decisions in a context of radical freedom no longer sustained by older ethical sanctions. Neither categories of reason nor feeling are adequate for understanding this human integrity.[1]

Here we have the exterior explanations of the types of concepts which Unitarian Universalists hold. However, it is important to remember that ours is a religion of individuals believing what makes sense to them. All of us recognize that the concepts *about* God are only ways of *explaining* God, and do not really touch the *existence* of God. This is beyond our knowing. In each and every way summarized by the commission on theology and the frontiers of learning, there are many religious liberals who hold a rational point of view, consistent not only with what seems logical, but also what psychologically is appealing.

Paul Tillich was one of the great modern theologians. In the first volume of his work, *Systematic Theology*, he discusses the fundamental problems. In doing so he says quite clearly, "God does not exist. He is being-itself, not a being."

To clearly understand Dr. Tillich's meaning we have to take his thought further, but let us first note the importance of the twist to thinking about God which he has given. God is not separable from existence. God is not an objective force beyond us that can be dealt with as though it were an entity or an individual. When we understand this, we are beginning to face up to the reality behind the God-image.

It is in this sense that an Anglican bishop, John Robinson, speaks not only for himself, but for all religious liberals whether they are of the Anglican, Protestant, or Unitarian Universalist Church. In fact, he told me on the occasion of our meeting that "many people think I am a Unitarian, and they accuse me of being one. Many Unitarians say kind things about what I have written and support me better than my fellow Churchmen do." When one turns to his book, *Honest to God*, they can understand why Unitarian Universalists support his position. Here is a clear rational popular explanation of theology that says well what we have been trying to say to a great extent. Our goals are somewhat different, but his understanding is most helpful to us. His scholarship and development are helpful. He points out clearly that the day is now past when we can say God is "up there" or "out there" somewhere in the universe. The space age has abolished the last hiding places in the ether for God and his heavenly kingdom. What is "out there" are more and more planets, stars, suns, satellites, et cetera, which we from the earth and other planets will be exploring until there is no place in the firmament where God could hide. We all know this. The Church needs today, he tells us, a Copernican revolution, howbeit a reluctant one, in its theology. This revolution, he finds, begins with the insight of Paul Tillich, who finds God not out there but "in here"—in the *depth of being*. God is the ground of being, and in this concept Dr. Robinson suggests a whole new orientation is open. He quotes from *The Shaking of the Foundations*, in which Tillich wrote:

> The name of this infinite and inexhaustible depth and ground of all beings is *God*. That depth is what the word *God* means. And

if that word has not much meaning for you, translate it, and speak
of the depths of your life, of the source of your being, of your
ultimate concern, of what you take seriously without any reserva-
tion. Perhaps, in order to do so, you must forget everything traditional that you have learned about God, perhaps even that word
itself. For if you know that God means depth, you know much
about him. You cannot then call yourself an atheist or unbeliever.
For you cannot think or say: Life has no depth! Life is shallow.
Being itself is surface only. If you could say this in complete seriousness, you would be an atheist; but otherwise you are not. He
who knows about depth knows about God.[2]

Robinson adds to Tillich's concept that of Dietrich Bonhoeffer,
whose *Letters and Papers from Prison* deals with "Christianity without salvation" as its central theme and compelling aspect. Finally,
Rudolf Bultmann's *New Testament and Mythology* leads him to see
that demythologizing the God-myth opens up a freshness in understanding. With all this study, the Unitarian Universalist is trav-
eling familiar ground, for all deal with the type of religious experience concerning the nature of God which we have been touching
for many years. However, for many of us our aim, like Dr. Robinson's, has been to save the God-image for future use, although
the full import of his study would seem to suggest that this cannot
be done in any conventional sense. The objective God "out there"
is not only dead, but the God who is separable from the individual
consciousness, from the mind and existence of the individual is
also not conceivable. The God who is "in here" is "the spark of
the divine in each human breast" of Channing. There is only a
divine essence central to life. It is not exterior to life as such. The
center of an individual's life is tied up with the center of life for
all beings, and in our need to deal with the issues at the center of
life, we come to grips with ultimate questions. Thus we are dealing
with that which properly is God, and only that is properly entitled
to be God. This, in essence, is what Drs. Robinson and Tillich are
both saying and is, I submit, the Unitarian Universalist, the religious liberal, and the humanist insight into the nature of the
theological concern.

However, as Sir Julian Huxley reminds us, we must be careful
of "semantic cheating." We should avoid the meaningless mouth-
ing of empty words. He points out that "God is a hypothesis
constructed by man to help him understand what existence is all
about." The God hypothesis for us cannot assert the existence of
some kind of purposeful power over the universe and its destiny;
and although this is what most people think, the religious liberal
must hold fast his insights, which do not come from this other-

directed force, but from inner effective power. Huxley fears we will confuse people if we talk about God without clarifying meanings. He suggests that God seemingly has lost its explanatory value and becomes a burden to thought.

Thus we end our discussion of God with the final note of warning: that concepts that make sense to us may elicit a quite different meaning in the minds of others. Hence, there is need for careful explanations of what we mean when we use traditional words for modern faith. We need to be circumspect and careful in our words, reserved in our affirmations of belief, and definitive in our choice of terms. Otherwise we appear sceptical. We must seek to overcome the greater scepticism which is found in noncommunication, because an isolation of minds occurs when there is a failure to "talk the same mythological language." Belief is personal; language is for the group. That which is of the heart is known by the heart.

Many Unitarian Universalists, however, place the emphasis on the internal and subjective feelings, psychological rather than logical, or perhaps poetical rather than theological. Dr. John Haynes Holmes, one of our greatest twentieth-century spokespeople, summed up the feelings of many in these paragraphs:

> When I am asked if I believe in God, I am either impatient or amused and frequently decline to reply. All I know, all I want to know is that I have found in my relations with my fellowmen and in my glad beholding of the universe a reality of truth, goodness, and beauty, and that I am trying to make my life as best I can a dedication to this reality. When I am in the thinking mood, I try to be rigorously rational and, thus, not to go one step farther in my thoughts and language than my reason can take me. I then become uncertain as to whether I or any one can assert much about God and fall back content into the mood of Job. When, however, in preaching or in prayer, in some high moment of inner communion or of profound experience with life among my fellows, I feel the pulse of emotion suddenly beating in my heart and I am lifted up as though upon some sweeping tide that is more than the sluggish current of my days, I find it easy to speak as the poets speak and cry, as so many of them cry, to God.
>
> But when I say "God," it is poetry and not theology. Nothing that any theologian ever wrote about God has helped me much, but everything that the poets have written about flowers and birds and skies and seas and the saviors of the race and God—whoever he may be—has at one time or another reached my soul! More and more, as I grow older, I live in the lovely thought of these seers and prophets. The theologians gather dust upon the shelves of my library, but the poets are stained with my fingers and blotted with

my tears. I never seem so near truth as when I care not what I think or believe, but only with these masters of inner vision would live forever.

When we speak of the value of Jesus of Nazareth, we may be referring to any of several aspects of his continuing importance and influence. Jesus appears under various guises. There is Jesus as the symbol and founder of a faith for countless millions, creating an image that is composed of many parts, legendary and mythical, devotional and believing. There is Jesus as a person, of his personality and impression on the world, the impression which grows out of the historical life he lived. There is the teaching of Jesus, who was a teacher expounding a way of life that has been recognized as religious. There is also the modern reinterpretation of Jesus growing out of the recent archaeological discoveries, that is modifying and expanding our knowledge of Jesus and his times. Finally, we cannot talk about Jesus without talking also about his continuing signficance for the modern world.

We shall look at this complex personality and symbol as generally interpreted by the religious liberal. At the outset we must note that changes and advances in scholarship have developed rapidly. There are many books about Jesus that are now outdated. We are fairly certain that the public career of Jesus lasted no longer than a year and that he died in his early thirties at the latest. We are now in possession of so much in the way of new manuscripts due to recent archaeological discoveries that Jesus is now appearing to us in clearer focus than ever before in a different cultural context than we had previously imagined. Chief among these discoveries are the Dead Sea Scrolls to which scholars of all faiths are making contributions, including Catholic, Protestant, Moslem, Jewish, and Unitarian. Scholars are now, for the first time, in possession of scrolls that were actually in use in the days of Jesus of Nazareth. These documents give us additional knowledge of the ideas, cross-currents, religious issues, and political tensions of his time.

In the past most of our knowledge has come from the four gospels. A noted Universalist Biblical scholar, Professor Rolland E. Wolfe, of Case Western Reserve University, has written:

Mark, the earliest gospel, written about 68 A.D., is perhaps 90 percent history. Luke was produced a few years later and may be

95 percent history. Matthew, originating around 85 A.D., drops to perhaps 85 percent history. In John, latest of all, written about 100 A.D., only 5 percent to 10 percent of its content can be classed as genuine history. Most of the generally accepted views concerning Jesus have been based on the portions of these gospels that are unhistorical, *i.e.*, the elaborations and idealizations of the first-century Christians.

In recent years scholars have delved back into the Aramaic origins of the gospels. The gospels from which our common English versions were translated were written in Greek, whereas Jesus spoke Aramaic. If we had an original Aramaic text we probably would know more of the real Jesus than is now possible. Artificialities in the gospels, as written in Greek, stand out even in English translation.

One example, indicating the problems the scholar encounters not only in textual criticism but in dealing with the sensitive issues arising from the symbolic nature of Jesus, will indicate the general issue.

The 18th verse of the 16th chapter of the Gospel of Matthew is to many people the key verse of the entire New Testament. Here, Jesus commissions Peter to found the church as a supernatural institution. Reading in the R.S.V. edition, the words are: "And I tell you, you are Peter, and on this rock I will build my church, and the powers of death shall not prevail against it." Here is the one verse by which Jesus is said to have intentionally established a church, his church. Scholars often note that the importance of the verse is found mainly in its Greek rendition, where the pun, or a play on words, occurs (Peter-*Petros* and rock-*petra*) and is a play on the similarity of sound meant to imply an identification of meaning: "Thou art *Petros* and on *petra* I shall found my church." Among students there is doubt as to the authenticity of this statement, as it does not appear in all the early manuscripts, so presumably it could have been interpolated by a scribe. The actual words of Jesus are in doubt, of course, as no gospel is known to have been written for at least decades following his death. Accordingly, the liberal interpreter is aware that it is questionable authority to assert that the precise words hold a divine commission, all ecclesiastical claims to the contrary. As Schweitzer pointed out in *The Quest of the Historical Jesus*, most theological meanings were read into the significance of Jesus long after the gospels were written, and, as we have just noted, these gospels were not even written while he lived.

We have already noted that recent archaeological findings, of which the Dead Sea Scrolls are the most widely publicized, are bringing a new impact to our knowledge of Jesus. This is primarily so because they deal with the historical context in which he appeared. We are learning more about his culture, its resources, literature, and language and the social and religious groups and divisions that existed. Jesus is being brought into a historical focus. Once our appraisal of Jesus was based entirely on the gospels. Today we have the growing field of newly discovered manuscripts, as well as the advancements in the study of language, paleology, and paleography.

One of the major problems of the ages was that people differed in their estimates of Jesus, even in the earliest records, just as they still do. Jesus meant different things to people who wrote about him in the first century, just as he means different things to different people today. There is no hope that a unified estimate of his significance will be forthcoming. But there is hope that we may find more truth and develop a better view of Jesus than did the earlier centuries and generations.

Here is Mark, picturing Jesus as a man who went about the business of preaching with dedication and purpose. Here is Luke, who pictures Jesus as a man of lowly origins, with a touch of the common people about him, and deeply sympathetic to the poor, the needy, and the peasant. Matthew, on the other hand, pictures him as the Jewish Messiah who is come to fulfill the Old Testament prophecies. John goes to the other extreme and pictures Jesus as wholly God, the Incarnate Christ, on which the great church of Rome and the orthodox Protestants have drawn their conception of him, blending this view with that of Paul's mystical Christ, who is still more remote from the Jesus of history and, hence, from reality.

Our main conception of Jesus, therefore, must come from the Gospels of Mark and Luke, recognizing the misconceptions in the other two that modified their reporting. Our view of Jesus, the person, will henceforth be tempered by the new knowledge we now have of the times, the contending forces, and the issues of his day.

What may we say of him as a man and as an historical personage?

We can say that Jesus was a leader of remarkable power, preeminently qualified to be a successor to the line of Hebrew prophets extending from Moses to John the Baptist. The differences to be noted are in degree only, the degree of his spiritual attainment, his ethical insight, and the attractiveness of his appeal and public performance. This last element must not be underrated.

On the one hand, he attacked with vigor such institutions and groups as he believed to be unworthy. On the other, he offered great assurances and summed up the attractiveness of life in meaningful terms. Thus, people were both aroused by a sense of righteous indignation and enchanted by the loftier view of life he offered. There was, in other words, a balance to his teachings and his utterances that made him possibly the best-rounded person to emerge in Hebrew history.

It has been said in many ways that Jesus did not offer much that was new or original in religious thinking. But in the power, the simplicity, the fervor with which he presented his message he made a striking impact on humanity. In addition, his life seemed to bear witness to his teachings, and this was the greater teaching. It seemed to be more than a theory or a philosophy and became a way of life, lived by him, and able to sustain him through agony and trial.

The message itself was simple. He believed "the time of the fulfillment of history had come, and that the acceptable day of the Lord was at hand." That is, he subscribed to the concept of the coming Messiah and of the reign of Yahweh in the eschatological end of the world. Therefore, he was imbued with a sense of urgency for people to rise above their inadequacies and shortcomings, their compromises with the material world—the world of Mammon, as he called it. This introduced the spiritual concept into the temporal Hebrew life in a more striking metaphor than had been done before. Previously, only within temple or monastic walls was this note really sounded. He saw the Messianic kingdom as not wholly political, but ethical. People had to fit themselves to live in it, and they, therefore, had to reorient their lives. This brought forth the ethical content of his message and gave meaning to his total effort.

He called upon people to go beyond the law, to find the spirit of the law. "The Sabbath was made for man, not man for the Sabbath." "The letter killeth, but the spirit giveth life." "I am not come to destroy the law and the prophets, but to fulfill." "Beware of the leaven of the Pharisees and Sadducees." "Not that which goeth into a man defileth a man, but that which cometh out."

He fought against the tendency for legalism in the life of his times and sought to call the people back to the spirit that should move through the laws and that was greater than the letter of the law. This was his first principle of religious reform.

He called upon the people to substitute for formal religious practice the principle of love. He did not condemn ritual as such, but when ritual became the end of religion rather than a means to an end it interfered with the practice of religion. His remedy was to practice the principle of love. "Ye have heard that it hath been said, Thou shalt love thy neighbor, and hate thine enemy. But I say unto you, Love your enemies, pray for them which . . . persecute you, so that you may be the children of your Father which is in heaven . . . For if ye love them which love you, what reward have ye? Do not (others) the same?" (Matthew 5:43–46.)

This led to a principle of community and neighborliness. This second principle of religious reform carried his emphasis still further along the road of a greater humaneness in religion.

Finally, he sought to humanize the concept of deity. He turned God from the forbidding image of the Old Testament tribal deity into a friendly and benign parent. Instead of the austere, fearful, stern, God of Judgment—the Lord God of Hosts—he presented God as a loving parent to whom children could turn and return. All people, like children, could rely upon such a loving God, find security in the concept, and know that when they called upon his name this type of God would be on their side if they were worthy children of their heavenly parent. This type of parent set the pattern for the relationships which should guide us in these relationships with others. This was the third reform in religious ideas he emphasized.

Thus, we find Jesus emerging from history not as a God, but as a teacher who, filled with the urgency of his times, called upon all to make their religion more humane. He brought a more humane and, hence, a more palatable conception of religion into the mainstream of the developing religious tradition of the West. The narrow legalism, the blind ritual observance, and the stern and remote God were concepts he sought to reform. The religious spirit should be more flexible, loving, and generous. He stressed the primacy of the spirit, the power to love, and the benevolence of God and, hence, of life.

To the further question, "How did he develop such striking concepts?," there are two answers. One is that they are not so striking in his culture as the New Testament tends to lead us to believe. The second is that his was not an isolated voice.

The lore of our faith has held that Jesus Christ was a unique phenomenon in history and lived in an era in which no new idea had existed since the time of the prophet Daniel when the Old Testament was completed two centuries earlier. The time in which Jesus lived is traditionally presented as a vacuum. This view no longer is valid. Much is known about that period, and with modern archaeological discoveries more is being added to our knowledge. In addition to the Dead Sea Scrolls, there is the Coptic library from the ruined tombs near Nag Hamadi in Upper Egypt, discovered in 1945, which includes the Gnostic manuscripts and most notably *The Gospel According to Thomas*. This Gospel possibly contains sayings of Jesus previously unknown, and may supply the missing link in the study of ancient manuscripts and texts that connect the Gospels with Gnostic, Patristic, Manichean, and even Cathare literature. It is an exciting prospect that archaeology holds out to learn more than was previously known about Jesus. Other sources often neglected and overlooked by our scholars, such as the Apocrypha, Pseudepigrapha, Mishnah, and Tannaitic literature, as well as the writings of Pliny, Josephus, Philo, and other historians of the period can increase our awareness. The road to the *Quest of the Historical Jesus* traveled by Albert Schweitzer and from which I have drawn copiously offers further insight.

The significance of Jesus for us today is the ethical teaching, timeless because timely, which still speaks. One of our outstanding Unitarian Universalist leaders, the late Dr. Robert Killam, has summed it up for us:

> Jesus' life was not bounded by the time, the country, or the community in which it was lived, for he knew and lived by the truths that are valid always and everywhere. Although many have thought to excuse their own dismal failures by calling him visionary and impractical, they have known in their hearts that it was they who were impractical, for everything they have touched has turned to ashes.
>
> It is true that Jesus knew nothing of modern conditions of life. He never saw a factory or heard its clatter. He never listened to a radio or watched television or rode in an automobile. He never visited a hospital or worked in a scientific laboratory. But these are only the gadgets of life! Life itself Jesus knew. Birth and death, work and wages, sickness and despair, poverty and blessings and hardships that make up life are not new to us. They were not new in his day. They have been present in every age. Every human goodness and evil, dream and failure which we know he also knew. He spoke to a world like ours. Despite our unwillingness to pay the price of discipleship, we believe in him, not because he was God, but because he was man, at man's best.

Notes

[1]Unitarian Universalist Association, *The Free Church in a Changing World*, (The reports of the Commissions to the Churches and Fellowships) 1963 published by the UUA.

[2]John A. T. Robinson, *Honest To God*, 1963. Westminister Press, Philadelphia, p. 22.

9
Accent on Religious Education

In visiting one of our churches or fellowships you will perhaps join in the lively discussions that take place along the corridors and in the halls of a Unitarian Universalist church school on a Sunday morning. It is here that parents meet other parents, confer with teachers, and have the opportunity to put questions to the director of religious education. You, too, may join in a serious conversation about religious education during a typical coffee-hour after-church gathering, which may include parents, teachers, and minister.

We have progressed from the conventional Sunday school to a new departure in religious instruction, taking forward strides, and the dialogue now taking place between parents and educators is largely concerned with this.

Such conversations often begin with key questions: "What is authentically religious about a curriculum that seems to focus on values and ethics?", "Where in the curriculum do our children learn about the Bible?", "Where do they learn what the Unitarian Universalist church really believes?"

Other questions raised: "How does the church school help our children understand why we rejected orthodoxy and affirmed the Unitarian Universalist position?", "How does it help our children understand why we cannot 'accept the Bible' as do their grandparents, aunts, and neighbors?", "How does our church school help our children become confident religious liberals in a sea of orthodoxy?"

One set of questions grows out of uncertainty about the liberal religious curriculum, and the other grows out of an assurance that our religious approach is confident and valid.

Often the attitude of nonparents (perhaps grandparents or great-grandparents) of the current church school is more difficult. They are an older generation, and during the years since their own education the world has shrunk unbelievably. They regarded the other side of the Atlantic, Pacific, and Caribbean as being a remote area that if they were lucky they might someday visit, whereas children today think of the moon, Mars, and constellations as places they may possibly visit some day. Instead of the standard for values of the quiet years before World War II the present generation knows the good life as something tenuous, something they must expect to achieve in the future if they survive. The older generations had a backdrop of security. They could say, "The sun never sets on the British Empire." Today, however, the British Empire is secondary to the great powers, and our children must live in a world where the difficult and precarious struggle among China, the Soviet Union, and the United States gives no clear picture of how the future will be shaped. The older generations could accept Kipling's challenge to take up with the white man's burden, but today the approximately two dozen African nations can outvote the American hemispheric nations or the NATO alliance in the United Nations General Assembly. The claims of a Christian civilization ring hollow to the millions in Asia and Africa and are becoming the marks of a Western provincialism. The world may no longer be looked upon as divided between Christians and pagans, but rather as composed of co-equal, self-respecting cultures.

It is a different world in many respects, and it is not surprising that the changes and confusions often cause uncertainties and insecurities. When religion, the church, and the church school are also in rapid transition, and our world no longer holds fast to the old certainties, it is understandable that many are puzzled. Because the church is an institution that is "person-sized," some think it ought to stand still. However, we see its role as helping our children orient their lives to the changing world in which they live, and to do this it must to a certain extent change in itself. Unless we help prepare our children for their world, not ours, we will fail them. Consequently, an understanding of faith must be offered them. The old stories of David and Goliath, of Moses in the Bulrushes, of the loaves and fishes, of "the rich and the poor, we have them always," are lessons illustrative of yesterday's faith. These and stories from other cultures are presented not as historical facts, but as legends expressing our search for meaning. Our children go into a classroom and see maps of interplanetary space; they see mounted leaves and crystals, gardens, and snow-making machines! They see seaweed and shells and Oriental motifs. Some people may ask," What do these things *have to do* with religion?" All of these things that bind together our cultural heritage express the unity of life that our religious education emphasizes.

There is a new creative element operating in religious education today, brought into play by the urgency of events and the loss of confidence in an older orthodoxy. The religious liberal has responded with a definite and clear-cut answer which is unique. For instance, Donald Harrington, speaking to the assembled Unitarians and Universalists in Boston's famed Symphony Hall at a service of celebration, following the vote to consolidate the two denominations, said:

> What we have seen emerging in Unitarian Universalism in this twentieth century is nothing less than a new world faith, formulated by and fitted for this great new world-age that is coming to birth in our time.

Of no aspect of our corporate religious life is this more certainly emphasized than in religious education. These seem to be bold words, exaggerated views, and a far cry from our religious education projects with plasticene and modeling clay, with stories and fishes, with questions that are barely answerable. While the most creative thinkers of other faiths have been preoccupied with questions of dogma, doctrine, theology, and apologetics, the creative and challenging concern of Unitarian Universalism often appears centered in rethinking and redefining the role of religious education in nurturing the spiritual and intellectual growth of youngsters. Today's methodology is a *process* approach that is frequently applied to problems selected by the students themselves.

Unitarians and Universalists are participating in this great adventure of creating a new world faith. It is an emerging faith, not a revolutionary faith, that is in process, and its clear outlines are not yet fully formed. It is emerging bit-by-bit and slowly, and it may not seem like a startling new development to us. Yet our religious education program is a new vanguard movement in religion.

Some time ago Dr. Harry Meserve wrote of an experiment with college students which led him to this conclusion:

A new faith is in the making in our world today. It is nothing anybody in an ivory tower has dreamed up. It must come because without it the world cannot continue, except on the present path which leads toward suicide.

This new faith is evident in the type of religious education program being evolved in Unitarian Universalist churches. Dr. Meserve continued:

> It must affirm before all else the mystery and the holiness within each. It must proclaim the sacredness of life, the right of all life to its highest possible material, moral, and spiritual development. The prophets and disciples of this new faith must be more than lovers and servers of humanity in the mass. They must be lovers and servers of men and women.

This I think is part of our goal: to create a faith that makes us responsive to men and women as people, not en masse, not in the abstract, but as individuals. Such a faith will increase the humanity of all; it will add to our capacity for kindness and sympathy.

It will also make us responsive to the great ideas of history and of the slow development through the ages to understand the whole drama of life.

To help bring about this we will seek and teach the great ideas. And we will interpret them, analyze them, so that we know what to accept and what to reject, until we learn how to live with and utilize humanity's vast storehouse of knowledge and experience.

"But," some may respond, I am sure, "if we are concerned with the total heritage why is it that our schools and curriculums are doing so much that is experimental and so little that is traditional? Why is it that we have so little teaching concerning the Bible and the doctrines and theology of biblical religion? If it is important that we teach the great ideas of our religious heritage, could we be mistaken in the type of curriculum we are relying upon?"

It is possible to answer these questions by saying, "Oh, but we do teach something about the Bible," but this, frankly is merely to avoid the heart of the question.

First of all, there is an implied assumption in the type of questions being raised: the assumption that orthodox church schools or Bible schools do a better job of teaching the Bible. This assumption is debatable.

A few years ago a now famous study was conducted which indicated that traditional and orthodox religious instruction fails woefully in its efforts to teach the Bible.

This study was made by a group of researchers with a group of fifty college sophomores who had orthodox religious backgrounds and had just completed a five-week course of study of the Bible in a course on religion, in a Bible belt university.

Results showed that out of the fifty students, only eight or nine, that is, less than twenty per cent, had a really adequate knowledge of the Bible. Among the other eighty per cent there was no understanding of the difference between the Old and New Testaments, between Jesus and God, and they wrote that Jesus appeared throughout the Bible, that he gave Moses the Ten Commandments and appeared to Job.

The fact that the Bible is a conglomeration of knowledge and literature collected over a long period of time, say 1,500 years, that it contains books of various types, such as history, fiction, poetry, prophetic and biographical, was not disclosed. To these students, all the books of the Bible were of equal merit and all of a uniform spiritual, historical, and religious value!

Now we know, or should know, that this is simply not so. There is no uniform ethical code or uniform spiritual quality to the Bible. Historically, some of it is a faithful representation of the events recorded, but some of it is wide of the mark. Rather than a logical sequence of events, systematically compiled and brought together, we know the Bible is an accidental collection of existing manuscripts that lack a coherent unity and help explain the fractured and obtuse nature of Christian theology.

This study also showed that whether students were Roman Catholic, Southern Baptist, Presbyterian, Episcopalian, or Lutheran there was little difference in their understanding of the Bible. All of them had had years of Sunday school training in orthodox denominations, and, except the twenty per cent earlier noted, none of them indicated competent Bible knowledge.

These findings would indicate that religious liberals should stop yearning for more of the disciplined and traditional teachings of the orthodox schools and become familiar with the Unitarian Universalist presentation of the Bible.

Our approach, based on comparative religions, on archaeological findings, on the historical method of criticism, deals with history as history, legend as legend, and fantasy as the product of imagination.

"This is all very well," some may say. "But granted that orthodox schools are not doing well, how do you know that we are more successful?" Others may ask, "Is there a better method or approach to teaching religious values than the Bible with its accumulated legacy of the spiritual quest?"

These questions lead us into taking a look at just what it is that we are trying to do and how our religious instructions vary from the traditional methods. The personnel of the Department of Education have often answered similar questions.

Unitarian Universalists recognize the universality of the religious approach. Any experience may be religious if it has the quality which touches personality at its core. An experience is religious if it gives a person insight into his actions and motivations, good or bad. An experience is religious when it relates a person to his fellows in ways that are mutually satisfying. Such experience can strengthen life and give a sense of purpose.

An experience is religious when it leads a person into intimate relationships with nature to appreciate its vitality, its variety, its predictability. An experience is religious when it awakens the young child to wondering, questioning, searching, discovering. Oh, the thrill of discovery and of personal identification!

The approach of learning from experiences is possible at home, using the materials available to liberal families and can foster greater religious growth than would be realized in any other way. Unitarian Universalists have long said that the church school is only an adjunct to the home, seeking in an hour or two a week to bring into focus the process of growth and identification that goes on all week at home, in the playground, and in the school. Too often, however, "The right hand knoweth not what the left hand doeth," and church and home fail to work harmoniously toward the same ends. This difficulty is avoided when the home is the center of religious instruction. It will not be a shortcut, but it will help you create and build values not otherwise possible.

Religious education is a process that starts with the birth of the child, indeed, before birth in the attitudes which the parents bring to marriage, in the concept they have of a home, in the type of values around which they organize their lives, and in the response they make to life situations. It continues with their child's first notice of the natural world. It is further developed as the simple and abundant things of nature are brought into the experience of life; the character of that development depends on how the child responds to them and how his parents react. It is enhanced by the wonder of birth and growth. It is increased when the child is allowed to stop a moment with adults and consider, naturally and freely, the fact of death. All these are part of religious education, and the sensitive parent may lead the child naturally into such growing experiences.

This kind of experience is best when it remains informal and when it is a normal, natural part of family life. Obviously, therefore, parents are often the best teachers, and, indeed, the child's principal teachers. However, parents usually find that they can't go it alone in the teaching process and for this reason turn to the school and the church. For many years now, Unitarian Universalist churches have been developing a distinctive and different type of religious education curriculum, which does not aim at indoctrinating, but at awakening; not at dogmatics, but at creative development; not at supernatural interpretations, but at natural acceptances. This course of study is the basic tool of our religious education. It will help lead parents and child into new experiences and discoveries together, and it will encourage the life-affirming and world-accepting philosophy which is most congenial to religious liberalism.

To use this course effectively the parent needs first to grasp the philosophy and simplicity of its conception and then use it as a guide to help in the natural religious orientation and development of the child. This curriculum is amazingly different from the teaching tools of the traditional church schools. It is a vastly significant departure from the curriculums of orthodox Sunday schools, not merely because of its educational methods but because of its religious content. Religious education has been one of the fields of greatest advance in the Unitarian Universalist movement during the past few decades. In some recent years, one way in which our churches differed from others was that the religious educators, rather than the theologians, were shaping the content and meaning of the movement.

Accordingly, when we talk of religious education we are not referring to the traditional type of church-centered indoctrination of other communions. Rather than indoctrinate children, we will help them develop a religion of their own, a religion that will have meaning to them. We will not be able to teach our religion as though it were a closed system with all questions neatly answered. Instead we will keep in mind the warning of the aged William Ellery Channing that there is always the danger that religious liberalism will be taught as a set of established truths and become a new type of orthodoxy. This is a danger we still must guard against.

When people ask me what Unitarian Universalists believe, I

cannot give a specific answer. In the same way we must be as fair with our children's questions and not close their minds in this matter. We teach truths, not the truth; laws, not the law; about churches, not the church; about lives, not the life; and about doctrines, not the doctrine.

Dr. Sophia Lyon Fahs, the former editor of the Beacon curriculum, once said that we wanted our children to begin at the place we stopped and implied that we expect our children to go beyond us.

Dr. Rufus Jones, the great Liberal Quaker, once wrote, "We do not want our children to become little theologians." Perish the thought! Rather we wish to make them eager, expectant, challenging, and creative children, able to enter into life and enjoy its rich rewards and able to find a place in the sun for themselves. We do not want them to accept the secondhand clothes of ancient theologians (as Carlyle said), but from firsthand experience to develop their own religion which will grow as they grow and be flexible to the multiple purposes of their lives. A second-hand religion, an external religion, does not always stand up in the face of life discoveries.

A physician (who was a warden in his church) once came to me after a service club luncheon and said, "Can I talk with you about my religious problem? I found my son's Bible in the ash can last week, and when I spoke to him he said, 'It is only a pack of lies. I am learning the truth in science at school.' My own church has failed my boy. How could the Unitarian Universalist church have helped him?" Here was a youngster whose faith, his religion, could not be adjusted to his experiences and his growing awareness of life. It was purely an external thing that did not square with his experience and learning; therefore, in discarding the Bible, an external object, he was discarding an external religion. If the father had not come to me immediately, so that something internal and personal could be developed, this youth might have gone on for years, floundering without a sense of religious value. He would have been another of the hollow men.

The family cannot escape providing religious instruction for its children. Religious education goes on all the time—in the way the family treats outsiders, neighbors, help, workmen, in the family attitudes toward foreigners and strangers and in their attitudes toward one another. Religious education is implicit in the method used in solving problems in the family and in the way decisions are made. The quality of religious instruction is evident in the response of family members to small creatures—to snakes, bees, frogs, beetles; it is apparent in the way they treat dogs and cats, whether their own or someone else's or just strays. They provide still another facet of religious instruction in their attitude toward music and art and in the type of response they make to the television programs that express violence, disregard of human values, unfair representation of husband-wife relationships, and lack of moral sensitivity and intellectual awareness.

A family can further its own religious growth by taking an honest look at the kind of responses each member makes to the ordinary situations of daily life—during the early morning rush to get off to school and work, for instance or at the dinner table— and at the differences in response when members are under stress or in the midst of an emergency. Furthermore, the family can look for opportunities in everyday life to foster religious growth and strengthen its constructive attitudes.

As part of the everyday routine, are there opportunities for children to throw off tensions and relax? Have parents time to listen to children's enthusiasms and their troubles? Is there a period for the whole family to be together so that parents and children can enjoy each other's company? Are there chances to be together on all levels from chores to fun? Is there a pattern of freedom and democracy, of responsibility and discipline so that they do not deny one another, but establish an orderly, consistent pattern for the development of values?

Mealtimes, bedtimes, week-ends, vacations, all offer opportunities for family experiences. Conflict situations—among siblings, with neighbors, at school—present a different, but important, opportunity for meaningful experiences. The way in which a family meets the problem of its child in trouble will deepen or weaken its religious life.

These give but the barest indication of possibilities in ordinary family life for experiences that can be profoundly religious. Such experiences are likely to be important determinants of individual character. Parents will find it worthwhile to compare these possibilities with the kind offered by a formal Sunday school education.

It is necessary, however, to make explicit for the child the values inherent in the experiences of everyday living; furthermore, as the child grows older, there are many occasions for reaching beyond the range of everyday family activities to enlarge the scope of family views and values. In these processes, the Beacon curriculum and supplementary materials can be effectively used.

Building upon these concepts and insights, the UUA Department of Religious Education helps congregations to stimulate and support the religious growth and learning of children, youth, and adults through education and worship. This department's services include curriculum development, leadership education and teacher training, and a youth office for teenagers. There are various other programs and services carried on that are necessary for the guidance and development of essential resources for a liberal orientation in religious education. One of its major services is the regular stimulation of church and classroom activities through the packet of the Religious Education Action Clearing House (i.e., REACH Packet) and the previously mentioned Worship Arts Clearing House packets. These packets of suggested materials are useful week in and week out for planning at the local level.

Information on curriculum materials is listed following the Bibliography at the end of this volume. More current material, as well as a more inclusive listing, may always be received by writing to either the Religious Education Department or the Bookstore at the Unitarian Universalist Association, 25 Beacon Street, Boston, Massachusetts 02108-2800.

Some time back, one of the creative writers of America, Clifton Fadiman, wrote a guest editorial for *The Instructor* magazine, which I would like to quote. He was writing for public school teachers, and when I read it I thought it was a good statement of the philosophy of our curriculum, and I wrote him to this effect. I would like to share his words with you as a challenge to what the parent might hope to accomplish and to assure you that those of us in this fellowship are not alone in wishing these things for our children. We think this is the truest type of religious instruction and so commend these words to you.

> I should like to set before you what may seem a crackpot notion: that the best place to teach philosophy is not the university but the elementary school; and that the ideal student of philosophy is the child from eight to twelve. It is he, not you or I, who wonders about the world; why it was made, who made it, what makes people different from animals, how we think, what it means to be brave and good or truthful and so on. These are basically philosophical questions.
>
> I am not asking that the child be turned into a philosopher at the age of twelve. All I suggest is that somewhere along the route his fresh, active, inquiring mind be led to *wonder* about the universe, the world, his place in nature, and some of the statements that wise men have made about these matters. My conviction is that we have become a people who can *do* almost anything, but who are baffled when asked to consider the origins, meaning and consequences of our actions.

This national weakness in abstract thought is partly the result of never having been confronted in our formative years with its content and its fascinations. The elementary school should do much to remedy this deficiency.

Our liberal religious education can do much to remedy this deficiency. Our children confront these questions in formative years and have been enticed by their fascinations.

Our Beacon curriculum is designed for institutional use—for the classroom—even while recognizing the values for personal growth and enlargement. While it becomes as we have noted a valuable tool for the parent or home, its value for the church school class must also be pointed out.

There is a continuous relationship between religious experience and all other experience. This we need to remember. We try to relate the material of experience more directly to the youngster than does the public school, the mass media, or the chance association. To a large extent it is in the relationship that the religious education takes place. Hopefully ideas will be carried into experiences, changing ideas from objective knowledge to primary relationships. This is the reason why it is often so difficult for the child to tell you, the parent, what has been learned. This learning is not something outside of the mind, like a time-honored take-home leaflet, but what it did, which is too personal for explanation. The teaching in our project method of experiencing, at its best, becomes too subjective to be objectively explained by the young mind.

The emotional involvement of the youngster is grounded, however, in the intellectual continuum. It is through the mental process and intellectual formulation that the environment is related to the youngster. Beginning with simple questions that lead naturally from one to another the individual must find private answers.

"What do you mean?" is probably the first of these questions. If we can bring our children to raise questions and help them to find the meaning and nature of what we are dealing with, then religious experience will be crystal clear. The traditional curriculum is careful never to allow this question to be asked. Much about things is taught, but nothing of their essence or nature.

God, immortality, spirit, and soul are talked about in a traditional course, but never is the question "What do you really mean?" answered to the satisfaction of the religious liberal. For us, such issues should lead to honest explanations.

Then the young mind, satisfied with the meaning, must go on (or perhaps be led) to ask a second question, "How do you know?" Upon what basis do we base our knowlege of the essence of the subject matter? Is it something that bears examination? How do we find the answer in the first place? A meaningful answer must come not from tradition, not from authority, and not from say-so, but from experience, experimentation, observation, and it must be verifiable. Upon no other basis can a bona fide faith be created and developed for children.

Then, after being satisfied with meanings and justifications, the child is in a position to go on to the third question, "What difference does it make?" This question can only become meaningful after the first two questions have verified the basis for the religious category. The general tendency to short-cut the religious learning process and take up only this third question lies at the root of the failure of much religious instruction. For us, religious education begins long before it is related to the application of the teaching to our lives.

It begins with the articulate clarification and proof of that explanation. In dealing with the relationships of life we are dealing with primary associations. We seek to make faith personal, laying it upon a sure foundation, giving it an intellectual support, so that it can stand up under the buffets of fate and the challenges of new knowledge.

The Bible is a part of this educational experience we wish to have our children discover and explore. We should perhaps call it the Judeo-Christian Bible, for in a broader sense all religions have their Bibles, and we will want our children to learn something of them, too. We want our children to know this eclectic book as scholars have unscrambled it for us, as a human document containing crude ancient beliefs, as well as some of the most sublime concepts that transcend time and place. We want our children to come to know this amazing book by degrees appropriate to their age and concomitant with their ability to fit it into the larger perspective of their related knowledge. Then the Bible is part of the growing experience.

All life is an ongoing experience. We move forward, and in the end it is our hope that our children will take up the pilgrimage we began and move beyond us. Our hope is that our children will not make the same mistakes, not be limited by our experience and knowledge, which is of yesterday. Rather we hope that they will grow with the new experience of tomorrow, which is to say the new experience of their age, of a world that came to birth in the day of interplanetary flight, of the struggle for the stability of the United Nations, and the control of atomic power, and of the new knowledge of science, as well as of its technology.

"All life is going out," wrote Harold Scott. "Under the watchful eyes of love we took our first infant step. Perhaps we fell and were bruised, but in time we learned to walk. This process is the symbol of all our lives . . . All about us are the inviting roads of new experience. We can loiter in the familiar paths, or we can go out. If we will, we can travel far; and that, too, within the confines of our own homes and accustomed work. Life calls us to go out, out of our uninteresting selves into new selves of fulfillment."

No lesser experience can serve us or the faith we would pass on to our children.

Our approach to religious education is, therefore, a unique experience that has broken free from the old stereotypes of Sunday school, church school, Bible school. We offer a flexible and growing experience-oriented approach to religious education. The education of the young does not take place in a vacuum, however, and the parent cannot leave this activity to the church or its teachers. For the child it begins with the earliest responses in the home and is intensified and altered with contacts with his contemporaries. All people, including children, learn much from their peer-group, and because children strive to belong and to relate actively with their equals, the approach of home attitudes is always in jeopardy. There is, therefore, no room for complacency. One of our Universalist leaders, Dr. Clinton Lee Scott, who wrestled with this problem through a long and illustrious career, gives us a lesson in the form of humor. In this "Parish Parable" he tells of the parent who postponed religious instruction until his child was old enough to choose his own church:

> And there was a certain man that had a son whom he greatly loved. And he thought within himself saying, None is wise enough to instruct my son in the mysteries of the eternal: neither priest nor Levite shall tell him what is good and what is evil, lest his mind be corrupted with error. And he saith, This shall he do: he shall wait until he is a man, then he shall know of himself what to believe.
>
> But it was not as the father thought. For the son did grow and wax strong. Keepeth he his eyes open for seeing, and his ears for hearing. And his teachers were neither priests nor Levites. Neither did he come to the Temple for instruction. But his teachers were them that speaketh into the air, and them that were seen in the pictures of Babylon, and messengers in bright colors that were brought into the household on the morning of the Sabbath day.

And when the father was old he understood that the mind of his son had not been as an empty vessel that waiteth for a day to be filled, but that it was like unto a parched field that drinketh of that which falleth upon it.[1]

The mind of a child will be filled with impressions; he will develop attitudes, will find a way to relate meaningfully to the world, to people and to society. In consequence, we must remember first and foremost that the church is a supplement to the home, not an alternative to the home. The superstitions of playmates, the fearful morbidities of hell and judgment, of devils and damnation, which children share in confidence, may be locked in the minds of our own youngsters if we have not given them something else to believe. The trite formality of conventional piety which is implicit in public school assemblies, public prayer recitations, and Bible readings, without comment or clarification (giving the impression it is God's Word, not to be approached with reasonable questions), creates an orthodoxy without the parents' awareness. Many children hold the idea that religion revolves exclusively around the question "Which church do you attend?" or such challenges as "I'm more religious than you, because I go to church more often."

These ideas are not those of the religious liberal, and we need to creatively build a more helpful scaffolding for our children's religion. This, of course, is done in many ways. The schools can help, and the church can help, but the parents must become the teachers of religion to their children. They do so unwittingly, as in numerous ways their insignificant gestures become a means of conversation that show their attitudes toward life. Fortunately or unfortunately, our children will acquire our response to life with a certainty almost equal to that of heredity.

Note

[1]Clinton Lee Scott, *Parish Parables*, 1946, Boston, Beacon Press, p. 34.

10
A Church of Your Own

When the author was a college student, a teacher commented that one could find Unitarians and Universalists in old New England towns, on college campuses, and in large metropolitan centers. He implied that except for certain heritage and intellectual interests, Unitarian Universalists were so few that only a large city could maintain a church, and none of us challenged him. We failed to note the obvious flaw in his analysis, which was that Unitarian Universalists depended upon the accident of geography rather than on a state of mind. To be a Unitarian Universalist is not dependent upon a pile of bricks and stones or a hollow lumber pile, no matter how gracefully arranged. Whitehead wrote, "Religion is what a man does with his solitariness." And Tom Paine proclaimed, "My own mind is my own church." Today, religious liberals, wherever they are, may identify and participate in the programs of the Unitarian Universalist Association.

The Reverend William P. Jenkins reported that on attending a Western Canadian Unitarian Conference, he was intrigued to find a Church of the Larger Fellowship member who had traveled 500 miles from a small crossroads community in the state of Montana. Under no circumstances could Mr. Jenkins presume that that tiny town would some day have enough persons to organize a Unitarian Universalist Church, but here was a committed Unitarian Universalist, whose contact was through the mailings of the Church of the Larger Fellowship of the denomination. He was every bit as informed, concerned, and vitally involved as those who came from the large churches in Winnipeg, Calgary, or Vancouver.

These members in the privacy of their own homes, through their "church by mail," receive sermons, bulletins, periodicals, an opportunity for directed reading courses, materials to carry on a religious education program with their children, the use of a lending library of over two thousand volumes of liberal religious literature, and the opportunities to raise questions and find answers through correspondence with the church's minister and the appropriate committee members. While it is often true they may never see a fellow member, most of them look forward to such an opportunity.

"I will be returning to the United States in the fall and hope to see in the flesh a Unitarian or Universalist for the first time," wrote a United States serviceman stationed in Germany.

Carol Donovan, a housewife in Massachusetts, wrote, "For years my family and I believed we had no religion, which is a strangely lonesome position in a well-churched community. We felt a need for a religious connection of some sort, but one liberal enough for us to agree with and love. When we discovered the Church of the Larger Fellowship, we were overjoyed, for it brought us just the faith and knowledge we needed. It gave us a secure religious background; the feeling of belonging to a worldwide, intelligent group of lonely Universalists; and thoughtful monthly sermons, introduced to us by a sympathetic, deep-thinking, intellectual whose quiet, friendly letters answered our deepest needs."

Winslow Sisson of Arizona reported, "A few days ago a truck drove into our ranch at sundown, and the driver introduced himself and his wife as Mr. and Mrs. Charles Gritzner, members of the Larger Fellowship from Yuma. They had driven over here, a distance of about 200 miles, to see their first living Unitarian."

And Dr. James Fraser, who lives high in the mountains of Colorado, wrote, "I carefully note the correspondents and new members listed in the Larger Fellowship News Bulletin on the chance that I might see someone in my area. I haven't as yet: I am just another of the lonely 'black sheep' liberals who is surrounded by orthodoxy."

These are four comments from the thousands of larger fellowship members scattered throughout the world whose only contact with Unitarian Universalism is through the Church of the Larger Fellowship. This church is the frontier edge of the Unitarian Universalist Association.

Chartered by the board of directors of the American Unitarian Association in the fall of 1944 with but a handful of members, this correspondence church has grown year by year until it lists the largest church membership in the denomination. The program and services it provides did not come full-blown. From time to time the members make their hopes known, and those charged with administration endeavor to meet the needs which have been expressed. It was incorporated in 1970.

For over two decades the Church of the Larger Fellowship through the religious education committee has provided religious education services to families. The members of this committee are recruited from experienced church-school workers who are familiar with the Beacon curriculum and the philosophy of the Unitarian Universalist approach to religious education.

In the Church of the Larger Fellowship parents are the teachers, not only actually, as always, but also the acknowledged teachers. That the responsibility for the religious guidance of the child rests directly on the parent has profoundly affected the CLF religious education program. The members of the religious education committee have written and adapted materials specifically for isolated families and are responsible for publications for children and young people.

Anyone anywhere may join the church by mail. In 1975, this program was serving more than 5,000 adults and children and reaching untold others who see our materials in the home. To receive materials it is only necessary to drop a note to the association office building at 25 Beacon Street, Boston, Massachusetts.

Some of our inquiries are almost humorous. Recently a business executive in Tokyo wrote us this account: "I spent nine days in Nepal. I became well acquainted with a retired Episcopal minister from Massachusetts. One day I told him that what I wanted in church was sermons from time to time that would guide me in solving everyday problems. I cited, for example, how to face jealousy, meanness, spite, overaggressiveness, overambition, disagreeableness, quarreling, discord at the office, cheating in business, invitations to offer bribes, cruelty to children, cruelty to animals, laziness in offices, intimidations in business, threats to resort to violence, illness, excessive worry over any of the above problems, etc. The minister said: 'Your needs can probably best be met by going to a Unitarian church![1]"

On another occasion, a letter arrived which read, "In the encyclopedia I read that Thomas Jefferson was a Unitarian. Although I have never knowingly met a member of your church, his ideas sound so much like my own I would like more information." Another person wrote that he told his rector he could no longer recite the creeds of the service honestly, and this resulted in "a withering eye, a long pause, and the scorching condemnation, 'Sir, you talk like a Unitarian.'" This person wrote that he then went to the library and looked up the Unitarians, and continues, "I believe my rector was right. There are no Unitarian churches in our community. How do I affiliate?" This letter was passed on to us at the CLF offices, and we sent him some materials, including our bond of fellowship, which one signs and returns in order to join.

This bond of fellowship, our covenant, reads "We seek to build the community of human fellowship so that, united in love and in strength, we may together search for the truth." That is all; there are no required beliefs. The purpose of the Church of the Larger Fellowship is expressed this way in the bylaws of the church, as adopted by the board of trustees of the Unitarian Universalist Association: "The purpose of this church is to provide a spiritual home for isolated Unitarians and Universalists and their families and to transfer the allegiance of its members to local Unitarian and Universalist churches or Fellowships whenever and wherever possible."

Through this medium, persons who are alone may join together in a larger fellowship of religious liberals. The release and joy that come in finding that one is no longer alone and that there are countless others who share the same sense of affirmative freedom and who reject the limitations of orthodoxy give these people a religous experience. They watch eagerly for each new sermon, write excited letters, and bear personal witness with confidence in their own communities, because they know that there are many others doing the same throughout the length and breadth of the land.

There was a CLF family that ran a placer gold mine fifty miles north of the Arctic Circle; and until recently a navy officer in Antarctica kept in touch with Unitarian Universalist concerns while on remote duty there. Dr. Albert Schweitzer wrote some years ago that as a student he was attracted to Unitarianism, but that there were no organizations where he lived which he could join, "but through the means of the Church of the Larger Fellowship it is now possible for me to join the Unitarians. I thank you kindly. . . ." Thus CLF reached people in the equatorial jungles of Africa and isolated religious liberals whever they may be, the great and humble alike, for it is no respecter of persons. Most of our members, however, are around the corner, in a neighboring town or in the next county. Our members live in thousands of communities in the United States and Canada.

Our mail gives boundless and continuous emphasis to the

wide scope of our Fellowship. Mrs. Schreiner wrote from the Rocky Mountains, "It is good, indeed, to learn of a group where you can bring your very own beliefs and opinions and be welcome and, in addition, receive help in presenting ideas upon which your children can build. Every week you must get many letters such as this from concerned mothers—at least I hope you do. Many thanks, in advance, for any help you can give us."

From California, George Dirksen wrote, "If only I had found your church twenty years ago! I presume this tale is rather common—in cases where the parents have tardily 'found' the liberal way of life!!"

A check from a member arrived with this note attached, "I am sorry that this check could not be more; it would take at least a hundred times this amount to cover the joy and spiritual stimulation that the Unitarian Universalist Church has given me."

With the exception of a modest membership charge, the Church of the Larger Fellowship is financed entirely by the voluntary gifts of members in a once-a-year canvass (by mail). Through this means, a budget of over $100,000 is annually raised in large measure from the membership. After incorporation it established the Frederick May Eliot/Clinton Lee Scott CLF Endowment Fund to help finance its program of outreach. This fund honors the memory of the two principal founders of this ministry.

"Although we have been married forty-one years," writes a storekeeper in Washington, "my husband and I have never attended a church service together. We have found that we have been doing Unitarian Universalist thinking for all that time and could not go to orthodox churches and subscribe to all the creeds and beliefs. As we read all the CLF literature, we find ourselves saying, 'That's just what we've always said.' We live in a small town where there are too many churches for the population. Since we have the one large store, we have some pressure to belong. We can now reply that we do belong."

Here is a church to which anyone may belong—if his or her "mind is his (her) church" and its integrity brooks no compromise. A Canadian broadcast commentator wrote, "I never before had the courage to stand up for my convictions as strongly as I do now, knowing that I am not the only one who feels this way."

Some of the letters come from those who, having been in CLF for a number of years, now find themselves able to attend a local church or fellowship. One such letter recently received from Mr. and Mrs. Potter reads as follows:

It is with mixed emotions that we inform you that we have moved from Kenai, Alaska; to Stanford and having a Unitarian Church in Palo Alto, are resigning our membership in the Church of the Larger Fellowship.

We have looked forward for years to the time when we would be able to join the activities and enjoy the companionship of other Unitarians on a face-to-face basis. After having attended the beautiful Palo Alto church for the past two Sundays, we feel assured that our membership here will be stimulating and rewarding.

As fine as this church may be, we doubt that any church could communicate to its members the feelings of closeness and concern which we have experienced as members of the Church of the Larger Fellowship. We have always felt that we truly 'belonged.' For this comfort plus the many hours of thought-provoking, inspiring and informative reading we wish to extend our deepest appreciation.

We expect to be at Stanford University for the next two, or perhaps three, years. We have no plans beyond the two years but, should we again return to Alaska, we would certainly join once more in the Church of the Larger Fellowship.

Thank you again for your contributions to enriching our lives over the past six years.

Actually, of course, many of our members become the nucleus out of which new churches and fellowships of the Unitarian Universalist Association grow. One such member, persecuted by the Nazis in the days of World War II, fled to Argentina then to the United States, all the time receiving our sermons and bulletins. In Fairfield County, Connecticut, he yearned to meet other CLF members and wrote to our office. In response to this request, our clerk gathered names of other CLF members in Fairfield County, and, as a result, one of the first of the new fellowships was formed in 1948. This fellowship, the result of the seedling idea carried across the Atlantic to South America and then to these shores, had the distinction of becoming the first fellowship to graduate to church status, and in time it built the quarter-million-dollar Westport Unitarian Universalist Church in Connecticut.

Some of the credit for the growth of the Unitarian Universalist movement is shared by the Church of the Larger Fellowship, but most belongs to the churches and fellowships which in local communities give a valiant witness to the power and vitality of the liberal religious idea. Many CLF members, like the Potters, find an excitement upon visiting and becoming part of a local church or fellowship. Our churches and fellowships represent a rich variety and serve many different temperaments. Some are heritage groups in old established communities where the contributions of frontier or colonial days have established a rich Unitarian Universalist strain. Others are vital new groups making a fresh impact upon the congealed stratification of American or Canadian communites. Some are leaders in social action or civil rights programs in their local towns or cities. Some have taken the lead in fighting corruption, working for integration, standing up for the separation of church and state in schools and local municipalities. Our members often become the main supporters of unpopular although very necessary causes, such as Planned Parenthood clinics, programs to support the United Nations, to ban the bomb and bring nuclear weapons under international controls, and to uphold freedom from false accusations of Communism. Resisting Communism and using Communism as an insidious weapon to silence opposition are two different matters, and the unfair use of "smear and fear" must be exposed. In many communities only, or at least first, the Unitarian Universalist Church or Fellowship has had the courage to speak up and to stand up for sanity, for justice, for fairness, for due and proper consideration for important issues. Religious liberalism has been a major factor in maintaining the freedom of American society in recent decades. It was in this regard we earlier quoted Adlai Stevenson as noting the important role of Unitarian Universalists as standing up to the issues and stirring the waters.

Among the most courageous people in many communities have been the Unitarian Universalist ministers. When the Rev. Brooks R. Walker's home and study were bombed on two different occasions by rightist groups, most Unitarian Universalist ministers were not surprised. It was inevitable that some one of our ministers would be singled out. His stand, his activities, his participation in the smoldering embers of California extremism marked him as the target. Fortunately, he was away speaking in a synagogue when the first bomb exploded.[1]

In spite of such attacks and the fearlessness with which Unitarian Universalism has entered into the social concerns of our time, it has had an amazing growth. Both in Canada and the United States Unitarian Universalism constantly attracts new members. In November, 1962, the Dominion Bureau of Statistics reported, according to the *Toronto Daily Star*, that Unitarianism is the "fastest growing religious denomination in Canada." It reported that, in a decade figures released by the latest Canadian census showed a growth of 328 per cent, as the number of persons listing themselves as Unitarians jumped from 3,517 to 15,062.

In the 1964 Yearbook of American Churches, according to the *Boston Traveler*, Unitarian Universalist figures showed it to be the fastest growing denomination in the United States and "seven times that of the entire Protestant community." The membership increased at a rate more than twice that of the Roman Catholic. The article concludes, "Figures by the U.U.A. for 1963 show a membership of 257,021 compared with 243,033 in 1962. This is a gain of 5.7 percent. The figure does not include 37,827 church-school pupils who increased by 6.4 per cent over the 1962 figure of 32,547. The yearbook reported the membership gain of Protestants as 0.77 per cent and the Roman Catholic gain of 2.3 percent.

Unitarian Universalism is today largely composed of "come-outers" who are looking for a more modern, ethical, and universal faith. It has an appeal to free spirits. We have presented in the pages of this volume reasons why this religion is attractive to many persons and reaching still more. Its potential is unlimited; it is a free faith for the modern world. It is a democratic faith, a scientific faith, a faith that calls for affirmative social, political, and intellectual action. It is a realistic faith for a world in turmoil as well as in transition. It beckons the concerned person who wants to make life count, who needs a faith to help measure up to the challenge of our day, and who, seeing the new perspective required, is freed from the appendages of the past in order to act in the present to ensure the future.

The present day is fraught with danger on many fronts. Personal values, old ideas, national and international relations, the menaces of war and annihilation, the tensions of race and underprivilege, the growing threat of violence at home and abroad, the breakdown of governmental authority, all indicate that a new orientation is needed. The religions of yesterday have failed. Unitarian Universalism, an evolving liberal faith, has the capacity to move swiftly, to adapt adroitly, to bend and blend with the conditions and circumstances that call for a broader and more encompassing horizon. It faces the new day with confidence, because it sees clearly the shape of the new day, and knows it is different from yesterday. Hence it offers a new faith for the new day.

All one need do to join in this venture is to walk through the doors into one of our meetings, or write to the Church of the Larger Fellowship. You will be cordially welcomed and invited to study our offerings to see if it is for you. This must be your decision. We cannot make it for you, nor do we coerce people to join.

Perhaps then, you will agree with the great Dutch-American

writer, the late Hendrik Van Loon, who joined during World War II, and wrote:

> I had lived my sixty years without ever feeling the slightest need of becoming a member of any kind of religious organization. It is true that I had been baptized a Lutheran, but as this ceremony took place a few weeks after my birth, I can honestly claim that it was performed without my being in any sense an "active participant."
>
> Both my parents—like my grandparents and practically all my relatives—had been "liberals" in the eighteenth century sense of the word. Indeed, the whole country was still steeped in that peculiar kind of "liberalism" which was the direct successor to the "enlightenment" of the preceding century. Soon afterwards a reaction was to set in, which would put an abrupt stop to this delightful system of "live and let live," and once more turn the Low Countries into a battlefield between Rome and Geneva. But during the first dozen years of my life "institutionalized religion" was considered a thing of the past, and although the people with whom I was brought up were exemplary citizens in every reasonable sense of the word, they were completely indifferent to the claims of any church to provide the only dependable means of salvation.
>
> They did not fight the Church as their ancestors had done. They considered the Church as merely superfluous. The Church might still mean something to people who had no philosophical compass by which to set their course across the uncharted seas of life. Like the late and lamented Thomas Jefferson, each one of them had composed himself a little bible-of-his-own. In addition to culling certain bits of wisdom from the New Testament (the Old Testament they left to their Jewish neighbors with whom, however, they lived in perfect harmony and understanding), they were on a footing of easy familiarity with the ancient philosophers. But as for any kind of revealed religion—God forbid! They would have none of it. As a result of that kind of bringing up, I too never associated myself with a definitely organized religious group until last year. Then I asked my beloved friend, Laurance Neale, to let me join the Church of All Souls'. . . .
>
> Partly . . . this was due to a personal element of friendship and affection. Partly it was the result of having observed the behavior of a number of the young Unitarians who rendered such magnificent services to the cause of humanity in Nazi-stricken Europe. But my main consideration was of a slightly different nature; I felt that I was not doing right in keeping entirely to myself. The time would come (of this I was absolutely certain) when Reason and Reasonableness would need a few shock troops of their own, and I considered that the Unitarians would be among the first to enlist in such an advance guard of Human Decency. For within that strange and invisible structure which the world rather vaguely calls Unitarianism, there is room for every thought and every opinion, if it be

based upon the conviction that mankind can save itself only if it accepts the words of the greatest spiritual benefactor of all time, that humble but undaunted prophet from the village of Bethlehem, who first of all had the courage to proclaim these words, "My brethren, nothing can ever be accomplished in this world unless, first, you learn to love one another."

It seems perhaps a little too simple! But all the great things in life are really very simple. And this, to us, will be the greatest experience of our lives—to offer to the real founders of a new world, those who played an active part in destroying the old and outworn fabric of a society that had long since outlived its usefulness, a home where they will be welcome on their own terms, where no unasked advice will be forced upon them, where good humor and tolerance shall prevail and all religious tenets be reduced to one sublime expression of faith:

"We are all of us fellow travelers along the same road and, as such, it behooves us to work together for one common purpose, the greatest amount of happiness for each and all of our companions."[2]

We are following the great companions, and the fellowship of Unitarian Universalists is progressing towards the new horizon of a better tomorrow and a richer life today.

Notes
[1]Brooks R. Walker, *The Christian Fright Peddlars*, New York, Doubleday, 1964.
[2]Hendrick Willem Van Loon, "This I Believe," *The Christian (Unitarian) Register*, 1945.

DECALOGUE FOR RELIGIOUS LIBERALS

1. I will not exploit my fellow humans, using them as means to my own ends—neither my parents nor my children; my husband nor my wife; neither those in my service nor those whom I serve.
2. I will not let others do to me, insofar as I am able, what I would not do to them.
3. I will be forgiving: remembering that forgetting takes a longer time.
4. I will keep my promises.
5. I will be forthright with my opinions, but I will listen while others speak.
6. I will be honest in my thinking, as well as my acting, not only to others, but also to myself.
7. I will try to keep my head, even if I've lost my temper.
8. I will not fear changing my mind nor admitting to error.
9. I will not pretend, nor live beyond my means.
10. I will seek to have pride without arrogance; humility without cowardice.

Rev. Paul N. Carnes, D.D.

Study Guide to Chapter 1

Each study guide outlines the text. You may wish to add the page numbers as you refer back to the text for each outline point. Answer all questions and study all tables.

You may wish to begin by using the following checklist to check your own religious ideas. After you have finished them, make a mental note to recheck the answers when you have completed the book, and see if your ideas have changed. For each question, check as many as you agree with.

I believe that God is:
- a person
- a spirit
- a superhuman power
- a mystery
- an impersonal power that rules the universe by natural laws
- a fiction created by wishful thinkers to console themselves
- the creator of the world as stated in the Bible
- in some sense the creator and preserver of the best we know
- an outgrown idea in an age of science

I believe that people are:
- basically good
- basically sinful
- weak and indecisive, and need help to do anything worthwhile
- good, but still need God's help
- the highest form of earthly life
- beings who are able to choose between good and evil by their own native wisdom
- capable of building a better world
- created by God to aid in the progressive betterment of the world

I believe that Jesus:
- was a son of God in some special sense
- was a prophet, like Amos or Isaiah, but for a later time in history
- was a human being like ourselves
- was the greatest human being who ever lived, whose teaching and example sum up the best we know of the good life

- was only one of many great leaders like Confucius, Buddha, Mohammed, Gandhi, Schweitzer, etc.

I believe that the Bible is:
- true as no other book is true
- either all true or all false
- a collection of both good and bad, plus some that is indifferent
- interesting chiefly for historical reasons, like other old books
- a valuable record of the search for God, or for enduring truth, full of the fascinating story of our upward growth toward maturity in religious understanding
- a rule book for daily life
- a general guide to our own faith
- a unique library of religious books produced by a people who gave the world more basic individual and social religion than others

I believe that prayer is:
- a means whereby people can really talk to God, and receive help
- a technique for taking stock of ourselves
- talking to oneself
- a merely formal way of influencing other people's thoughts, as used in church services
- a power that can actually change the course of events
- a way of consulting one's own conscience
- I am undecided

I believe that the church is:
- the best means we have of bringing religious influence into life
- an old-fashioned institution that should be superseded by some newer and more efficient form of teaching religious and moral truth
- still useful as the guardian of our moral and spiritual welfare, but should not be placed first in a busy person's life
- important to the world-wide effort to secure peace and democracy
- indispensable to the attainment of a worldwide community among people everywhere
- badly needs to be improved
- all right as it is

I believe:
- that all people are of equal value in the sight of God or of history regardless of color, race, creed, or class
- that some people are inherently superior to others
- that while all people are equal, conditions today make racial equality impossible to attain, and that we must wait
- that the attainment of interracial good will is the first objective of the church today, especially the liberal church
- the church should say nothing about politics in any form
- that while the church should avoid party politics, it should express itself courageously on great social and moral questions that are being discussed by the agencies of government
- the church should never engage in controversial discussions, regardless of their moral significance
- the church should not hesitate to take a stand on controversial questions in which the physical, moral, and spiritual welfare of all people is at stake.

Study Guide to Chapter 2

Philosophic concept of religion as a determinant of one's way of life

Everyone worships something. Every person, whether conscious of it or not, loves, values, aspires to, in short, "worships" something. *Faith determines life.* What a person is genuinely devoted to (the faith he or she lives by) determines the kind of person he or she is.
Faith can be improved. While one is governed by a faith, whether one wills it or not, one can if he or she chooses influence and develop that faith.

Faith and affiliation—unity or diversity

Two aspects of religion. In addition to the faith by which one lives, almost everyone has some church to which they turn, at least for normal occasions, such as weddings, funerals, baptisms, perhaps religious education of children, etc.

Same or different? The two, the faith by which one lives and one's church affiliation, should be the same and sometimes are, but, alas, for a great many are not.

Reason for difference. One important reason for this is the authoritarian character of orthodox Christianity.

Pattern of growth of liberal religion in the Christian culture

Uncritical peace of mind. An authoritarian faith offers a safe anchorage for the unthinking who value repose more than truth.

Contradictions now difficult for many. But as people have acquired knowledge and understanding in secular fields, the contradictions with the factual premises and explanations of a religion developed in more primitive times have baffled many even when they tried to follow the two-fold path offered by St. Thomas Aquinas, whereby faith is viewed as supreme in matters of doctrine and reason prevails in secular affairs.

Anti-intellectual solution. Some have overcome this artificial and perplexing separation of faith and reason by giving up reason and retreating into the anti-intellectual vacuum of fundamentalism.

Nonreligious solution. At the other extreme some have given up all affiliation with any organized religion and live by some secular faith as sceptics or nonreligious.

Middle solutions. In between are many who have tried in a variety of ways to resolve the conflict by coming to terms with it.

Secular alternatives. The secular alternatives to an authoritarian faith include (a) a selfish interest in material wealth, power, prestige, comfort, etc., (b) some less selfish devotion to the welfare of another or others, (c) some social, professional, business, or cultural activity, (d) some political ideology such as Communism, fascism, democracy, nationalism, etc., or (e) some great cause such as abolition of slavery, civil rights, temperance, etc.

Liberal affiliated alternative. But since these frequently fall short of a permanently satisfying and meaningful faith some have affiliated with Unitarian Universalism, a liberal religious movement that imposes no dogmas, but encourages each to develop for oneself the faith that is most suited to him or her.

Liberal unaffiliated alternative. And millions more, unaware of Unitarian Universalism as an organized liberal faith more or less consciously parallel it by rejecting the dogmas of the authoritarian denomination in which they choose, for one reason or another, to retain a nominal membership.

Aspects of duplicity

Tragedy of separate faith and affiliation. Those who are conscious of a duplicity of faith and formal affiliation may rationalize that the beliefs to which they cannot subscribe may have some meaning for others that they do not comprehend, but tragically such a religion cannot be a living faith that is a part of their lives.

Another duplicity—true and imagined faiths. All, regardless of their faith, must guard against another form of duplicity involving beautiful ideals and their really operative faith.

Test of faith. The true test of faith is life; it is the beliefs we actually live by, not those by which we would like to live or to be thought to live that count.

Easy aspects of being a religious liberal

Liberal religion "easy." It is sometimes asked whether liberal religion is an easy faith and the answer is both yes and no, depending upon the point of view from which it is made.

No memorization. For anyone who views religion superficially as formal adherence to catechisms, creeds, and dogmas, liberal religion is easy because there is nothing to be memorized.

Not an alien faith. Again, from the point of view of the liberal who, on the other hand, takes religion with the utmost seriousness, it is easy because it is not something alien, but an integral part of being.

Courage multiplies strength. But above all, a liberal's religion may be said to be easy in the sense that to meet a challenge courageously through supreme effort affords an exhilaration of spirit that multiplies one's strength.

Difficult aspects of being a religious liberal

Difficulties more revealing. But it is perhaps more revealing to describe the courage required of the present day religious liberal in terms of the difficulties that must be faced.

Full-time faith. For one thing, in identifying religion with a way of life one foregoes the convenience of a part-time faith and assumes an obligation to courageously live one's ideals in all that one does and thinks throughout every moment of life.

Must decide for oneself. Then again, the liberal cannot turn to others for moral, intellectual, or social decisions, but must possess the courage to make his or her own, adopting a delicately balanced course between excessive complacency about the state of the world, excessive fright over the highly explosive issues that surround us, and excessive impulse to take premature, confused, and ill-considered action.

Truth never static. As a final evidence of courage, the liberal is denied the comfort of fixed and absolute truth and must submit to the inconvenience of suspense and imperfect opinion, since the search for truth is endless, and as our knowledge and insights grow so will our religious understanding.

Dr. Channing's apprehension. This is the basis of Dr. Channing's worry over the tendency toward orthodoxy and is aptly summed up by Mr. Marshall's observation: "The Bible of tomorrow has not been written, is not completed."

Essential character of Unitarian Universalism as a liberal religious movement

Constant change. The religious liberal views all religion as a universal expression of the human spirit constantly renewing itself.

Primacy of daily moral responses. The genuine test of religion for a liberal is in terms of courageous moral and social responses by individuals to daily life, because one does not separate one's secular life from one's religious life.

A single commandment. For all theological complexities are substituted one single commandment: "We are commanded at every moment and in every condition of life to do the duty of that moment and to abstain from doing the wrong."

Direct relationship. The religious liberal rejects the need for external props, mediators, or atonement and has a one-to-one relationship with life and the divine.

Test of Unitarian Universalism. The criticism sometimes voiced that Unitarian Universalism is a sterile intellectual religion is refuted by the many Unitarian Universalists in the forefront of the great social and political struggles, and by the proportion of eminent Americans who are regarded as Unitarian Universalists as compared with the proportion of Unitarian Universalists in the entire population.

Test for individuals. To measure up to one's faith a religious liberal is not afraid of a new orientation of values, and can try to *live* the answer to "What can I do?" Which Horace Traubel summed up in his Chant Communal: "I can give myself to life when others refuse themselves to life."

Choose your answers

As we face the question of one's real religion and one's alternative faith, the either/or questions prepared for the Department of Education several years ago by Mrs. Dorothy Duffee of Evanston, Illinois, may be helpful. Her question was: What is liberal religious education to you? She gives alternative replies, "Is it this?" or "Is it this?" Check your answers. In subsequent chapters you will find clarification on the liberal religious answers or attitudes.

1. It teaches that Jesus was just human.

   Or: *It teaches that the human race is capable of producing Jesus.*

2. It doesn't teach that Jesus was divine.

   Or: *It teaches that all people are the children of God.*

3. It does not teach the doctrine of original sin.

   Or: *It teaches that people love and yearn for good. They make mistakes in their efforts to attain good, but they continue to seek. Children are born not of or in sin, but of their parents' love of life and their desire for fulfillment. Children want to be good and want to be loved, wanted, accepted, considered good. They learn to love and understand others.*

4. It teaches that human beings are related to other animals.

   Or: *It teaches that all forms of life are related, that there has been steady growth and development throughout the ages, that this growth and development are in process now and must continue always.*

5. It does not teach personal immortality.

   Or: *It teaches that life is unending, that death is a phase of life, that the forces of life are present everywhere, at work constantly, neither beginning nor ending ever, at any point in time.*

6. It does not accept the Trinity.

   Or: *It teaches that God is One; that God is present everywhere in all things and in all persons and at all times. No figure or representation or limitation is great or broad enough to contain God. To present God as a Trinity is not very different from presenting God as a many-headed hydra. Either figure limits God: neither figure contains God.*

7. It does not teach a personal God, caring for each.

   Or: *It teaches that all so-called personal Gods are determined by the ideals of people in different places at different stages of growth. They change as we change. We respect these human ideals and human yearnings. We do not defy them. We try to reach outward and beyond.*

8. Each person can believe what he or she wants to believe.

   Or: *Everyone not only has the right and the privilege, but also bears the burden and the responsibility of thinking honestly or examining experience for oneself, of speaking in accordance with his or her words. Each individual is morally bound to think what must be thought in the light of one's own experience and understanding. It is one of the functions of government and of religion alike, socially, legally, and civilly to guarantee the freedom of each individual to fulfill this moral responsibility. It is the duty of each parent and teacher to free the child to accept, understand, and live in accordance with this universal human responsibility.*

9. It does not teach that the Bible is holy.
   Or: *It teaches that the religious books of all peoples are to be respected and revered as the products of their aspirations and as their interpretations of the meaning of life.*
10. It is not Christian.
    Or: *It honors Jesus and his teachings. Its adherents seek to honor God and love other people.*

There is always an easy, trite answer that can be given, a nonbelief statement, but Mrs. Duffee whets our appetites to see that a more meaningful answer is available in each instance.

Questions on the text

1. Was the Emerson quoted (a) a Unitarian minister; (b) the brother of the famous literary figure; (c) was Emerson, the famous literary figure, a Unitarian minister?
2. Do Roman Catholics tend to think our membership figures are inflated? Do they recognize far more people are Unitarian Universalists than are counted as such?
3. Have you read Emerson's essays, "The Over Soul," "The Preacher," "Self-Reliance," "Nature," or the "Divinity School Address?" Are all important documents for helping develop a philosophy of life? Reflect on their importance; it will pay to peruse a volume of Emerson's essays.
4. Consider the statement: "Channing wanted the religion to remain unchanged once he had defined it." Is it true or false? What incident and quotation clarifies his point of view? Is this a genuinely liberal position?
5. Is everyone's alternative religion Unitarian Universalism? Do many people need a different type of religion than Unitarian Universalism? Is it true that religious liberalism makes its strongest appeal to certain types of people, and none to other types?
6. Everyone has two religions: the one professed and the one lived by. If a person is fortunate the two will coincide. Can one hope to find a church with a faith by which it is possible to live?
7. When some people reject the faith of their family they sometimes latch onto social movements as substitute for faith. In days past abolition, suffrage, et cetera, became such substitutes. Do you think it is possible that Civil Rights or peace movements today can become substitutes for faith? Do they? What is important in order to have a faith?

8. Not only social causes, but people (*i.e.*, heroes, lovers, family, etc.) become the medium of one's devotion. What is the danger of such substitutes? Will such last a lifetime? Are they well enough rounded to satisfy the needs of the whole person? If people or issues change, is there an assurance of continued growth, or is a vacuum apt to remain? Can one create a flexible faith that provides the opportunity for great causes, personal involvement, and deep devotion? Is this not better? Many people find it best to write an essay that answers such questions on paper, to help them think through and articulate their thoughts. Even if you never show such an essay to anyone, it can be a valuable experience.

9. Who said, Unitarian Universalists are "rocking the boat"? Who said "This is not a time for liberals of the genteel tradition"? Who wrote the *Chant Communal*? Go back to the end of the chapter and reread it. Is this something that a religious liberal might find valuable in adding to an anthology of quotations for purposes of meditation? If you were going to gather your own personal anthology, would this be included? (Scattered throughout this volume are passages that might serve such purposes.)

Study Guide to Chapter 3

Nature of religion

What religion is. What we call religion is in fact a number of things, each with its own system.

What theology is. While theology is a systematic organization of the concepts and doctrines of a religion, a religion can exist without a theology, and many thoughtful people have no theology.

What a system of ethics is. A system of ethics is an organization of principles of human conduct upon which to judge one's own conduct and that of others and may be held without accepting a conventional religion.

What a philosophy of life is. While a philosophy in the abstract is a system of knowledge by which principles can be organized and explained, a philosophy of life embodies the working principles by which one does live and is, in other words, a way of life.

Constant change. Despite the insistence of traditionalists on absolutes and external verities, religions are always in a process of
change, there is always a choice between an older and newer faith.
Religion concerns all the facts. It is important to realize that religion
is not, as many seem to think, a way of handling the unknown
and irrational, but is an adjustment of all the facts and their
relations to each other.
Purpose of religion. The purpose of religion is an endless search for
ever-increasing understanding that will enable us to face with
greater serenity the inner stresses and outer disasters we encoun-
ter in life.

Importance of a religion appropriate to its time

Different problems. Every age is an age in transition with different
problems to solve.
Many controversies. And the differences have at many times and in
various places provoked controversies over the need to liberalize
existing religions.
Example. At times the inadequacies of old dogmas and ancient
doctrines become clearly apparent, for example, the religious bias
against birth control is now a dangerous doctrine and a threat to
civilization itself.
Needs evoke fresh approaches. Fortunately the needs of the times seem
gradually to evoke new appraisals of age-old questions, forcing
fresh insights on religion.

Special needs of an emerging and possibly "post-Christian" era

Nature of our age. We live in an exciting age, full of great promise
of reducing man's inhumanity to man, yet also an age of fear,
witnessing cruelty beyond comprehension; in sum, a new day is
being born for which we are ill-prepared.
Aim of western religions. The aim of all western religions is to help
people find meaning in life and to escape being hollow.

The liberal trend—away from orthodox authoritarianism

Orthodox emphasis on externals. To the authoritarian the externals of
religion, heavily centered about theology, and what Carlyle called
Hebrew old clothes, are all important.
Revival of orthodoxy. The challenge of the revival of orthodoxy in
our day can be summed up in its insistence upon the absolutes of

religion, the unchanging standards, the eternal values, as authoritatively revealed long ago for all time.

Liberal contrast. On the other hand, liberal religion represents a movement away from formalities of structure and theoretical expressions of doctrine toward a personal way of living.

Nature of difference—is it religion? To a considerable extent the orthodox objection to the liberal philosophy of life is that it is not religion in a narrowly accepted sense, and the liberal response tends to be one of satisfaction that liberal concerns are so closely related to the world of practical affairs and the insights of the intellectual disciplines.

The liberal trend—toward elements of agreement

This life the basic concern. Unitarian Universalism and most liberal religion takes as its basic concern human existence on earth rather than in afterlife, and it focuses on the controversies of its times and on the conduct appropriate to them. Hence such expressions as "deeds not creeds," and "salvation by character."

Universal nature of religion. It views religion as a universal experience rather than one limited for cultured or ideological reasons to a segment of the human race and tends to view Jesus as simply one of the great saviors of humanity.

Responsibility of self-control. It emphasizes that we cannot by pretensions of unworthiness or sin dodge our responsibilities to control ourselves.

Goodness of humanity. But it asserts the perfectability of all standing high on the evolutionary ladder, with great potential for further growth.

Institutional ends. Its main ends are not to build an organization or to seek wide dominion for itself. It simply asks for liberty of access for its faith and an opportunity to help people escape the nightmare of being "hollow men" by making their lives meaningful.

Nonexclusive. It separates itself from no believers, Christian or otherwise, except as they deny its claim to freedom.

Freedom will prevail. It trusts that in time its devotion to freedom will be claimed by all denominations.

The challenge of a modern faith for the modern mind

Purpose of the liberal way. The mission of the liberal way is not to promote one single religion, Unitarian Universalism or any other, but as Adlai Stevenson pointed out, to welcome and encourage differences, free interchange of ideas, fresh approaches to the problems of life, and vigorous critical self-examination.

Proof of soundness. That such a mission can be accomplished is evident from the histories of come-outers who have made their own religious journeys to religious liberalism.

What is needed. The equipment needed to develop one's own religious philosophy includes (a) scepticism for theologies, (b) scorn for empty forms and ritual, (c) respect for one's own reason, (d) hatred for every form of injustice, (e) abhorrence for falsehood even in established religions, and (f) a real love of truth.

Unitarian Universalism as a bridge. While it shares many things with other liberal religions Unitarian Universalism is deeply rooted in Western culture, and thus relates both to the past and the future, can comfortably serve for many as a bridge between the two.

Answer these questions

Dr. Peter Samsom, having served distinguished ministries in San Diego, Cleveland (West Shore), and metropolitan New York, now devotes his time to assisting churches without a settled minister by acting as an interim, so that he travels the continent in the service of our churches. Several years ago he proposed ten key questions that sometimes assist a person to discover whether he or she has passed beyond orthodoxy to religious liberalism. We offer his questions, and suggest that you answer them.

1. Do you believe the Bible to be an often inspiring human document and a product of its age, rather than the literal word of God?
2. Do you believe the individual is not condemned by original sin, but is inherently capable of a good and meaningful life by exercising innate natural powers?
3. Do you believe Jesus was a gifted religious teacher rather than a pre-existing or a present-day deity?
4. Do you believe that the development of human character to its finest utmost is more important than accepting a savior or a creed?
5. Do you believe that when reason and creed conflict, creed should give way to reason?
6. Do you believe that religious truth, to be acceptable, must be in harmony with truth in other areas of life?
7. Do you believe that you are profoundly kin to all human beings irrespective of nation, race, or creed and that their well-being is inevitably bound up with your own?

8. Do you believe that lay people should be free to question or refute the opinions of clergymen, even in church-reserved areas of faith and morals?

9. Do you believe that the function of religion is to help people live this life happily and usefully, rather than to prepare them for an afterlife?

10. Do you believe that the primary responsibility for human progress rests upon people themselves, whatever may be our personal belief concerning forces greater than humanity?

Dr. Samsom's key answer is that if you can answer these questions affirmatively then you are indeed a Unitarian Universalist, in spirit and outlook, whether or not you are affiliated with us. He points out that there is no Unitarian creed, for each is free to use one's own freely chosen undertones and overtones to all these points. But they do describe in a general way the Unitarian Universalist approach to religion.

Questions on the text

1. Would you say that Unitarian Universalism, as a religion for modern minds, has roots that go back as far as the American Revolution? The landing of the Pilgrim Fathers? The Enlightenment? The Reformation? Into Christian beginnings? Before the Christian era into ancient Greece and Egypt? If you check any of these eras before the modern, how do you acount for the *modern* nature of Unitarian Universalism?

2. Is Unitarian Universalism, then, just another old-time religion?

3. If not, why not? What makes the difference? Can we have it both ways (that we are a modern religion and that we have deep roots in the past and in mankind's heritage)?

4. Some people say before there was Unitarian Universalism there was unitarianism and universalism (spelled with small u's), by which they mean people with free spirits who were open-minded on questions of dogma and doctrine; who faced the future in religion unhampered by the dead hand of the past and who rejected specific orthodox tenets of faith that brought them into a Unitarian or Universalist position, even before there was an organized movement. Do you agree that they might be called Unitarian Universalists? Do you think the name Unitarian Universalist must be retained for official members of an ecclesiastical organization? If we so insist are we in danger of becoming as parochial as the orthodoxy we reject? On the other hand, if we use the term Unitarian Universalism for people,

such as ancient Greeks (Socrates), Egyptians (Akhnaton), Hebrews (Amos or Micah), Chinese (Confucius), Medievalist
(Huss), Renaissance men (Erasmus and Copernicus), etc., are
we in danger of falsifying history? Perhaps it may be said,
"There were Unitarians before Unitarianism was organized and
Universalists before Universalism was established, and though
we walk in their shadow we cannot walk in their shoes."

If religion is more a frame of mind than an organizational
membership we must consider the prehistory as well as organizational history of the movement.

5. Harry Meserve's six points that bind together Unitarian Universalism are: (*make a list in your own words of what he said, after
rechecking his quotation*). Are these six points an adequate yardstick? Do they explain why many Unitarian Universalists look
upon persons who never entered a Unitarian Universalist
Church as kindred spirits?

6. Does the scientific principle of probability have anything to do
with Freud's principle of the irrational concept in human be-
havior or the religious concept of free will? Do you find a
relationship? If so, does it then follow that the individual is not
a wholly rational creature? Does the thesis that Unitarian Universalism is a rational faith have to be rethought? Can liberal
religion serve the whole man: body, mind, and spirit, or rational
and emotional?

7. A number of American authors have been writing about our
post-Protestant culture. Perhaps of more importance is the post-
Christian culture which is clearly presented by the great English
historian, Arnold Toynbee, in his book *Christianity Among the
Religions of the World*. We refer you to this small book for a
broader perspective if this concept is new to you.

8. What do you think about the idea that modern religion must
pose questions rather than give answers? Is the quest for values
rather than stable positions the goal of liberal religion? Some
people as a psychological defense in the light of unhappy experiences, others because of religious teaching that only the
church has the answers, are hesitant about affirming their own
competency in the face of religious issues. Do you know where
to turn for further assistance? Are you confident of your ability
to find your own answers and develop your own values once
the opportunity for integrity, the use of reason, acceptance of
advancing knowledge, and the freedom to make choices is
granted to you?

Study Guide to Chapter 4

Tests of faith

False tests. Fervor of Sunday devotions, frequency of church meetings or pious expressions are not genuine tests of faith.
Crises as tests. One important test of faith is how it enables us to meet life's adversities of all kinds, most notably death.
Death as an ultimate test. A person who can face death, either one's own or of others, with strength, can face up to life.
Life and death. It is interesting to ponder the fact that the words life and death are almost synonymous, and in some instances substitution of one for the other may increase the meaning of that which we face and endure.
Social conscience as a test. Another important test of faith is how we accept good fortune in a world where others have less, how, in other words, we give expression to a social conscience.

Ways of facing life and death

Alternates. There are two ways of facing life and death—with an external faith or with an internal faith.
Traditional Christianity. Orthodox authoritarian Christianity invites us to lay our burden on the Lord and to seek peace safe in the arms of Jesus, as it is sometimes phrased.
External faiths. Great emphasis is put on the formal aspects of faith, church attendance, religious ceremonies, pious expressions of belief, etc., in short, on external things.
Internal faiths. Religious liberalism, on the other hand, encourages one to carry one's own burden through the exercise of self-discipline and thus may be described as an internal faith.
Powers of the soul. Emerson not only showed the force of an internal faith by his life, but voiced it in his unforgettable dictum, ". . . the powers of the soul are commensurate with its needs, all experience to the contrary notwithstanding."

Arguments for an internal faith

Ready availability. An internal faith that one constructs for oneself is a part of one's being available at all times and in all places whenever an unexpected crisis occurs.

No external props to lose. Nor can such a faith be stolen or otherwise taken away.

The need to grow. Adults no less than children need the opporutnity enjoyed by those cultivating an internal faith to grow through facing up to their problems and making their own decisions.

Psychologically sound. An internal faith predicated upon the belief that our problem is not one of living *without* tension but of living *with* it through internal self-control is in accord with the views of modern psychiatry.

A curious paradox. The purpose of religion is to overcome tension, but for some the idea of human sinfulness, the need to seek forgiveness or to believe regardless of reason, often emphasized in external faiths, may compound existing tensions.

Encourages reflection. An internal faith by its nature helps one to become sensitive to the fundamental issues of life.

Fundamental issues—purpose and meaning in life

Reason for being. One of the great issues of life for thoughtful persons is "For what do we live?"

Concept of God. To many religious liberals God is not an external force, but is the meaning and purpose of life.

Searching for God. When they say that religion is a search for God, they are in fact saying it is a quest for purpose and for the fulfillment of meaning in life.

Fundamental issues—reverence for humanity

Great underlying issue. One of the great, perhaps the greatest, of underlying issues is the proper respect for human dignity.

Significance of human nature. Channing said with regard to human nature, "In its vast potential lie all the attributes of the godlike we may ever know."

Safeguard against evil. Where a proper sense of human dignity is present, neither violence, bigotry, hatred, lust, nor carnage can triumph.

Fundamental issues—use of reason

Primacy of thinking. Reliance upon human reason is fundamental to liberal religion.

Reason and religion. Albert Schweitzer called upon liberal Christianity to proclaim that thought and religion are not incompatible and observed, "All deep religious thinking becomes thoughtful; all truly profound thinking becomes religious."

Accept the indisputable. He further wrote, "Faith which refuses to face indisputable facts is but little faith. . . . To linger in any kind of untruth proves to be a departure from the straight way of faith."

Fundamental issues—individuality

Self-assurance promotes it. Awareness of the other great issues leads to self-assurance and this in turn makes one freer to resist the pressure of overorganization.

Liberals resist conformity. Religious liberals throughout history illustrated the truth of Emerson's observation, "Whoso would be a man must be a nonconformist."

Great historic examples. The religious liberals among the Hebrew prophets, Confucius, Buddha, and Jesus were all nonconformists in their times.

Facilitates maturity. A self-developed internal faith makes it more likely that one can be a nonconformist without being an extremist.

Goals for the religious liberal

Ultimate end. For many religious liberals the following excerpt from Channing's letter to his conscript son in the army expresses the ultimate values which guide them. "Whatever you may suffer, speak the truth. Be worthy of the entire confidence of your associates. Consider what is right as what must be done. It is not necessary that you should keep your property, or even your life, but it is necessary that you should hold fast your integrity."

Choice of means. To pursue that end we are well advised to strive for the balance in our selection of means which William L. Sullivan caught in these lines:

> To outgrow the past, but not to extinguish it;
> To be progressive, but not raw;
> To be free, but not mad;
> To be critical, but not sterile;
> To be expectant, but not deluded;
> To be scientific, but not live in formula that cuts us
>   off from life;
> To hear amidst the clamor, the pure, deep tones of
>   the spirit;
> To turn both prosperity and adversity into servants of
>   character;

This is to attain peace; this is to invest the lowliest life
with magnificence.

For further reading

Have you ever picked up a Gideon Bible in a hotel room? It
tells you where to turn in the Bible to read "if you are in trouble
and discouraged," "if overcome and defeated," "if lonesome and
restless," "if you desire peace, power, and plenty," and "if you
are losing confidence in men." The religious liberal cannot thumb
a Bible and find answers, but must face life squarely and, with
sensitivity, judgment, and courage, find a means of salvation. "The
powers of the soul are commensurate with its needs, all experience
to the contrary notwithstanding," Emerson once wrote. This is
our experience. Many psychiatrists suggest that liberal religion can
be helpful to those facing crisis. We refer you to the books of Harry
and Bonaro Overstreet, Karl Rogers, Erich Fromm, and to two
books—Abraham Maslow's *Religion, Values, and Peak Experiences*
and Roland Gittelsohn's *Man's Best Hope*.

Read, if interested, John Gunther's *Death Be Not Proud, A
Memoir* (Harper, 1949)—a heroic account of the final days of the
sixteen-year-old son of John and Frances Gunther and of how this
son of divorced parents, one Jewish and one Unitarian, faced life
and death.

Also read Lael Tucker Wertenbaker's *Death of a Man* (Beacon
Press, 1957). She tells of the facing and final end of life of her
husband, Charles, who knew he was dying.

Samuel Goodstone's *The Doctor Has a Heart Attack* (Beacon,
1964) is a surgeon's account of his own heart attack and slow
recovery.

Harry Meserve's *No Peace of Mind* (Harcourt Brace, 1955) is a
valuable book by a Unitarian Universalist minister who has served
as director of the Academy of Religion and Mental Health.

Read Marshall's *Before the Family Faces Death* (originally published as *When a Family Faces Death*), (UUA Pamphlet Commission)
Unitarian Universalist Association.

Clinton Lee Scott's *These Live Tomorrow: Twenty Unitarian Universalist Lives* (UUA, 1987) is an excellent study of religious liberals
facing life.

Abraham H. Maslow's *Religions, Values, and Peak Experiences*
(Columbus, Ohio: Ohio State University Press, 1965) is a valuable
exploration of the psychology of religious motivations and values
by a humanistic psychologist.

These books should be available in church or public libraries if they are out of print.

Study Guide to Chapter 5

Early Christian History
325 Nicene Creed adopted at Council of Nicaea establishes dogma of the Trinity.
544 Belief in universal salvation condemned as heresy by a church council.

The Reformation Period
1511 Birth of Michael Servetus (the most famous of the sixteenth-century anti-Trinitarians).
1527 Martin Cellarius publishes *On the Works of God* (the earliest anti-Trinitarian book).
1531 Michael Servetus publishes *On the Errors of the Trinity*.
1553 Michael Servetus is burned at the stake in Geneva.

Polish Socinianism
1539 Birth of Faustus Socinus (leader of the Polish Socinian or Unitarian movement).
1546 Anti-Trinitarianism appears in Poland.
1579 Faustus Socinus arrives in Poland.
1585 Founding of the Rakow press (the first official Unitarian press).
1591 The Socinian Church in Krakow is destroyed by a mob.
1658 The Polish Diet banishes Socinians.

Transylvanian (Hungarian) Unitarianism
1520 Birth of Francis David (leader of Transylvanian Unitarians).
1566 Francis David preaches against the doctrine of the Trinity.
1568 King John Sigismund (the Unitarian King of Transylvania) proclaims the earliest edict of complete religious toleration.
1579 Francis David, condemned as a heretic, dies in prison.
1821 English and Transylvanian Unitarians discover one another.

English Unitarianism and Universalism

1550   The Church of the Strangers (Socinian in influence) is established in London.

1615   Birth of John Biddle (the father of English Unitarianism).

1654   John Biddle is banished to the Scilly Isles.

1662   Execution of Sir Henry Vane.

1703   Thomas Emlyn is imprisoned at Dublin for anti-Trinitarian beliefs.

1703   Birth of George de Benneville (one of the leaders of American Universalism) in London.

1723   George de Benneville undertakes first preaching mission on the European continent.

1723   Birth of Theophilus Lindsey (one of the founders of the English Unitarian movement).

1733   Birth of Joseph Priestley (one of the greatest scientists of his age, a founder of both the English and American Unitarian movements).

1741   John Murray (the founder of American Universalism) born in Alton, England.

1741   George de Benneville emigrates from Europe to Pennsylvania.

1750   James Relly, an associate of the evangelist George Whitefield, withdraws from the connection and establishes himself as an independent preacher of Universalism.

1759   *Union* (a theological treatise on universal salvation by James Relly) published in London.

1774   Essex Street Chapel opened in London (marking the beginning of permanently organized Unitarianism in England).

1791   Riots against Joseph Priestley and his fellow Unitarians in Birmingham.

1794   Joseph Priestley emigrates to America.

1825   The British and Foreign Unitarian Association founded.[1]

This chapter covers the period from the earliest preChristian times—through the Christian beginnings until the seventeenth century in England and the Reformation on the continent. Three great figures carried Unitarian Universalism across the Atlantic to the New World. These people were active in the period before the organization of Unitarian Universalism as we know it.

Joseph Priestly (1733–1804) said that "Christ and the Apostles were the first Unitarians." A Canadian Reform rabbi said recently, "The Hebrew prophets were the first Unitarians." Others have said that Unitarian Universalism was found in the ancient religions of Asia. While we recognize the deep rootage of the free mind, of the search for freedom and reason in religion, of the inclusive spirit which always identifies the religious liberal, we nevertheless must confine our study to the historical stream that came out of the Christian heritage.

Begin by noting Origen (185–251), a church father—the *Encyclopedia of Religion* says "one of the greatest of all." Bratton says he was "the most liberal thinker in the first 1,000 years of the Christian church." He was born in Alexandria. Note early struggle between the Greek and African schools. He was called the leader of the Alexandrian school. He believed in the universal salvation of all souls and the humanity of Christ. He was an opponent of St. Augustine, the leader of the African school. Arrested during the Decian persecutions, Origen died on his release. He is called the first great modern because he believed in free will, denied miracles, and paved the way for Arius. Look him up in other books.

Clement of Alexandria (150–200) sought a union of Hellenism and Christianity. Adapted Christian thought so that it did not remain a Jewish cult, but fitted the broader culture. He was concerned with Christianity developing a meaningful philosophy of religion rather than in remaining merely an ecclesiasticism.

Anti-Trinitarianism flourished in the heresies of Monarchism, Nestorianism, Pelagianism, and Arianism. During the first four centuries a conflict between these two poles—Trinitarianism and Anti-Trinitarianism (often a primitive Unitarianism) flourished. The concept of "the faith once for always delivered to the saints, unchanged," is simply not true and never existed. The Early Church history is a period of great conflict and struggle between contending positions—between Trinitarianism and Unitarianism or between Universalism and salvation religion, between liberalism (heresy) and conservatism (orthodoxy). For us this is climaxed in Arius (died in 336 A.D.) and the Councils of Nicea and Constantinople.

Ideas of Erasmus (1466–1536), an ecumenical figure of the Renaissance who saw the error of the Trinitarian doctrine, but never joined the Reformation, remaining independent in thought, and of Zwingli (1484–1531), the leader of the Anabaptists, who was anti-Trinitarian, may be studied with profit by those wishing a deeper understanding into the background of Unitarian Universalist ideas and their development. Servetus (1511–1553) published in 1531 his *Errors of the Trinity* and, a few years later, his *Reconstruction of Christianity*. Note the influences of the Spanish Inquisition, of the opportunity for a student to actually read the Bible, of the effect of his service in Rome, and his fugitive life thereafter. Did these events help shape his thought and temperament? What was the contribution and what the real tragedy of his life?

Faustus Socinus (1539–1604), Francis David (died 1579), and King John Sigismund (crowned 1540) were all important in Unitarian beginnings in Eastern Europe. Note their relationship, sequence of events, and the continuing heritage of Transylvanian Unitarianism. Why, do you suppose, Unitarians for the next century were called Socinians?

Now relate Unitarian thought to the Reformation of Calvin and Luther. The rethinking of religious ideas was taking place in Western Europe which became the movement known historically as the Reformation. Consider the action, reaction, and interaction of Protestant Reform on the rational and liberal reform we have been exploring. Why do some historians consider them different movements? Do you now consider the Protestant Reformation and the Rational Reformation to be identical, related, or distinctive?

In England, the transition to a modern Unitarian Universalism began. In 1689 two important events occurred in England: the Acts of Toleration were passed, and Locke's "A Letter Concerning Toleration" was published. Relate these two events to earlier beginnings in England, to the contemporary seventeenth century situation, and to its influence on the future. What was the Trinitarian controversy taking place in the Church of England? What is the importance (and content) of Locke's *The Reasonableness of Christianity*?

Before studying Joseph Priestley (1733–1804) you should know about the translation of the Racovian Catechism into English, and the lives of Theophilus Lindsey, John Biddle, as well as the scope of the Deistic and Enlightenment movements in England. Then turn to a specific study of Joseph Priestley, the first undisputed Unitarian whose religious liberalism spanned both sides of the Atlantic. Coleridge called him the first modern Unitarian. The broad scope of his life and cultural interests indicate a continuing characteristic of Unitarian Universalists. List his various careers and achievements. Note important people and movements he influenced. Look up in a library the books and articles concerning Priestley published in recent years—thus noting his continued importance and broader influence. Read the chapter "Joseph Priestley and the Socinian Moonlight" in Basil Willey's *The Eighteenth Century Background*.

George de Benneville (1703–1793) was a pioneer who made his way to these shores before Priestley or Murray. He brought a continental strain of religious liberalism and Universalism here before the English influences of Murray and Priestley were felt. Study this influence for a broader understanding. Huguenot, statesman, diplomat, heretic, physician, preacher—a man of wide culture and experience, he influenced the growth of Unitarian Universalism in Pennsylvania. Note the geographical tendency that will follow in history: from Philadelphia, to Boston, to New York to the West and then the South in subsequent episodes.

John Murray (1741–1815) was the man whose name became identified as the founder of American Universalism. Why him? Study his life, his thought, his organizational ability, and you will understand.

Note
[1]Reprinted from *The Unitarian Universalist Pocket Guide*, edited by Harry B. Scholefield. Boston, Beacon Press, pp. 56-57.

Study Guide to Chapter 6

American Unitarianism and Universalism

1637 Samuel Gordon (a pioneer of Christian Universalism) driven out of Massachusetts for his political and religious radicalism.

1684 Joseph Gatchell has his tongue pierced with a red-hot iron for his statement "All men should be saved."

1740 High point of the Great Awakening (which, by its emotional excesses, stimulated a desire for a more rational religion).

1743 Christopher Sower (a Universalist Quaker), with the assistance of George de Benneville, prints the first Bible in America translated into the German language. Passages supporting the universal character of religion produced in heavier type.

1770 John Murray arrives at Good Luck on Barnegat Bay, New Jersey.

1770   On September 30 Murray preaches his first sermon in America in the meeting house of Thomas Potter.

1771   Birth of the great Universalist Hosea Ballou, in Richmond, New Hampshire.

1774   John Murray preaches in Gloucester, Massachusetts.

1778   Caleb Rich organizes the General Society (Universalist) to ordain ministers and issue preaching licenses.

1779   Gloucester Universalists organize the first Universalist church in America and call John Murray as minister.

1785   Liturgy of King's Chapel, Boston, is revised (omitting references to the Trinity and prayers to Christ).

1785   The first Universalist convention (with delegates from churches) held in Oxford, Massachusetts.

1786   Gloucester Universalists successfully contest the right of the state to raise taxes for the established church.

1786   A Universalist church (called the Universal Baptist church) organized in Philadelphia.

1788   Murray wins the right of Universalists and dissenting ministers to be recognized as ordained ministers with authority to perform marriages.

1790   The Philadelphia Convention of Universalists adopts a declaration of faith and a set of principles of social reform.

1796   Joseph Priestley advocates Universalism and Unitarianism in Philadelphia. Founding of the First Unitarian Church of Philadelphia with the encouragement of Franklin.

1802   The oldest Pilgrim church in America (founded at Plymouth in 1620) becomes Unitarian.

1803   Winchester Declaration of Faith adopted by Universalists at Winchester, New Hampshire.

1805   Hosea Ballou writes *A Treatise on Atonement* (the first book published in America openly rejecting the doctrine of the Trinity).

1819   William Ellery Channing delivers his Baltimore sermon (a landmark statement of Unitarian principles).

1819   *The Christian Leader* (Universalist) begins publication.

1821   *The Christian Register* (Unitarian) begins publication.

1825   The American Unitarian Association is organized.

1833   Formation of "The General Convention of Universalists in the United States" (advisory powers only).

1838   Ralph Waldo Emerson delivers his "Divinity School Address" (a major event in the history of religious liberalism).

1841   Theodore Parker delivers his South Boston sermon, "The Transient and Permanent in Christianity" (a sermon in defense of natural religion).

1847   The Universalist General Reform Association is organized.

1852   Tufts College founded by Universalists at Medford, Massachusetts.

1852   The Western Unitarian Conference is organized in Cincinnati, Ohio.

1854   Publication of the first book under American Unitarian Association imprint—*Grains of Gold or Select Thoughts on Sacred Themes* by the Rev. Cyrus A. Bartol, Jr.

1856   St. Lawrence University and Theological School founded by Universalists at Canton, New York.

1856   Children's Sunday started, Universalist Church, Chelsea, Massachusetts.

1862   The Universalist Publishing House established.

1863   Ordination of Olympia Brown, first woman to be ordained by any denomination.

1865   The National Conference of Unitarian Churches is organized.

1866   Organization of the Universalist General Convention (renamed in 1942 The Universalist Church of America).

1867   The Free Religious Association is organized.

1869   Women's Centenary Association formed. (In 1939 it became the Association of Universalist Women.)

1880   The General Alliance of Unitarian and Other Liberal Christian Women (originally called Women's Auxiliary Conference) is organized.

1884   The American Unitarian Association becomes an association representative of and directly responsible to its member churches.

1889   Young People's Christian Union formed (later called Universalist Youth Fellowship).

1890   Universalists establish churches in Japan.

1896   Unitarian Young People's Religious Union organized.

1899   Essential Principles of Universalism adopted at Boston, Massachusetts.

1899   First Merger Commission.

1900   The International Congress of Free Christians and Other Religious Liberals is formed.

1902   The Beacon Press is launched (broadening the American Unitarian Association's book-publishing program). First title: *Some Ethical Phases of the Labor Question,* by Carroll Wright.

1904   Starr King School for the Ministry is founded in Berkeley, California.

1908   The Unitarian Fellowship for Social Justice is organized.

1913   The General Sunday School Association is organized at Utica, New York.

1917   The first denomination-wide Unitarian Youth Sunday held.

1920   The Unitarian Laymen's League is organized.

1921   Universalist women acquire Clara Barton homestead (developed into camp for diabetic girls).

1931   Second Merger Commission.

1933   Free Church of America formed.

1935   Washington Statement of Faith adopted by Universalists.

1937   The Unitarian Sunday School Society is merged with the Religious Education Department of the American Unitarian Association.

1938   The Beacon Press begins a series of pioneer publications in the field of religious education.

1940   The Unitarian Service Committee is organized.

1941   Young People's Christian Union organized into Universalist Youth Fellowship.

1942   The Young People's Religious Union is reorganized into American Unitarian Youth.

1942   The Universalist General Convention is renamed the Universalist Church of America.

1943   The Unitarian Service Committee makes plans for medical missions to war-devastated countries.

1944   The Church of the Larger Fellowship is organized to serve Unitarians living in areas without Unitarian churches.

1945   The Universalist Service Committee is formed.

1948   A continental program to establish Unitarian fellowships is begun.

1950   American and English Unitarians jointly celebrate the 125th anniversary of their respective denominational organizations.

1953   Liberal Religious Youth, Inc., is formed by the merger of American Unitarian Youth and Universalist Youth Fellowship.

1953   The Council of Liberal Churches (Universalist-Unitarian), Inc., is organized for the federation of the departments of publications, education and public relations.

1953   *The Christian Leader* is renamed *The Universalist Leader.*

1956 Unitarians and Universalists create Joint Commission on Merger to examine feasibility of merging the two denominations.

1958 *The Christian Register* is renamed *The Unitarian Register*.

1961 The American Unitarian Association and The Universalist Church of America officially consolidate and organize the Unitarian Universalist Association. Rev. Dana McLean Greeley, first president.

1961 *The Unitarian Register* and *The Universalist Leader* are merged as the Unitarian Universalist *Register-Leader*.

1962 The Unitarian Laymen's League and the National Association of Universalist Men join to form the Laymen's League (Unitarian-Universalist).

1963 The Alliance of Unitarian Women and The Association of Universalist Women join to form the Unitarian Universalist Women's Federation.

1963 The Unitarian Service Committee and the Department of World Service of the Unitarian Universalist Association unite to form the Unitarian Universalist Service Committee, Inc.

1968 The Black Affairs Council (B.A.C.) organized and funded at the General Assembly. B.A.W.A.—the Black and White Action—is affiliated with U.U.A.

1969 Rev. Robert Nelson West elected second president.

1977 Rev. Paul N. Carnes elected third president.

1979 Rev. O. Eugene Pickett elected fourth president.

1985 Rev. William A. Schulz elected fifth president.

Prof. Bratton, in his *Legacy of the Liberal Spirit*, notes that any references to liberalism in the first four centuries of the Christian era must be thought of as relative to that age, a comparative liberalism that usually went under the label of heresy. Until Unitarian and Universalist organizations existed this continued to be so; a relative position, a radical approach to religious doctrine, a heresy or dissent outside of established doctrines often personifies the free mind of the religious liberal. Possibly the Pilgrim Fathers' venture in Holland and Plymouth, Massachusetts, was of this nature. John Robinson, the Pilgrim pastor in England and Holland, will be recalled because of his Delftshaven farewell address. When he said, "The Lord hath more truth and light yet to breakforth from out his Holy Word," he was expressing a liberal religious sentiment. Robert Weston, the representative of the Pilgrim Fathers, had to negotiate with the merchant adventurers of London who underwrote the Mayflower expedition of 1620. He answered the charge that in Leyden these religious dissenters did not seem like good economic risks because they lived in impoverished, humble homes, by saying they lived in homes that "they could set afire and flee by the light" if necessary.

Thus, the liberal religious story in America may begin with these earliest settlers who were nonconformists and dissenters. Joining the Pilgrims soon were such Puritans as Ebenezer Gay of Hingham and Charles Chauncy of Boston who rapidly were emancipated and spoke freely on theological as well as liturgical questions.

How did New England Liberalism evolve from Calvinism? Consider the importance of the Halfway Convenant, the Great Awakening, the New England theocracy and the reaction which set in. To what extent did this reaction, with its concern over the nature of humankind and the goodness of God, help prepare the way, intellectually, for the American Revolution?

Note the distinction between the relative positions of Murray and Ballou. There has always been a tension within Universalism between a more conservative and a more liberal outlook—a right wing and left wing of the movement. In Unitarianism this also is to be noted. Parker Unitarians were more radical than Channing Unitarians (indeed, as was Channing himself, who complained of those who made an orthodoxy of his position).

Note the relationship of the liberal religious ferment with the political spirit of freedom which brought forth the American Revolution. Patriots, such as Ethan Allen, Tom Paine, John Adams, and Thomas Jefferson, were all religious liberals and possibly this philosophy fed and helped ignite their political liberalism. What do you think? Does religious liberalism help give a philosophical platform for democratic freedom? Does the dignity of life lead to human rights? If everyone is created equal are we entitled to equality of treatment? Do you find a relationship, or believe the patriot fathers of the American Revolution did? In this connection, Norman Cousins' study, *In God We Trust* (Harper, 1958), is valuable reading as he discusses the religious beliefs and ideas of the American Founding Fathers.

Note the early course of free thought, infidelity, the separation of church and state, and the establishment of nonestablishment (religious liberalism) in the early decades of the American Repub-

TIME CHARTS SHOWING TWO WAYS OF STUDYING UNITARIAN UNIVERSALIST HISTORY

Which have we used, and why?

185 A.D.	Universalism	1961
(Origen)		
325 A.D.	Unitarianism	Unitarian
(Nicea)		Universalism

Old View of Unitarian Universalist History
(Institutional Approach)

Ancient Times	Sixteenth Century	Seventeenth Century	Eighteenth Century	Nineteenth Century	Twentieth Century
Akhnaton	"Radical Reformation"	English Puritanism	John Relly	Ballou	Atwood
Socrates	Free Churches	Separatist movement	John Murray	Channing	Capek
The Prophets	Zwingli	The Enlightenment	T. Lindsey	Parker	Scott
Confucius	Servetus	Act of Toleration	De Benneville	Kneeland	Skinner
Origen	Francis David		J. Priestley	Starr King	Eliot
Arius	Socinus		C. Chauncy	Emerson	J. H. Holmes
etc.	etc.		T. Jefferson	Thoreau	Davies
			etc.	etc.	Schweitzer

New View of Unitarian Universalist History
(Contemporaneous Approach)

lic. Why was Thomas Jefferson's expectation of every young person becoming a Unitarian not fulfilled?

Note practical applications of Unitarian Universalism to social problems: the communitarian groups, social reform movements, personal improvement, education, humane societies, et cetera. Catalogue and list known examples and known leaders in social, educational, philanthropic, civic, and political endeavors. Identify some of the following names and their relationship to our movement: Brook Farm, Salubria, Owen, Wright, Ballou, Theodore Parker, Bronson Alcott, Abner Kneeland, Horace Mann, Henry Bergh, Dorothea Dix, Susan Anthony, and Clara Barton. Name the founders of the first peace society in Pennsylvania and first peace society in Massachusetts. Identify: Julia Ward Howe, Thomas Mott Osborne, Samuel Gridley Howe, and Joseph Tuckerman.

Place in chronological sequence: Channing, Parker, Ballou, Thomas Starr King, Kneeland, de Benneville, Murray, Emerson, James Freeman Clark, and Edward Everett Hale.

Define Deism, Transcendentalism, humanism.

Find dates and give scope of the following organizations (place in a chronological sequence): Universalist General Convention, American Unitarian Association, Berry Street Conference, Free Religious Association, National Conference of Unitarians, General Conference of Unitarians, the Free Religious Fellowship, the Council of Liberal Churches, and the Unitarian Universalist Association.

Study Guide to Chapter 7

Introduction

A warning. To attempt to understand Unitarian Universalism by simply considering it in terms of principal Judeo-Christian concepts, such as prayer, the Bible, God, and Jesus, is to risk gaining a wholly false impression that it is predominantly negative faith. *Scope of this chapter.* Consequently this chapter will consider the nature of religious beliefs, some dangers therein, the purposes behind Unitarian Universalism, a notable flexibility in its worship, and some major background assumptions, and will leave its position on the major Judeo-Christian concepts for the following chapter.

Liberals more affirmative than traditionalists. The purpose of this preliminary approach is to show that Unitarian Universalism is not simply negative, that, indeed, it affirmatively accepts life here and now in contrast to the negative subordination of this life to some afterlife by orthodox Christianity and affirmatively welcomes new truths which the orthodox summarily negate.

Broader basis of comparison. If one is tempted to generalize solely on the basis of attitude one should consider the observation of Dr. Charles Edward Park that ". . . in its main features Christian theology is the work of ill-balanced and nervously overwrought men, laboring at times of passionate feeling and under great emotional pressure, and influenced by just the forces that should be kept out of the picture . . . ," naming Paul, Athanasius, Augustine, and Calvin.

Nature of religious beliefs

What beliefs are. An individual's religious beliefs are the assumptions that really determine what he or she thinks and does.

Historic duality of religious beliefs. Two broad categories under which beliefs may be grouped were graphically portrayed long ago by the contrast between Lao Tze and Confucius, the former counseling against worldly involvement and stressing the way of the divine, the latter concentrating on better ways of living this life.

Persistence of duality. In the present day this difference remains in the tendency of salvation Christianity to stress the hereafter, while liberal religious thinkers put primary emphasis upon the meaningful values of their everyday lives.

How beliefs are formed. One's intellect, voluntary will, social experience (what others do and say) and emotional reactions all contribute to the establishment of one's beliefs.

Validity of beliefs. We must accept most beliefs without adequate proof of their validity and, therefore, nonauthoritarian religious liberals should remain alert to change their religious beliefs for persuasive reasons as their understanding grows.

Basis of faith of religious liberals. Religious liberals believe the true basis of belief is to take this world religiously.

Meaning of living religiously. To take this world religiously means to ground one's beliefs not on meaningless dogmas, handed down from others, but on living values in terms of simple things and to live with fidelity to one's chosen values.

Discovering one's true beliefs. One can gain insight into one's actual

operative religious beliefs by asking oneself about everyday atti-
tudes, convictions, and practices through questions such as these:
How did I spend my time today? How should I have spent it?
What were my contacts with others? Were they for better or worse?
What do I enjoy most? Least? Why? etc.

Questions and answers—catechism—have been a major procedure in religious instruction over the years. The authoritarian
churches use catechisms that have the full weight of ecclesiastical
sanction behind them, so that they become not merely informative
but disciplinary and restrictive. With Unitarian Universalists there
are no definitive answers to questions: only questions that each
must answer for oneself. True, Faustus Socinus offered a catechism
published in Racow, Poland, in 1605 (hence called the Racovian
catechism), and John Biddle offered an English-language children's
catechism, which was published in London in 1652, but these were
for matters of information only.

Theodore Parker published a list of questions as a defense,
and Parker's Twenty-eight Questions became historic in their own
right. They were argumentative, and with them he took the offensive against those who were attacking him. Parker (1810–1860)
became the stormy center of a great controversy over advancing
liberalism in New England Unitarianism. He undeniably was a
great architect of the movement into modern religious liberalism;
a prodigious scholar of tremendous energy, of acute sensitivity
and keen mind, he was attuned to all the currents in the intellectual winds of his time. In consequence, he was ahead of his time
and suffered accordingly. His questions pointed up the issues of
an older approach to liberalism and the advancing liberalism of
the mid-century.

Professor Conrad Wright of Harvard Divinity School wrote,
"He remained a persistent irritant within the Unitarian community; and he suffered the customary fate of nonconformists who
decline to withdraw politely, despite pointed suggestions that they
are not entirely welcome."[1] He tells us how the Boston Association
of (Unitarian) Ministers sought to expel Parker in what Wright
calls "the closest the Unitarians ever came to a heresy trial." Dr.
Parker's rebuttal was the famous Twenty-eight Questions with
which he challenged the Boston Unitarian ministers to search their
own minds. He offered no answers; each should answer personally. So thorough was the scrutiny of religious truth that little
doubt remained in most minds that they, as Unitarian ministers,
no longer believed these conventional Christian beliefs. Today we,

without the heightened drama of a near-heresy trial, need to also ask and answer such questions. Theodore Parker's are offered to assist us, as well as recall an epic occasion. For us, as for Parker's listeners, they imply the necessary answers of liberalism rather than the ancient theological answers. They expose the bankruptcy of the old theology and must lead us to reconstruct a new one for ourselves. With these questions, Parker took the offensive against his persecutors and those who attacked him, articulated the doctrines and dogmas they defended, and by exposing them to the clear list of reason opened the way for a new rationalism in liberal religion. He not only prevented his own expulsion, but so impressed the bulk of religious liberals that never again could a Unitarian, and now Universalist, be cast out due to the lack of orthodoxy in belief. A new natural religion, based on rational examination, came into being. Thinking won out. What Parker's questions asked were "Do you *really* believe . . . ?" or "Do you *really* think . . . ?" We suggest you put in the "really" as you read questions seven on. Parker's questions follow:

Parker's 28 questions

Class 1. *Scholastic questions relating to the definition of terms frequently used in theology.*
1. What do you mean by the word SALVATION?
2. What do you mean by a MIRACLE?
3. What do you mean by INSPIRATION?
4. What do you mean by REVELATION?

Class 2. *Dogmatic questions relating to certain doctrines of theology*
5. In questions of theology, to what shall a man appeal, and what is the criterion whereby he is to test theological, moral, and religious doctrines, are there limits in theological inquiry—and if so, what are those limits? Is truth to be accepted because it is true, and right to be followed because it is right, or for some other reason?
6. What are the conditions of salvation, both theoretical and practical, and how are they known?
7. What do you consider the essential doctrines of Christianity; what moral and religious truth is taught by Christianity that was wholly unknown to the human race before the time of Christ? And is there any doctrine of Christianity that is not a part also of natural religion?
8. Do you believe all the books in the Bible came from the

persons to whom they are, in our common version thereof, as-cribed? Or what are genuine and canonical scriptures?

9. Do you believe that all or any of the authors of the Old Testament were miraculously inspired, so that all or any of their language can properly be called the word of God, and that their writings constitute miraculous revelation? Or are those writings to be judged of, as other writings, by their own merits and so are to pass for what they are worth; in short, what is the authority of the Old Testament, and what relation does it bear to man—that of master or servant?

10. Do you believe the law contained in the Pentateuch, in all parts and particulars, is miraculously inspired or revealed to man? Or is it, like the laws of Massachusetts, a human work in whole or in part?

11. Do you believe the miracles related in the Old Testament, for example, that God appeared in human form, spoke in human speech, walked in the garden of Eden, ate and drank; that he commanded Abraham to sacrifice Isaac; and made the verbal dec-larations so often attributed to Him in the Old and New Testament; that Moses spoke with Him "as a man speaketh with his friend"; that the miracles alleged to have been wrought for the sake of the Hebrews in Egypt, the Red Sea, Arabia, and Palestine, and re-corded in the Bible, were actual facts; that the birth of Isaac, Samson, and Samuel, was miraculous; that Balaam's ass spoke the Hebrew words put into his mouth; that God did miraculously give to Moses and others mentioned in the Old Testament the com-mands there ascribed to him; that the sun stood still as related in the book of Joshua, that Jonah was swallowed by a large fish and while within the fish, composed the ode ascribed to him; and do you believe all the miracles related in the books of Daniel, Job, and elsewhere, in the Old Testament?

12. Do you believe that any prophet of the Old Testament, solely through a miraculous revelation made to him by God, did distinctly and unequivocally foretell any distant and future event which has since come to pass and, in special, that any prophet of the Old Testament did thereby and in manner aforesaid distinctly and unequivocally foretell the birth, life, sufferings, death, and resurrection of Jesus of Nazareth, so that Jesus was, in the proper and exclusive sense of the word, the Messiah predicted by the prophets and expected by the Jews?

13. What do you think is the meaning of the phrase, "Thus saith the Lord," with its kindred expressions in the Old Testament?

14. Do you believe that all of or any of the authors of the New

Testament were miraculously inspired, so that all or any of their language can properly be called the word of God and their writings constitute a miraculous revelation, or are those writings to be judged of as other writings by their own merits and so are to pass ,for what they are worth; in short, what is the authority of the New Testament, and what relation does it bear to man—that of master or servant?

15. Do you believe the Christian apostles were miraculously inspired to teach, write, or act, with such a mode, kind, or degree of inspiration as is not granted by God, in all time, to other men equally wise, moral, and pious; do you think the apostles were so informed by miraculous inspiration, as never to need the exercise of the common faculties of man and never to fall into any errors of fact and doctrine, or are we to suppose that the apostles were mistaken in their announcement of the speedy destruction of the world, of the resurrection of the body, etc?

16. What do you think is the nature of Jesus of Nazareth; was he God, man, or a being neither God nor man, and how does he effect the salvation of mankind; in what sense is he the Savior, Mediator, and Redeemer?

17. Do you believe that Jesus of Nazareth was miraculously born, as it is related in two of the gospels, with but one human parent; that he was tempted by the devil, and transfigured, talking actually with Moses and Elias; that he actually transformed the substance of water into the substance of wine; fed 5,000 men with five loaves and two fishes; that he walked on the waters; miraculously stilled a tempest, sent demons out of men into a herd of swine; and that he restored to life persons wholly and entirely dead?

18. Do you believe that Jesus had a miraculous and infallible inspiration—different in kind or mode from that granted to other wise, good, and pious men—informing him to such a degree that he never made a mistake in matters pertaining to religion, to theology, to philosophy, or to any other department of human concern; and that, therefore, he teaches with an authority superior to reason, conscience, and the religious sentiment in the individual man?

19. Do you believe that it is impossible for God to create a being with the same moral and religious excellence that Jesus had, but also with more and greater intellectual and other faculties, and send him into the world as a man; or has Jesus exhausted either or both the capacity of man, or the capability of God?

20. Do you believe that from a state of entire and perfect

death, Jesus returned to a state of entire and perfect physical life; that he did all the works and uttered all the words attributed to him in the concluding parts of the gospels after his resurrection and was subsequently taken up into heaven, bodily and visibly, as mentioned in the book of Acts?

21. Do you believe that at the death of Jesus, the earth quaked, the rocks were rent, that darkness prevailed over the land for three hours, that the graves were opened, and many bodies of saints that slept arose and appeared to many?

22. Do you believe that Jesus or any of the writers of the New Testament believed in and taught the existence of a personal devil, of angels good or bad, of demons who possessed the bodies of men; and do you, yourselves, believe the existence of a personal devil, of such angels and demons; in special, do you believe that the angel Gabriel appeared to Zacharias and to the Virgin Mary and uttered exactly those words ascribed to him in the third gospel?

23. Do you believe that the writers of the four gospels and the book of Acts never mingled mythical, poetical, or legendary matter in their compositions; that they never made a mistake in a matter of fact; and that they have, in all cases, reported the words and actions of Jesus, with entire and perfect accuracy?

24. Do you believe the miracles related in the book of Acts— for example, the miraculous inspiration of the apostles of Pentecost; the cures effected by Peter, his vision, his miraculous deliverance from prison by the angel of the Lord; the miraculous death of Ananias and Sapphira; the miraculous conversion of Paul; that diseased persons were cured by handkerchiefs and aprons brought to them from Paul; and that he and Stephen actually and with the bodies' eye saw Jesus Christ, an actual object exterior to themselves?

25. Do you believe that Peter in the Acts correctly explains certain passages of the Old Testament, as referring to Jesus of Nazareth, his sufferings, death, and resurrection; that Jesus himself—if the gospels truly represent his words—in all cases applies the language of the Old Testament to himself in its proper and legitimate meaning; was he never mistaken in this matter, or have the passages of the Old Testament many meanings?

26. Do you think that a belief in the miraculous inspiration of all or any of the writers of the Old Testament or New Testament; that a belief in all or any of the miracles therein mentioned; that a belief in the miraculous birth, life, resurrection, and ascension of Jesus; that a belief in his miraculous, universal, and infallible

inspiration is essential to a perfect Christian character, to salvation and acceptance with God, or even to participation in the Christian name? And if so, what doctrine of morality or religion really and necessarily rests, in whole or in part, on such a belief?

27. Do you believe that the two ordinances—baptism and the Lord's Supper—are, in themselves, essential, necessary, and of primary importance as ends, valuable for their own sakes, or that they are but helps and means for the formation of the Christian character and, therefore, valuable only so far as they help to form that character?

28. Do you think it wrong or un-Christian in another to abandon and expose what he deems a popular error or to embrace and proclaim an unpopular truth; do you count yourselves, theoretically, to have attained all religious and theological truth and to have retained no error in your own creed, so that it is wholly unnecessary for you, on the one hand, to reexamine your own opinions or, on the other, to search further for light and truth, or do you think yourselves competent, without such search or such examination, to pronounce a man an infidel and no Christian solely because he believes many things in theology which you reject and rejects some things which you believe?[2]

Notes

[1]Wright, *Three Prophets of Religious Liberalism*, 35.

[2]These form a quotation in Parker's own words. No effort has been made to modernize them. *From a letter to the Boston Association of Congregational Ministers, written by Theodore Parker, Minister of the Second Church in Roxbury, March 20, 1845.*

Study Guide to Chapter 8

In 1966, the committee on goals arranged with the National Opinion Research Center to conduct a sampling of contemporary attitudes and beliefs of Unitarian Universalists. The results are considered somewhat startling in showing the nature of pluralistic dissent among Unitarian Universalists. *Time* magazine, April 14, 1967, reported on the "Growing Avant-Garde Unitarians," observing, "Most of them seem to deny the major tenets of Christianity: less than three percent think that God is a supernatural being, 90 percent do not believe in the existence of life after death, 64 percent say that they seldom pray." *Newsweek*, April 17, 1967 reported, "To many mainstream Christians, Unitarians are largely atheistic intellectuals who can't kick the habit of going to church," and concluded that the poll showed this observation to be accurate, but that Unitarian Universalists are not only intellectuals but activists. Following is a summary of the goals committee report.

Personal beliefs and attitudes

(1) 2.9 percent defined God as a supernatural being revealing himself through history, whereas 23.1 percent see God as the ground of all being, while 44.2 percent find God to be a name defining some natural processes within the universe, such as love or creative evolution. On the other hand, 28 percent found God to be an irrelevant concept while 1.8 percent felt God to be a harmful concept.

(2) Unitarian Universalists pray in the traditional Christian sense infrequently: 36 percent marked never, while 27.8 percent chose seldom, and only 11.6 percent pray often. Twenty-three percent do not find the term prayer useful, while 54.8 percent define prayer as meditating, auto-suggestion, or communion with the inner self.

(3) Eighty percent believe that science strengthens their religion, while 19.1 percent say it has little effect.

(4) Not only did 56.9 percent feel that their religion was not Christian, but 36.7 percent of Unitarian Universalists preferred that their own denomination ten years hence be "closer to an emerging, universal religion," and 52.0 percent preferred that it be "closer to a distinctive, humanistic religion."

(5) Most Unitarian Universalists (89.5 percent) do not accept the traditional Christian concept of immortality.

(6) Unitarian Universalists are optimistic, 95.2 percent agreeing that there has been progress in the history of human civilization. They chose the following to support that belief:

Growth of science and knowledge	88.5%
Increase in moral sensitivity	44.0%
Emergency of a world community	50.8%
Decrease in poverty and disease	37.2%

(7) That everyone's potential for love can overcome the potential for evil was checked by 89.5 percent.

Social attitudes and beliefs

(8) On our military policy in Vietnam, Unitarian Universalists were in favor of a negotiated settlement in Vietnam: 9.2 percent supported escalation of the war, 31.8 percent hoped the U.S. would not extend the war, 33.6 percent believed we should take further initiatives to stop the war, and 21.7 percent indicated that the U.S. should unilaterally withdraw militarily from South Vietnam.

(9) Very much in the liberal tradition, Unitarian Universalists approve of civil disobedience when laws are unjust (62.3 percent), while only 28.3 percent disapprove of civil disobedience under any circumstances.

(10–11) Unitarian Universalist attitudes toward divorce, abortion, and sexual mores are very much in their tradition of individual choice. The questions asked and answers are as follows (each person could choose only one). On divorce: (a) If one partner to a marriage wishes a divorce, he or she should be able to obtain it without any legal obstacles, 17.4 percent; (b) If the partners are incompatible and both wish to end the marriage, they should be able to do so, 67.1 percent; (c) If the other partner has practiced mental or physical cruelty, a divorce should be granted, 9.6 percent; (d) Only if the other partner has deserted, is mentally ill, or has engaged in adultery or criminality should a divorce be granted, 5.4 percent; (e) There are no valid grounds for divorce, 0.6 percent. Their reactions to the abortion questions were all yes: (a) If there is a strong chance of serious defect in the baby, 97.0 percent; (b) If she is married and does not want any more children, 61.8 percent; (c) If the woman's own health is seriously endangered by the pregnancy, 99.0 percent; (d) If the family has a very low income and cannot afford any more children, 75.6 percent; (e) If she became pregnant as a result of rape, 97.3 percent; (f) If she is not married and does not want to marry the man, 71.9 percent. (Of those responding to the questionnaire, 55.6 percent felt that the matter of sexual intercourse between unmarried persons should be left to free choice; and 80.2 percent felt that homosexuality should be discouraged by education, not by law.)

(12) Of the Unitarian Universalists tested, 99.7 percent agreed that married persons should be able to receive contraceptive information, devices, or pills if they wanted them; 86 percent approved them for engaged couples; and 83 percent for any adult. Fifty-five

percent felt that any young person should be able to acquire contraceptive devices legally.

(13) Listed below are percentages of some of the major programs in the area of social controversy voted by Unitarian Universalists:

	Approve	Disapprove
Peace activities ——————	86.1%	13.9%
Civil rights ——————	90.6%	9.4%
Civil liberties ——————	92.8%	7.2%
Legislative activity ——————	82.3%	17.7%

(14) For Unitarian Universalists, previous religious values usually ceased to be meaningful during high school (25.6 percent), or college and/or before marriage (26.0 percent). (Incidentally, 60.1 percent of all Unitarian Universalists turn out to be college graduates, with 25.4 percent of them holding graduate degrees.)

Conclusion

It should be obvious that Unitarian Universalists are not all things to all people. No religious group can make such a claim. Although everyone is welcome in the churches and fellowship, not everyone will share their views. But for that growing group of people who are looking for a religion based on reason and experience, Unitarian Universalism provides an opportunity to continue the quest for meaning and hope in a modern world.

—News service release

Study Guide to Chapter 9

The needs of today's children

Between two worlds. The world is changing with unbelievable rapidity. It is shrinking as we prepare to invade outer space, the older sense of security fades as empires come and go and peoples and cultures can no longer be classified smugly as Christian or pagan.

One set of questions. For some of the older generation who can't comprehend the extent of change, the important questions in the current dialogue over religious education are about the adequacy of today's liberal religious curriculum.

Another set of questions. For others who sense today's realities, the questions center about how our church schools can help our children to understand why we have rejected orthodoxy and can best assist them to become confident religious liberals in a sea of orthodoxy.

Only a pack of lies. The needs of members of today's generation to attain internal faiths is well illustrated by the boy who threw his Bible in the ash can as a result of his science courses.

Orientation for their world. If, as we believe, the role of the church is to help our children orient their lives, we must prepare them for *their* world, into which they are moving, not *ours*, hence the church school cannot stand still and try to preserve the old certainties as some would wish.

Who should teach them?

Primary responsibility. Parents should be and often are the best and principal teachers, however, they usually find they can't go it alone and turn to school and church.

Responsibility of church. The Unitarian Universalist church school attempts to be an adjunct to the home in religious instruction in the broadest sense.

Our response to today's needs. Parents, teachers, directors of religious education are uniting to break free from old stereotypes of Sunday school, church school, Bible schools to create a flexible growing experience-oriented approach.

Break with tradition. Our religious education program is amazingly different from the teaching tools of the traditional Sunday schools.

Denominational emphasis. Religious education for youth has been one of the fields of greatest advance in the Unitarian Universalist movement during the past few decades and religious educators, rather than theologians, are shaping its content and meaning.

What should they be taught?

Universality of religion. We believe any experience may be religious if it touches personality at its core.

Examples. An experience is religious if it gives one insight into oneself, relates to another in a mutually satisfying way, leads into an intimate relationship with nature, awakens a child to wonder, leads to the thrill of discovery and personal identification, and thereby strengthens life and gives a sense of purpose.

Unity of life. We seek to emphasize the unity of all things.
Comparison of subjects. Unitarian Universalism:

teaches:		*does not teach:*	
	truths		The Truth
	laws		The Law
	about churches		about the Church
	about lives		about the Life
	about doctrines		about the Doctrine

Many adults who reject the religions of orthodoxy live without formal church affiliation until their children raise theological questions. When it becomes necessary to correct the attitudes of youngsters who quote, parrot-fashion, religious superstitions or supernatural ideas of playmates, parents often realize they must make arrangements for religious instructions. Oftentimes the questions children raise may be natural for their age: "Mommie, who made life?" "What is love?" "What was before there was anything?" "Where is God?" Such questions must be answered, but often they bewilder parents. Parents often need help in projecting a rational philosophy of religion that will help their children grow without the frustrations, the negation, and the emptiness that often result from giving childish answers which will be soon outgrown. Accordingly, many parents make a decision about church affiliation which leads them to Unitarian Universalism. What are the values of the nondogmatic, rational, and natural religious approach of religious liberalism and modern ethical teachings for such families? What other reasons lead many people not themselves raised in the Unitarian Universalist movement to it for aid in the religious instruction of their children?

Can parents turn their children over to our churches, fellowships, and schools of religion to do the job for them? Do you agree that the school and institution are merely an adjunct to the home, and the attitudes found there?

We believe that books, such as *Today's Children and Yesterday's Heritage,* and *Worshipping Together with Questioning Minds* by Sophia L. Fahs are important background material for all parents. What do we mean when we say the real teachers of religion are the parents? To what extent does this also apply to playmates? To public school teachers? To nursery school teachers? To church school teachers? Is there ever a vacuum where children are safely insulated from religious influences and attitudes?

Are there hard and fast lines separating the teaching of religion from science? From nature? From history and citizenship concerns? Consider the elements of our past heritage, our role and relationship to our natural environment, our place in a world of growing insights and new knowledge. Our conduct including our civil and moral rights and our ethical commitments must also be considered.

Consider the importance of religious education in relating the modern child to the cultural patterns of the world. In studying comparative and complementing cultures and religions of the East and West, how important is it to emphasize the inherent values of each? Reflect upon the dangers of giving the impression that our ways are superior and others are inferior, more primitive, or more superstitious. Is this opportunity for appreciating the inherent qualities of each not a part of the value of the religious educational approach of Unitarian Universalism? Yet, what are the role and responsibility of selective judgment? How can the religious liberal make judgments?

What is the role and place of the Bible in our religious education? Turn back to Chapter 8 and reconsider the basic problems confronted in dealing with the questions about the Bible, Jesus, God, et cetera.

Study Guide to Chapter 10

The following questions are often first asked by an inquirer without benefit of a reading course. Many of these questions are recurring, and the answers can almost be ground out of a mill. Yet for each one they could be different. The essence of such answers put in cryptic form might be as follows. You, however, have now graduated and are qualified to give your own answers. How would you differ from the following? This is now your privilege.

History

Who is a Unitarian Universalist?
He or she is a freethinking adherent of a member society of the Unitarian Universalist Association. In religion he or she is a freethinker who would be considered a heretic, radical, infidel, or nonconformist in other churches. Being independent in thought,

he or she is basically an anti-institutionalist who, nevertheless, has combined with others of like mind to develop and maintain an institution based on individual freedom, convinced that the nurture of the free mind is necessary for the improvement of the human lot.

What is Unitarian Universalism?

Unitarian Universalism is the religion reflected by the organizations, churches, fellowships, and adherents of the Unitarian Universalist Association. Incorporated in the U.U.A. are a number of preceding organizations: notably the American Unitarian Association (1825); the Universalist Church of America (including predecessor organizations in continuity since 1785); the Council of Liberal Churches (1953); and the earlier organizations incorporated into the A.U.A.—the General Conference of Unitarian Churches (1865) and the Free Religious Association (1867), together with various state and regional bodies.

What does a Unitarian Universalist believe?

One is free to believe what one's conscience, mind, experience, and emotions lead one to affirm. In later questions we shall discuss specific beliefs, rather than merely believing. Our fellowship is founded upon the free-mind principle, and ours is an association that seeks to help a person develop the religion that is within each, rather than merely to give an external religion that can be put on like a suit of clothing. What can be put on can be taken off, and we feel too many people find they have no religion when the chips are down. What makes sense when we have background organ music or the filtered light of colored windows often escapes us when we are involved in the hustle and bustle of everyday life. Accordingly, if we can develop our own religion in terms of our beliefs they can assist us in meeting the issues of life.

What are the principles and purposes of a Unitarian Universalist Church?

The purposes of the Unitarian Universalist Association are set forth in Article 2, Section C-2.1 of the Bylaws of the U.U.A.:

We, the member congregations of the Unitarian Universalist Association, covenant to affirm and promote
• The inherent worth and dignity of every person
• Justice, equity and compassion in human relations

- Acceptance of one another and encouragement to spiritual growth in our congregations
- A free and responsible search for truth and meaning
- The right of conscience and the use of the democratic process within our congregations and in society at large
- The goal of the world community with peace, liberty and justice for all
- Respect for the interdependent web of all existence of which we are a part.

The living tradition which we share draws from many sources:

- Direct experience of that transcending mystery and wonder, affirmed in all cultures, which moves us to the renewal of the spirit and an openness to the forces which create and uphold life
- Words and deeds of prophetic women and men which challenge us to confront powers and structures of evil with justice, compassion and the transforming power of love
- Wisdom from the world's religions which inspires us in our ethical and spiritual life
- Jewish and Christian teachings which call us to respond to God's love by loving our neighbors as ourselves
- Humanist teachings which counsel us to heed the guidance of reason and the results of science, and warn us against idolatries of the mind and spirit.

Grateful for the religious pluralism which enriches and ennobles our faith, we are inspired to deepen our understanding and expand our vision. As free congregations we enter into this covenant, promising to one another our mutual trust and support.

The Unitarian Universalist Association shall devote its resources to and exercise its corporate powers for religious, educational and humanitarian purposes. The primary purpose of the Association is to serve the needs of its member congregations, organize new congregations, extend and strengthen Unitarian Universalist institutions and implement its principles.

Section 3 then says in part, "Nothing in this Constitution or in the bylaws of the Association shall be deemed to infringe upon the congregational policy of the churches and fellowships, nor upon the individual freedom of belief which is inherent in the Universalist and Unitarian heritages." While no church is bound by these purposes, their intentions may be assumed to be roughly compatible with those of the larger denomination.

Is Unitarian Universalism a new religion?
Yes and no. It is new in the sense that it is discovered anew by each adherent, and constantly redefined and recreated in the light of our new experiences and increasing wisdom. It is also new in the sense that with the merger of the Unitarian and Universalist denominations in the United States and Canada a new denomination came into being. However, it is a religion that is as old as the first protest against conformity and the unthinking acceptance of other men's religions. In a broad sense, Akhnaton (Ikhnaton), the Egyptian Pharaoh who first perceived an ethical monotheism, may have been a Unitarian Universalist, as were Confucius, most of the Greek dramatists and philosophers (notably Socrates), the Hebrew prophets who protested the decadence of the religion of their day, and Jesus who was a minority of one in his time. Throughout history we find those who in the spirit represented the type of religious outlook we hold—a free mind, unbowed to tyranny, quietly proclaiming the dignity to think for oneself, no matter what the consequence. For Socrates it means the hemlock, for Jesus the cross, for Servetus the fiery faggot, and for many others it has meant personal abuse and cries of "heresy!" or "infidel!"

This question often is much more limited in its scope, however, and often is tied in with such questions as: are Unitarianism and Universalism identical? Is there a separate Unitarian church? . . . A separate Universalist church? Has the Unitarian church split into smaller denominations, the Unitarian and Unitarian Universalist? Has the Universalist church been split so that there is a Universalist and a Unitarian Universalist movement? The answer to all of these questions is no. Happily the Unitarian and Universalist churches, growing out of separate heritages, have found themselves so close together that they have been able to join into a united movement. Since May, 1961, there has only been one consolidated movement. Some of our churches continue to call themselves by a historic Universalist name or a Unitarian name or by the Unitarian Universalist name. Also, as a matter of convenience or preference, our members often refer to themselves as Unitarians, Universalists, or Unitarian Universalists. There is no hard and fast rule in their regard, and each person and congregation is free of ecclesiastical control.

What makes a Unitarian Universalist different?
He or she is one who believes that in religion, as in everything else each individual should be free to seek the truth for oneself,

unhampered by official creeds. We are supported in a meaningful way by Unitarian Universalist membership which assures us of both a past heritage and present fellowship of vast numbers who, like us, are committed to the proposition that in religious and intellectual matters the rights of the individual are superior to those of the organization, so that we find a strength through membership, reading, and participation. The "loner" who lacks this sense of fellowship and continuity with an ongoing stream of heresy, martyrdom and individualism can be overcome or paralyzed into inactivity or silence. The Unitarian Universalist is encouraged to hold the head high proudly as a member of an ongoing stream of religious liberalism that has paved the way for progressive advances throughout the centuries.

What is the meaning of the word "Unitarian"?
Theologically, the word Unitarian means one who believes in the Unity of the Godhead, rather than the Trinity of the Godhead. We often say that "one in a Unitarian church *may* believe in the Trinity," but most likely if one did so believe he or she would choose a church that supported that position. It is not that we reject the doctrine or other doctrines, but that we ask for a different approach to religious fellowship. Historically, rather than theologically, the name Unitarian was first used in the sixteenth century in Transylvania where a group of religious liberals made a pledge not to persecute each other because of differences of opinion on religious questions. Thus they were united together, hence, Unitarian. Eventually, those who believed it was necessary to believe in the Trinity to hold Christian worship withdrew, leaving only those who were not concerned over the Trinity as a matter of doctrine; hence, the name Unitarian came to be identified in the common mind with the non-Trinitarians or Unitarians. In the United States and Canada, early Unitarians rejected the rigid orthodoxy of Calvinism and were influencing religious thought by the time of the American Revolution. They traced it back to the fourth century heresy of Arius (256–336 A.D.) and the Reformation heresy of Socinus, Zwingli, and later of Arminius. The first Episcopal church in Massachusetts, King's Chapel, Boston, became the first Unitarian church in the United States.

What is the meaning of the word "Universalist"?
"Universalism—the biggest word in the language," said Elizabeth Barrett Browning. Since the beginning of recorded time and, no doubt earlier, men have created exclusive cults that said, "We hold

the secret of eternal life, and the mystery of life itself." Undoubtedly there have always been those, though few in number, who have said, "Truth, knowledge, life, and meanings cannot be restricted to cult, tribe, race, or nation. Truth and life are universal, and many are the pathways that lead to it." Even some within the cults who said, "This way we shall be saved" may very well have thought, "For others there may be other ways to find salvation." This broader view was Universalism.

Universalism, as an historic movement in the United States and Canada, was brought to these shores by an Englishman, John Murray, who became a chaplain in the Continental Army of General Washington, and by others with German or French backgrounds, who resisted the rigid conformity of Calvinism and religious establishment. They found early Christian agreement particularly in the great church father, Origen (185–254 A.D.), who believed in salvation for everyone whether or not they were within the Christian church. The rejection of the specific Calvinist doctrine of election as the sole means of salvation, solidified the area of concern. Later generations have found that the liberalism inherent in the free mind approach and the universal outlook evolved in the Universalist movement led logically to a concern for humankind and gave a new and broader content to Universalism as a faith for one world and for a united world community in which the diversity and cultural contributions of all people create a universal bond.

Beliefs

What do Unitarian Universalists believe about Jesus?
We may love the person and message of Jesus of Nazareth, but we find the concept of the Christ to be an abstraction, which is unnecessary for those who would live according to the teachings of the simple Galilean. He appears to us as a great teacher, rather than as a member of the Trinity. We find inspiration and guidance in his prophetic utterances, and we turn to his words as recorded in the gospels for insight, strength, and inspiration. The gospel record, as interpreted by sound scholarship with the aid of archaeological research, helps us to understand the man, Jesus, better. The discovery of the Dead Sea scrolls and Egyptian manuscripts help us make informed judgments today that former generations could not make. We believe the accumulated evidence shows that Jesus did not think of himself as a Savior offering a blood atonement, or that he regarded himself as a person in a

Trinity, although during the last days of his life, he may have come to think he was the Jewish messiah. It is the ethics of Jesus, rather than the doctrines about him, that are attractive to us. We find this same ethical concern in other great leaders (Socrates, Confucius, Buddha, Mohammed, etc.), so that we do not regard him as unique and set apart from all others, although we may consider him superior.

What do Unitarian Universalists believe about miracles?
It is unnecessary for Unitarian Universalists to believe in miracles, because the proof of religion for us does not require an outward manifestation of God, but rather an intelligent understanding of life. For us, miracles seem to contradict the orderliness and assurance of natural law. As the holy scriptures of all religions were written long ago in prescientific times, we ascribe the account of miracles to misconceptions or ignorance of natural occurrences that people innocently sought to explain when they could not understand.

What then do Unitarian Universalists believe about God?
We hold a multitude of beliefs, because there is no set dogma or doctrine. It is probable there may be some Unitarian Universalists who believe in the type of jealous, nationalist God of Old Testament accounts, and some who believe in the loving parent of Jesus' concept. Some would agree with Jesus, "God is love." Others would join with Gandhi in saying "God is truth." Others join with scientists in saying God is "the first cause," or with philosophers in calling God "the center of focus in the universe." Others define God as the integrating force, that which makes meaning in our experience, that which makes sense out of life, the power for good, etc. Generally speaking Unitarian Universalists find God within the natural order, not outside of it. God becomes a natural force rather than supernatural.

All Unitarian Universalists do not agree in the necessity for belief in God. Some are humanists who feel it is more important to deal with human and social concerns and to apply their attention to the ethical issues of life, rather than draining it off in theological and philosophical speculation. Many say it is not a matter of rejecting the idea of God, but that this idea means many different things to different people, and in different churches so that one person does not really know what another means when saying "I believe in God." Accordingly they often feel that as a matter of intellectual honesty we should try to say in specific terms what we mean, rather than use so subjective a term.

What is the source of authority for Unitarian Universalists?
Ours is a religion that does not require an outside authority. For some churches the authority is supernatural, coming through revelation from God, such as holy scriptures (the Bible), a Mediator (Jesus Christ), a church creed (Apostles' or Nicene Creeds), the conscience (the Inner Light). For the Unitarian Universalist authority lies in the mind, drawing upon knowledge and experience which lead to the beliefs that guide us. As our knowledge increases and our experiences bring wisdom or new insights, our religious outlook will grow and change, but will be consistent because it is part of our continuous development.

What do Unitarians and Universalists think about the Bible?
As already indicated, it is not necessary as a source of divine authority, nor is it regarded by us as a verbally inspired book. It is looked upon by us as a body of literature, composed of many books, not one, and covering many fields of knowledge including legendary stories, poetry, history, drama, prophetic books, and biographical accounts. Different parts of it are to be taken more seriously than others, and we should use our intellect in interpreting and judging its contents. While it is quoted by us and may be used in our services, it is often read in conjunction with other books, including those from other religious traditions and secular fields.

What do Unitarian Universalists believe about hell?
Universalism began with an emphasis on the belief that God would condemn no one to eternal hellfire and damnation. This quickly evolved into the popular belief that Universalists denied the existence of hell. Unitarians, believing in the divine element in each individual, could not accept the concept that a just and loving God could allow a human personality to suffer eternal or supernatural torment. Thus early in the evolution of religious liberalism, both rejected hell, holding a concept of compensation, stressing that the deeds we do upon this earth are compensated for in this life. This became the principal belief of both Unitarians and Universalists in the nineteenth century. There is enough hell in this world without creating an imaginary hell in another world.

What do Unitarian Universalists believe about immortality?
Unitarian Universalists believe that this life, rather than a future life, is our main concern. We are living now and should make this life count, do the best, experience the most, and achieve the highest we can now in this natural life. If we do this, we will have no regrets, no matter what the ultimate issue of life is.

If life ceases with this existence, then we will have lived fully. If there is another life we will have better prepared ourselves for it. The undue concern with salvation in an afterlife which we observe in others sometimes strikes us as a selfish preoccupation with self, rather than an ethical concern for improving the conditions of living. Many different types of ideas regarding afterlife are held by our members, but in general, Unitarian Universalists tend to avoid absolute conclusions about that which, by its very nature, must be conjecture, since no one has really returned from the dead to give us an account.

Other churches talk about such beliefs as Virgin Birth, Resurrection, the Ascension, etc. What do Unitarian Universalists say about them?
Consistent with the statements made above, we say there is no need for such beliefs.

If you have no creeds, what holds you together?
As stated, Unitarian Universalists do not rely on external authority. We are bound together by the free-mind principle, which encourages everyone to develop their own religion. To us, creeds are negative; they say "no" to new truth. They imply that truth belonged to some period now past. We say truth belongs to the living. For us, the bond of union is not conforming ideas, but the sincerity of the quest for the good life. Everyone who honestly joins in the search for the way to a better life is welcomed, and only the individual can be the judge of personal integrity to the best and highest known. Consequently we do not pass judgment on one another, and we have a richer fellowship because we know that we say what each believes for there is no correct or incorrect position among us. Ours is what William Ellery Channing called a church from which "no man can be excommunicated . . . but by the death of goodness in his own breast."

Without creeds, etc., how can you be Christians?
We say that Christianity should be a religion that seeks to put into practice the ethical principles taught by Jesus of Nazareth and the Hebrew prophets, and this we try to do, tempering our actions with our best insights. However, most Christian bodies say that Christianity to them requires acceptance of certain beliefs. Accordingly, because we do not have a mechanism to require concurrence, we are not admissible by their standards as Christians. This is their judgment on us, not our own. We point out that Unitarian and Universalist movements, as we know them, began as liberalizing movements within Christianity, seeking to keep it open to new truth and contemporary—true to the practice of Jesus who sought to liberalize the orthodoxy of his own day. However, we note that, having begun as a liberalizing movement within Christianity, we have moved to a position that brings us close to those who have carried on liberalizing movements in other world faiths, so that the liberal mind often has more in affinity with liberals of other traditions than it has with the closed mind of orthodoxy. Nevertheless, in practice, our forms of worship, our observance of religious holidays, such as Christmas and Easter, show that we still are in a broad sense part of the Christian heritage. The historical roots of modern Unitarian Universalism are to be found in the Reformation of the sixteenth century and the Enlightenment of the eighteenth century.

What is the Unitarian Universalist relationship to other religions?
We are not an exclusive religion, so we do not have to deny the truth of other religions in order to prove our own. Rather, we inclusively accept the good of all religions, and join in mutual efforts whenever possible. For us the great monotheistic world religions and the ethical religions of the East have much merit which we in the Christian tradition should draw upon. We actively seek to do so. Judaism, Islam, Buddhism, Hinduism, and Shinto all have liberalizing elements that come close to the Unitarian Universalist point of view. The group we are closest to in the United States and Canada, is naturally, Judaism, and Unitarian Universalists find much in common with the Reform Jews particularly. Our common social concern as non-Trinitarians and, consequently, as opponents of a church-state establishment leads into a common sense of fellowship with many Jewish groups. At whatever point we meet other world faiths, we find similar concerns to band us together in practical programs.

Practices

Do Unitarian Universalists pray?
Yes, in our own way, though we might call it meditation. There is no thought we can influence God to "change his mind" or do what "he" would otherwise not do. The good effects of prayer are upon the one praying, in being drawn into closer relationship with one's God through the thoughtful consideration involved. Prayer lifts the mind to a higher level than ordinary, reminds us of deeper needs, raises standards and ideals, and nurtures our higher nature. A Unitarian Universalist does not need an intermediary between him and God and, in fact, a Unitarian Universalist might even pray beneficially whether or not there is a God to listen. The value of prayer is personal and intimate.

Do Unitarian Universalists practice christening of children?
Yes, many do. The service of bringing children, a gift of God in their innocence and in our sense of dedication, to the church as we share our joy and undergird our hopes and seek the support of the values by which we live, is a beautiful and inspiring service for many of us. It has none of the connotations of original sin, of the need to be washed in the blood of the lamb, however, of the orthodox theologies, and so some of our members prefer not to christen, lest it be misconstrued. It is a service of dedication, a naming service, a presentation of parent and child under solemn considerations, whenever practiced, free of theological implications. To us it is an ethical, thankful, and dedicatory occasion.

What do Unitarian Universalists do about weddings?
We hold wedding services in the church, whenever possible and prefer to have a liberal minister of religion solemnize them, because nothing is more sacred to us than the vows we take at the time of marriage. We want our service to be ethically and socially meaningful, however, and so we often alter the words of traditional services making them contemporary, and state the beliefs, resolves, and commitment that each brings to the service. The wedding partners are usually invited to join in the preparation of the service and the choice of wording and music, the form and style to be followed. The minister, in conferences, discusses the sociological, psychological, physiological factors, as well as the spiritual implications of marriage. There are no ecclesiastical commitments required, however. The members are not questioned nor required to state their religious affiliations or forced to undergo

religious instruction in the faith of a Unitarian Universalist church. It is reprehensible to a Unitarian Universalist that such an occasion would be used to coerce a person to join a church.

What about funerals?

Unitarian Universalists conduct Memorial Services for the departed in dignity and simplicity. Usually the coffin is closed and the form of service is simple and pertinent to the person and the family without sentimental elaboration. Cremation is a method often preferred by our people. Unitarian Universalists have been leaders in the movement for simple and rational funeral arrangements, and many of our churches and fellowships have formed memorial societies to advance in the community the education and thinking leading to more rational, less ostentatious funerals.

What is the Unitarian Universalist attitude toward ordained ministers?

Unitarian Universalism, emerging out of the Protestant tradition, emphasizes that every person is his or her own priest. Unitarian Universalists try to practice this belief. We follow the congregational practice of ordaining ministers who are the religious leaders and church administrators, guides, and teachers for the believing congregation. For us, however, the minister is one among many, a chosen member of the congregation, a man or woman trained for the work of professional leadership. He or she is one of those to whom one ministers and has no special efficacy, no sacred position, no key to the kingdom that separates him or her from others *per se.* Church policy is something that is not created, but which grows, is adapted, and altered by the wisdom of passing generations. In this wisdom, the tradition of the ordained minister of liberal religion has proved effective. Our ministry is a carefully developed, organized profession. Many other liberal religious movements have appeared in history, and for the most part have passed from the scene within a generation. Unitarian Universalism has survived because it has held to a congregational policy, although evolving, so that its practices have remained consistent.

Ordination is practiced as a beautiful service of resolve and intention, marking the completion of a seven-year university program and the entrance into a career. This service identifies the professional church leadership.

Lay leadership is important in our churches, and our fellowship program could not exist without it. Continued evolution will alter the course of this leadership, we confidently predict, as liberal religion, drawing on its heritage, adapts to new conditions.

Can only a minister conduct a Unitarian Universalist service, and how are the congregations governed?
It is not necessary to have an ordained minister in order to hold a worship service, funeral, or christening service, although many lay people prefer to have one in charge. Lay people themselves can conduct such services, give prayers, and preach sermons. Usually the conditions set for marriage services by the respective state governments require an ordained minister.

The minister, in keeping with congregational polity, as apart from episcopal or presbyterian polity, has no special standing in decision making on fiscal policy for the local congregation. The election of parish committees or boards of trustees is by the membership in a face-to-face meeting to which the minister reports. He or she is not the moderator or chairman and usually is without vote. The raising of the budget and the responsibility for it lie with the lay members. Naturally, prudence and good business dictate that the responsible administrator—the minister—be involved and consulted in the decisions and be turned to for views and advice.

How does the denomination control the local congregation or fellowship?
Its control is by tradition and polity only. A Unitarian Universalist society is an independent, self-governing body that relates to the denomination first of all through the intangible, but very real, practices, polity, and heritage of the movement. Membership in the denomination is through the Unitarian Universalist Association, which has assisted and guided in the organization of districts, which service, give counsel and guidance, and hold conferences and meetings where local groups may benefit by conferring with neighboring bodies on their mutual concerns. The Association has no power to enter and involve itself in the internal affairs of a local church or fellowship. Its officers and staff members may enter only upon invitation of ministers or lay officers. This is a highly unrestricted congregationalism, guaranteeing the utmost freedom possible in religious organization. It appears to be a weak system, and perhaps it is, but it works surprisingly well. This may be due to the fact that no one in our free association has anything to fear from the others, and the destiny of each is safe from the other. This makes for mutual accord and respect of a very high order.

Our Unitarian Universalist Association has a loose affiliation with the I.A.R.F.—renamed in 1969 the International Association for Religious Freedom—with offices in Frankfurt, Germany. We cooperate with other Christian, Hindu, Buddhist, Jewish, and free religious groups around the world. Through the Church of the

Larger Fellowship, individuals in nearly ninety countries as well as in hundreds of American communities, affiliate directly with the Unitarian Universalist Association. The Church of the Larger Fellowship offers a home program for individuals unable to identify with a local society. Through it, sermons, bulletins, religious education programs, a library service, etc., are available directly to individuals who lack similar services from a local church or fellowship.

What is the missionary emphasis of your church?
The Unitarian Universalist church is nonmissionary. We believe that every person has a right to his or her own religious position so long as it does not trespass upon the rights of others. Further, we believe that all cultures, including primitive ones, develop a religious orientation that is necessary to bind together society.

Accordingly, it is a mistake to break down the religion unless one is prepared to transform the entire culture. The Unitarian Universalist Association carries on extension and publication programs in which are set forth the purposes, programs, range of thinking, etc., that exist among us. This dissemination of background material serves the double-pronged purpose of extending information about Unitarian Universalism to avoid misunderstanding and also gives inquirers knowledge about our way of religion so as to ensure all kindred spirits of a welcome among us. This is not missionary activity, however, for we never seek converts, nor do we try to coerce people to agree with us. Rather, we simply make known our position, and one is free to join or not to join us.

Is Unitarian Universalism a salvation religion?
No. We are concerned about this life, not an afterlife. We are concerned with the ethical relations and understanding of life, not about the salvation of souls. For us, salvation is by character; religion is a matter of deeds, not creeds; and this natural world is the center of our lives.

What is the Unitarian Universalist idea about the religious education of children?
We believe that the purpose of religious instruction is to share knowledge and experience that will help children grow into whole personalities, with an understanding of the religious heritage of the ages, able to make discriminating distinctions between higher and lower forms of religion, and able to develop a religion that

makes sense for themselves. We teach truths, not the truth; and we give knowledge, not indoctrination. We do not try to make little Unitarian Universalists, but young people able to think and respond affirmatively for themselves. This calls for a different type of religious education from that which Bible-centered curriculum offers or than an old-fashioned approach can offer. Our schools of religion are pioneering adventures into a new approach toward education.

Questions on social concerns

Do Unitarian Universalists believe in controlling the state or society?
No. Unitarian Universalists are committed to the separation of the church and the state. We believe that the first article of the Bill of Rights (First Amendment to the Constitution of the United States of America) is the cardinal principle for religious freedom. Living in a pluralistic culture we support the wall of separation between state and church. Unitarian Universalists have been active in many efforts to ensure the continued freedom of both state and church from the encroachments of the other.

What is the Unitarian Universalist attitude toward modern knowledge, education, and the control of ideas?
Unitarian Universalists believe that the truth shall make us free and that the free mind can develop only in a society where knowledge is open, education is free, and all ideas are subject to study and consideration by persons who have the right, duty, and privilege to examine all sides of an issue and arrive at independent decisions. Horace Mann, the "father of American public education," was a key layman in the Unitarian movement, and many important, independent educational institutions, free of control, have been founded or amply supported by Unitarian Universalists, individually or in groups.

What is your attitude toward history? Have Unitarian Universalists a special interpretation of history, as do some sects?
Unitarian Universalists accept the findings of secular knowledge in all fields, including history, the social sciences, education, science, etc. There are no church doctrines that limit the freedom of belief. Rather we expect everyone to think individually in any and every field of human endeavor.

*Do Unitarian Universalists have special doctrines in regard to health
and medicine as do some faiths?*
No. We accept the competency of the medical profession, and
believe it represents humanity's experience, wisdom, and knowledge in regard to physical and psychical health. We believe in the
intelligent acceptance of the results of research, experience, and
wisdom. We rely upon the medical profession. We think it good
sense to maintain good health.

*What do Unitarian Universalists believe about abortion, artificial
insemination, and euthanasia?*
In general, Unitarian Universalists believe that more research will
add to humanity's knowledge and wisdom in dealing with socially
controversial questions, and we favor such research. We also believe that, when a body of knowledge indicates a probable position, people should be encouraged to follow it. For instance, the
general assembly of the Unitarian Universalist Association has
repeatedly passed overwhelmingly resolutions setting forth circumstances in which abortion is justified. We, therefore, believe
in a courageous facing of such issues.

What do Unitarian Universalists believe about divorce?
Divorce has become an established pattern of modern life, and in
many cases it can save men, women, and children from unjust
and unhappy situations that are unendurable. Accordingly, intelligent thinking indicates a divorce is often to be preferred to enduring a life of frustration.

What stand does Unitarian Universalism take on birth control?
Birth control is the wise use of medical knowledge for family
planning and the proper spacing of children, which is a necessity
for most families. In view of the dangers of the exploding world
population it becomes increasingly evident that more thought
must be given to birth control, and Unitarian Universalists encourage facing this issue.

*What are Unitarian Universalist attitudes in regard to such social
customs as the use of tobacco, alcohol, or card-playing, etc?*
Where medical science has said social habits such as smoking,
drinking, or overeating are harmful, Unitarian Universalists would
say the prudent person learns from science and cuts down harmful
habits. To this extent these are medical or health questions rather
than social or moral questions. There is no moral question involved

beyond that of our duty to take care of the body. Unitarian Universalists from the early part of the nineteenth century have called for advanced facing of social questions without ecclesiastical reprisals. Card playing, social dancing, and other harmless social diversions have never been denied by Unitarian Universalists in the name of religion. In our judgment, religion has spent too much time in fighting against harmless social conventions while greater issues of social injustice have been avoided. Racial discrimination, bigotry, poverty, war, and ignorance are the real enemies of humanity which the churches should have been resisting.

What is the Unitarian Universalist attitude in regard to discrimination, bigotry, war, and other major social issues?
Unitarian Universalists hold to the principle of the supreme worth of every personality and the dignity of the individual. We see these ideals requiring a human rights' society, made possible through government guarantees of civil rights. Accordingly, the general approach followed may vary in specific instances for specific individuals or groups, but the main concern is always that of finding the solutions which guarantee the supreme worth of every personality.

What stand do you take on peace?
The Unitarian Universalist Association has gone clearly on record as favoring all efforts leading toward peaceful solutions of world problems. We support fully the United Nations, disarmament efforts, and international safeguards for peace. Atomic, biological, and gas warfare are regarded as monstrous perversions to be eliminated. The U.U.A. maintains a Registry of Conscientious Objectors for pacifist members, and, on the other hand, membership on the General Commission of Army and Navy Chaplains, to represent our members in the Armed Forces. Thus all points of view are held by our members. At least two of our members (Albert Schweitzer and Linus Pauling) have received the Nobel Peace Prize.

Who have been some of the Unitarian Universalists we have heard about?
Great Unitarian Universalists of the past have been Presidents Thomas Jefferson, John Adams, John Quincy Adams, Millard Fillmore, and William H. Taft. Great literary figures have included Longfellow, Whittier, Thoreau, Emerson, etc. Great scientists have included Locke, Benjamin Rush, Priestley, Steinmetz, Throop.

Great modern Unitarian Universalists include Adlai Stevenson, Albert Schweitzer, Dr. Benjamin Spock, Dr. Paul Dudley White, Linus Pauling, five U.S. Senators, and numerous leaders in the field of education, science, industry, public life, and literature.

How definitive are these answers? Are Unitarian Universalists expected to agree with all these answers?
No. There are no set positions required by anyone to be a member of a Unitarian Universalist organization. Rather, membership is a matter of common interest and spirit. If you agree with the general tone of this material, then you would be a welcome addition to our gatherings. At all points there are differences of opinion. The free mind is an open mind, and we do not have final answers because tomorrow morning's headlines have not yet been written. We simply do not have enough knowledge or experience.

In all answers above, there is room for variation, and no single answer can be considered definitive. These are answers actually given to inquiring members of the Church of the Larger Fellowship by the author, who constantly must stress that all Unitarian Universalists are entitled to their own opinions on all matters of conscience and faith. There is freedom of practice as well as belief.

The value of the questions above is simply that it shows how some of us in a conversational way have asked and answered questions. As we ask these questions we can find our own answers. The Unitarian Universalist way is not to accept someone else's answers, but to find them for ourselves.

Bibliography

Bainton, Roland, *Hunted Heretic: The Life and Death of Michael Servetus* (Boston: Beacon Press, 1953)

Bell, Albert D., *The Life and Times of Dr. George deBenneville* (Boston: Universalist Church of America, 1953)

Boynton, Richard W., *Beyond Mythology* (New York: Doubleday, 1952)

Bratton, Fred G., *Legacy of the Liberal Spirit* (Boston: Beacon Press, 1961)

Channing, William E., *Unitarian Christianity* (Bartlett, ed.) (Indianapolis, Ind.: Bobbs-Merrill, 1957)

Commager, Henry Steele, *An Anthology of Theodore Parker* (Boston: Beacon Press, 1960)

Cousins, Norman, *In God We Trust* (New York: Harper & Row, 1958)

Davies, A. Powell, *Faith of an Unrepetent Liberal* (Boston: Beacon Press, 1965)

Delbanco, Andrew, *William Ellery Channing: An Essay on the Liberal Spirit in America* (Cambridge, Mass.: Harvard University Press, 1981)

Douglas, William O., Ed., *The Mind and Faith of A. Powell Davies* (New York: Doubleday, 1959)

Frank, Mary and Lawrence, *Your Adolescent at Home and at School* (New York: Viking Press, 1961)

Frothingham, Octavius B., *Transcendentalism in New England,* (New York: Harper & Row, 1959)

Hewitt, S. C., *A Brief Sketch of the Life of John Murray* (Boston: Bela Marsh, 1852)

Holmes, John Haynes, *I Speak for Myself* (New York: Macmillan, 1959)

Howe, Daniel Walker, *The Unitarian Conscience,* Harvard Moral Philosophy 1805–1861 (Cambridge, Mass.: Harvard University Press, 1970)

Hutchinson, William R., *The Transcendentalist Ministers,* Church Reform in the New England Renaissance (New Haven: Yale University Press, 1959)

Koch, Adrienne, and Peden, William, eds., *The Life and Selected Writings of Thomas Jefferson* (New York: Modern Library, 1944) Jefferson's letters to Dr. Benjamin Rush and James Smith on pp. 566, 700, 703, and 705 document his concern for Unitarianism.

Marshall, George N., *An Understanding of Albert Schweitzer* (New York: Philosophical Library, 1966)

———, *Buddha, The Quest for Serenity* (Boston: Beacon Press, 1978)

———, *Church of the Pilgrim Fathers* (Boston: Beacon Press, 1950)

———, *Facing Death and Grief,* (Buffalo, N.Y.: Prometheus Books, 1981)

Marty, Martin E., *The Infidel, Freethought and American Life* (New York: Living Age Books, 1961)

Mills, Betty and Hasley, Lucille, *Mind If I Differ?* (New York: Sheed & Ward, 1964)

Park, Charles E., *We Hold in Common* (Boston: American Unitarian Association, 1946)

Patton, Kenneth L., *Beyond Doubt* (Ridgewood, N.J.: Meetinghouse Press)
———, *Man's Hidden Search* (Meetinghouse Press)
———, *A Religion for One World* (Meetinghouse Press)
———, *The Way for This Journey* (Meetinghouse Press)
———, *Strange Harvest, Collected Lyrics and Sonnets* (Meetinghouse Press)
Persons, Stow, *Free Religion* Second Edition (Boston: Beacon Press, 1963)
Poling, David, *The Last Years of the Church* (New York: Doubleday, 1969)
Robinson, John A. T., *Honest to God* (Philadelphia: Westminster Press, 1963)
Schweitzer, Albert, *Out of My Life and Thought* (New York: Henry Holt, 1947)
Scott, Clinton Lee, *Parish Parables* (Boston: Beacon Press, 1946)
———, *Religion Can Make Sense* (Boston: CLF Book Service, 1982)
———, *Some Things Remembered* (Boston: CLF Book Service, 1977)
Skinner, Clarence R. and Cole, Alfred S., *Hell's Ramparts Fell: The Biography of John Murray* (Boston: Universalist Publishing House, 1941)
Van Loon, Hendrik W., "This I Believe" (Printed in the *Christian Register*, 1945)
Voss, Carl H., *A Summons Unto Men* (New York: Simon & Schuster, 1972)
Walker, Brooks R., *The Christian Fright Peddlars* (New York: Doubleday, 1964)
Wilberforce, William, *A Practical View of the Prevailing Religion Systems* (London, 1797)
Wilbur, Earl Morse, *History of Unitarianism, Vols. I & II.* Third Edition. (Chicago: Meadville/Lombard Theological School, 1972)
———, *Our Unitarian Heritage* (Boston: Beacon Press, 1925)
Willey, Basil, *The Eighteenth Century Background* (Boston: Beacon Press, 1961)
Williams, George H., ed., *The Harvard Divinity School* (Boston: Beacon Press, 1954)
Wright, C. Conrad, *The Beginnings of Unitarianism in America* (Boston: Beacon Press, 1955)

Books Available from the UUA Bookstore, 25 Beacon St., Boston, MA 02108-2800

Cassara, Ernest, *Hosea Ballou: Challenge to Orthodoxy* Second Edition. (Washington, D.C.: University Press of America, 1982)
Cassara, Ernest, ed., *Universalism in America* Second edition (Boston: Unitarian Universalist Association, 1984)
Church, F. Forrester, *Born Again Unitarian Universalism* (New York: All Souls Church, 1981)
Commager, Henry Steele, *Theodore Parker, Yankee Crusader* (Boston: Skinner House Books, 1982)
Davies, A. Powell, *America's Real Religion* (Boston: CLF Bookservice, 1976)
Fleck, G. Peter, *The Mask of Religion* (Buffalo, N.Y.: Prometheus Books, 1984)
Hewett, Philip, *Unitarians in Canada* (Toronto: Canadian Unitarian Council, 1978)

Hitchings, Catherine F., *Universalist and Unitarian Women Ministers* (Boston: Unitarian Universalist Historical Society, 1985)

Howlett, Duncan, *The Critical Way in Religion* (Buffalo, N.Y.: Prometheus Books, 1984)

Marshall, George N., *Schweitzer, A Biography* (New York: Doubleday, 1971)

Mendelsohn, Jack, *Being Liberal in an Illiberal Age* (Boston: Beacon Press, 1985) Formerly *Why I Am a Unitarian Universalist.*

Miller, Russell E., *The Larger Hope: History of the Universalist Church in America, 2 vols.* (Boston: Unitarian Universalist Historical Society, 1986) Modern scholarship in a thorough retracing of Universalism from its inception in this country to its merger in 1961 with the Unitarians.

Rankin, David O., *So Great a Cloud of Witness* (San Francisco: Strawberry Hill Press, 1978)

Robinson, David, *The Unitarians and the Universalists* (Westport, CT: Greenwood Press, 1985)

Scholefield, Harry B., ed., *Unitarian Universalist Pocket Guide* (Boston: Unitarian Universalist Association, 1983)

Scott, Clinton Lee, *These Live Tomorrow* Second Edition. (Boston: Skinner House Books, 1987)

Index of Names

General Index